Navigating Boundaries

A Comprehensive Study of Postcolonial Theory and Literature

Shuchi Agrawal
Professor, Amity University, Noida, India

Series in Literary Studies

VERNON PRESS

Copyright © 2025 Vernon Press, an imprint of Vernon Art and Science Inc, on behalf of the author.

All rights reserved. No part of this publication may be reproduced, stored in a retrieval system, or transmitted in any form or by any means, electronic, mechanical, photocopying, recording, or otherwise, without the prior permission of Vernon Art and Science Inc.

www.vernonpress.com

In the Americas:	*In the rest of the world:*
Vernon Press	Vernon Press
1000 N West Street, Suite 1200,	C/Sancti Espiritu 17,
Wilmington, Delaware 19801	Malaga, 29006
United States	Spain

Series in Literary Studies

Library of Congress Control Number: 2024949518

ISBN: 979-8-8819-0205-6

Also available: 979-8-8819-0095-3 [Hardback]; 979-8-8819-0204-9 [PDF E-Book]

Product and company names mentioned in this work are the trademarks of their respective owners. While every care has been taken in preparing this work, neither the authors nor Vernon Art and Science Inc. may be held responsible for any loss or damage caused or alleged to be caused directly or indirectly by the information contained in it.

Every effort has been made to trace all copyright holders, but if any have been inadvertently overlooked the publisher will be pleased to include any necessary credits in any subsequent reprint or edition.

Cover design by Vernon Press. Image by Freepik.

Contents

Acknowledgement	vii
About the Author	ix
Preface	xi
Introduction	xiii

Chapter 1
Key Concepts in Postcolonial Theory 1
1.1   Abrogation 2
1.2   Appropriation 3
1.3   Binarism 3
1.4   Centre/ Margin 4
1.5   Colonial Discourse 5
1.6   Counter Discourse 6
1.7   Colonialism 7
1.8   Contrapuntal Reading 8
1.9   Cartography 9
1.10 Cultural Diversity/ Cultural difference 10
1.11 Decolonization 11
1.12 Diaspora 12
1.13 Displacement 13
1.14 Ethnography 15
1.15 Eurocentrism 16
1.16 Fanonism 18
1.17 Globalization 19
1.18 Hegemony 20
1.19 Heritage 22
1.20 Home 23
1.21 Hybridity 24
1.22 Imperialism 25

1.23	Mimicry	25
1.24	Miscegenation	26
1.25	Nation/Nationalism	27
1.26	Nativism	29
1.27	Neo-colonialism	30
1.28	Other/other	31
1.29	Post-colonialism/Postcolonialism	32
1.30	Post-colonial Reading	33
1.31	Subaltern	34
1.32	Third World	36
1.33	Transculturation	36
1.34	Transnationalism	37
1.35	Universalism/Universality	38

Chapter 2
Postcolonial Theory: An Introduction — 41

2.1	Postcolonial Theory- Relevance	43
2.2	"Representation and Resistance"- Edward Said	45
2.3	"Thinking Otherwise: A Brief Intellectual History" (from Postcolonial Theory: An Introduction) – Leela Gandhi	49
2.4	"Cultural Identity and Diaspora"- Stuart Hall	51
2.5	"Colonialist Criticism"- Chinua Achebe	59

Chapter 3
History, Culture and Place: Writing Back — 65

3.1	"Postcoloniality and Artifice of History"- Dipesh Chakrabarty	66
3.2	"Writing in Colonial Space"- Dennis Lee	69
3.3	"Cultural Diversity and Cultural Differences"- Homi K Bhabha	72
3.4	"Literary Colonialism: Books in the Third World"- Philip G Altbach	77

Chapter 4
Body, Ethnicity, Subaltern and Language — 81

4.1	"The Fact of Blackness"- Frantz Fanon	84
4.2	"Can the Subaltern Speak?"- Gayatri Chakravorty Spivak	89
4.3	"Language of African Literature": Ngũgĩ wa Thiong'o	95
4.4	*Necropolitics*- Achille Mbembe	100

4.5 *Epistemic Freedom in Africa: Deprovincialization and Decolonization* - Sabelo J. Ndlovu Gatsheni ... 103

Chapter 5
Postcolonial Feminism, Third World Literacy, Nationalism and Education ... 107

5.1 "Under Western Eyes: Feminist Scholarship and Colonial Discourses"- Chandra Talpade Mohanty ... 108
5.2 "Minute on Indian Education": Thomas Macaulay ... 114
5.3 "The Beginning of English Literary Study in British India": Gauri Visvanathan ... 117
5.4 "The Nation and Its Fragments"- Partha Chatterjee ... 120

Chapter 6
Postcolonial Caribbean Literature: Works by Derek Walcott and Jamaica Kincaid ... 127

6.1 Postcolonial Literature: An Introduction ... 127
6.2 Postcolonial Caribbean Literature ... 131
6.3 "A Far Cry from Africa"- Derek Walcott ... 132
6.4 "A Small Place"- Jamaica Kincaid ... 140

Chapter 7
Postcolonial African Literature: Works by Chinua Achebe, Wole Soyinka, David Diop and Namwali Serpell ... 151

7.1 *Things Fall Apart* as a Postcolonial Novel ... 151
7.2 Narrative Threads in *Anthills of Savannah* ... 160
7.3 "Telephone Conversation"- Wole Soyinka ... 167
7.4 "Africa"- David Diop ... 171
7.5 *The Old Drift*- Namwali Serpell ... 180

Chapter 8
Postcolonial Voices from Indian Descent: Works by M K Gandhi, Jhumpa Lahiri, Mahashweta Devi and Kancha Ilaiah ... 185

8.1 *Hind Swaraj*- Mohandas K. Gandhi ... 186
8.2 "Interpreter of Maladies"- Jhumpa Lahiri ... 197
8.3 "Dopdi"- Mahasweta Devi ... 209
8.4 *Why I Am Not a Hindu*- Kancha Ilaiah ... 214

Conclusion	223
Works Cited	227
Index	237

Acknowledgement

"Navigating Boundaries: A Comprehensive Study of Postcolonial Theory and Literature" is a collaborative effort that benefited from the support, and inspiration of many individuals and institutions. First and foremost, I want to thank the scholars and theorists whose ground-breaking works lay the groundwork for this research. Their insights have lit my path, helping me through the complex terrains of postcolonial discourse. I owe the obligation of intellectual inspiration to them.

I convey my heartfelt gratitude to libraries, both physical and digital, as well as the persistent efforts of librarians and archivists. Their abundance of resources has been essential in the lengthy research and inquiry that has underpinned this comprehensive study.

I would like to express my gratitude to the publishers, editors, and peer reviewers who helped shape and refine the content of this book. Their dedication to academic rigour and constructive feedback has been critical in assuring the quality and coherence of this work.

My appreciation also goes to my colleagues, peers and students who participated in serious debates, provided significant insights, and a supportive academic environment. The exchange of ideas and perspectives has been critical in developing and expanding my arguments.

I want to thank my family and friends for their steadfast support and understanding throughout the research and writing process. Their encouragement offered the emotional and practical support required to complete this work.

Finally, I want to thank all of the readers-students, researchers and professors who have engaged with the concepts given in this book. I hope that "Navigating Boundaries" makes a significant contribution to the current discussion of postcolonial theory and literature. Each individual and organization mentioned has had a significant impact on the intellectual inquiry examined in this extensive study.

About the Author

Dr. Shuchi Agrawal is a passionate educator in the field of English literature, currently serving as a Professor at Amity University, Noida, India. With over 20 years of teaching experience, she has impacted countless lives, inspiring her students and guiding M.Phil and Ph.D. scholars toward achieving their aspirations.

Her academic interests are as diverse as they are impactful, ranging from American Literature and Literary Theory to Postcolonial Studies and Gender Studies. Dr. Agrawal's enthusiasm for exploring new ideas is evident in her body of work: eight insightful books and 62 research papers published in renowned peer-reviewed journals. These contributions reflect her dedication not just to knowledge but to the deeper understanding of the role of literature in society.

Her published works delve into significant topics like *Reconstructing Women's Identity, Fostering Integrity in Research, A Study of Communication in the Light of the COVID-19 Pandemic, Linguistics and Phonetics: A Complete Introduction, Business Communication: A Streamlined Approach, A Study of Philip Roth* and *Research Methodology*. Each book and paper is a testament to her belief in the power of words to shape perspectives and foster growth.

Beyond the classroom, Dr. Agrawal actively engages with international academic bodies and associations, always eager to share, learn, and contribute to research. Known for her zeal and commitment, she is more than a teacher — she is a mentor, a guide, and a lifelong learner who finds joy in the success of her students and peers. Dr. Agrawal actively continues to leave an enduring impact through her remarkable body of works, the meaningful relationships she builds, and the inspiration she provides to others.

Preface

Navigating Boundaries: A Comprehensive Study of Postcolonial Theory and Literature explores postcolonial landscapes through an intricate web of theory and literature, aiming to untangle the complexity inherent in the aftermath of colonial histories. This intellectual odyssey is a testament to the numerous voices that have emerged from the periphery, questioning dominant narratives and creating a greater knowledge of identity, power, and resistance. The desire to study postcolonial theory and literature stems from an understanding of the critical necessity to navigate the boundaries that have defined and continue to influence our world. As a result, I probe into the vast and often turbulent intersections of cultures, history, and societies. The metaphorical borders we encounter are not only geographical, but also pertain to language, identity, and power dynamics.

This book emerges as a careful investigation of the theoretical frameworks that have arisen in the aftermath of colonialism. From Edward Said's seminal writings to Homi K Bhabha's critical inquiries, the theoretical terrain is crossed in order to provide readers with a deep knowledge of the intellectual foundations that support postcolonial discourse. Furthermore, the theoretical inquiry acts as a compass for the subsequent analysis of literary works that navigate and test these boundaries.

As I begin this in-depth examination, the issues of resistance, hybridity, identity crisis and mimicry dealing with historical and emerging contemporary situations, which I further explore in the realm of gender, culture, memory, trauma, nationalism, religion, and politics, realizing that each of these subjects contributes to the complex and developing narratives of postcolonial literature. My goal throughout this journey is not just to illuminate the current canon, but also to draw attention to the lesser-explored and neglected voices of the subcontinent and diaspora. The use of vernacular languages adopted by postcolonial critics and theorists provides another degree of authenticity to investigation, reflecting the multiplicity of experiences and expressions found in postcolonial literature.

This book seeks to be more than just an academic exercise; it is an invitation to participate in the complex and multidimensional world of postcolonial literature. It asks readers to reflect, question, and eventually engage in the continuing debate about power, identity, and cultural representation.

As we cross these intellectual and literary borders, I hope that this in-depth study will be a significant resource for scholars, teachers and all those seeking a greater knowledge of the complex and intricate web of postcolonial theory and literature.

Introduction

Overview of Colonialism- The origins of colonialism can be traced back to ancient times, when many civilizations strove to expand their domains and establish authority over other people and places. However, modern colonialism as we know it today emerged during the Age of Exploration in the 15th century. One of the fundamental motivations behind contemporary colonialism was the desire for new trade routes to Asia, particularly for spices and other important goods. European powers such as Portugal, Spain, the Netherlands, France, and England set out on exploration and expansion trips to locate alternate ways to Asia, so evading the Ottoman Empire's monopoly over conventional trade routes.

Vasco da Gama's successful expedition to India in 1498 initiated European maritime exploration and the building of Asian commercial networks. Following this, Spain supported Christopher Columbus' travels to the America, resulting in the "discovery" of the New World and subsequent colonization of a huge territory in America (Canny 46). Economic incentives, such as the thirst for rich metals, agricultural resources, and cheap labour, drove the colonial enterprise even more. European powers established colonies in the Americas, Africa, and Asia, exploiting local populations and resources to their own advantage. The process of colonialism was aided by technological advances in navigation, shipbuilding, and military technology, which enabled European nations to establish dominion over faraway territories.

Furthermore, imperialist ideology, which justified the expansion of European power and the "civilizing mission" (Ashcroft, Griffiths, and Tiffin, *The Postcolonial Reader* 81) of spreading European culture and Christianity, played an important part in justifying colonial efforts. Overall, contemporary colonialism sprang from European exploration, economic interests, technological improvements, and ideological causes, eventually leading to the construction of colonial empires that profoundly changed global history and continue to influence the world today.

Algeria was colonized by **France** in the nineteenth century and remained under French authority until its independence in 1962, following a protracted liberation struggle. From the late nineteenth to the mid-twentieth centuries, France conquered sections of Southeast Asia, including Vietnam, Cambodia, and Laos, which became known as French Indochina. France built colonies in Senegal, Mali, Ivory Coast, and Burkina Faso, also known as French West Africa. These colonies were exploited for resources, including rubber, gold, and wood. Following Christopher Columbus' expeditions, **Spain** built significant colonies in Latin America, including what is now Mexico, Peru, Colombia, and Argentina (Hulme 108). Spanish colonialism in the America resulted in the oppression and exploitation of indigenous people, as well as the extraction of large amounts of wealth such as gold, silver, and other minerals. Spain invaded the Philippines in the 16th century, significantly influencing its culture, language, and religion. Spanish colonial rule lasted until the Spanish-American War in 1898, when the Philippines became part of the United States.

The Dutch East India Company built colonies in the East Indies, which included present-day Indonesia, in the 17th century. The Dutch colonial rule was distinguished by the exploitation of natural resources such as spices, coffee, and rubber, as well as the installation of forced labour regimes. The Dutch established a colony in Suriname, South America, in the 17th century. Suriname was predominantly used for plantation agriculture, particularly sugar and coffee, with enslaved Africans and, subsequently, indentured Asian labourers (Eltis et al. 503).

Portugal invaded Brazil (Bethell 345-350) in the 16th century, making it the largest and longest-lasting Portuguese colony. Portuguese colonization in Brazil included the extraction of resources such as sugar, gold, and diamonds, as well as forced labour by indigenous people and enslaved Africans. Portugal created colonies in Angola and Mozambique (Juang and Morrissette 872-873), Africa, in the 15th century. These colonies were exploited for resources such as ivory, minerals, and slaves, which added to Portugal's wealth and influence.

Italy colonized Libya in the early twentieth century and incorporated it into the Italian Empire. Italian colonial control in Libya was characterized by persecution, forced labour, and the suppression of resistance groups. Italy sought to colonize Ethiopia in the late nineteenth and early twentieth centuries, which culminated in the First Italo-Ethiopian War. Despite initial Italian triumphs, Ethiopia successfully resisted colonization and remained independent. In due course, British colonialism grew more powerful and expansive than other European colonial powers because of various reasons (Porter 1-7).

During the colonial era, the British Royal Navy was one of the world's most formidable naval forces. This enabled the British to gain **naval dominance**, control critical commerce routes, and provide effective protection for their colonies. Their maritime superiority made it easier to move troops, goods, and people to distant territories, allowing the British Empire to expand.

Britain's relative **political stability in comparison to other European powers** facilitated long-term colonial growth. The Glorious Revolution of 1688 and the institution of constitutional monarchy ensured political stability, creating a favourable environment for international undertakings.

British colonialism was distinguished by **mercantilist policies** designed to benefit the mother country. The British Empire enacted rules like the Navigation Acts, which limited colonial trade to British ships and ensured that colonies dealt exclusively with Britain. This economic exploitation increased British riches and power.

The Industrial Revolution, which began in Britain in the late 18th century, gave the British Empire a considerable competitive advantage over other colonial powers. Britain's industrial success stimulated demand for raw resources from its colonies while also providing manufactured items for worldwide trade. This **economic vitality** aided the expansion and consolidation of British colonial territory.

Unlike other colonial powers that were primarily concerned with resource extraction, the British founded a large number of **settlement colonies**, particularly in North America, Australia and New Zealand. The large-scale influx of British settlers to these colonies helped to establish a lasting British presence and cultural dominance. The British Empire used a reasonably flexible style of **colonial administration**, allowing for adaptability to local conditions and the co-optation of indigenous leaders. This pragmatic strategy allowed the British to maintain control over a wide range of regions, each with its own cultural, social, and political landscape. The spread of the English language and the acceptance of British legal systems in many colonies improved government and communication. **English language** became the lingua franca in many parts of the world, increasing British influence and soft power. **The British Empire** had colonies and territories spread across continents. Britain's strong territorial control and strategic posture allowed it to exert power and influence globally. Thus, naval power, economic domination, industrialization, flexible administration, and global reach all contributed to British colonialism's exceptional scale and power when contrasted to other European colonial powers.

Postcolonial theorists frequently focus more on British colonialism than other European colonial powers for many reasons. The British Empire was the **largest empire** in history, spanning continents and lasting several centuries (Jackson 100). Its extensive territorial domination and long-standing influence had a tremendous impact on world history, politics, and culture. Postcolonial theorists frequently emphasize the scope and duration of British colonialism as a key aspect in their analyses. British colonialism has had a significant impact on **global culture, communication, and identity**. Postcolonial theorists criticize the imposition of English as the dominant language, which has diminished indigenous languages and cultures in many former British territories.

British colonialism was linked to the expansion of British cultural standards, values, and institutions throughout the world. Postcolonial theorists investigate how **cultural hegemony** influenced notions of identity, race, and gender in colonial and postcolonial civilizations. Unlike other colonial powers that used direct rule, the British frequently used **indirect rule** and divide-and-rule techniques to keep control over diverse populations. Postcolonial theorists investigate the long-term social divisions and conflicts caused by colonial practices. Economic exploitation was the driving force behind British colonialism, with colonies providing as raw material suppliers, marketplaces for manufactured commodities, and outlets for excess capital.

British colonialism had a significant impact on indigenous cultures and traditions, frequently resulting in cultural absorption, language loss, and the extinction of indigenous knowledge systems. Postcolonial theorists investigate colonialism's consequences on cultural identity, as well as ongoing efforts to preserve and revitalize culture. While other European colonial powers had important effects on the regions they colonized, British colonialism's extent, longevity, cultural influence, and governance techniques have made it the primary target of postcolonial critique. However, it is vital to remember that postcolonial theory also investigates the legacies of other colonial powers, as well as their effects on world history and modern culture, recognizing the different experiences and effects of colonialism around the world.

Postcolonial Theorists and Critics- Postcolonial thinkers examine the colonial practices of several European powers, including France, Spain, Portugal, the Netherlands, and Italy. They look at the governance, economic exploitation, cultural imposition, and social control techniques used by colonial regimes around the world. Postcolonial theory investigates how colonialism, regardless of colonizing power, influenced indigenous cultures, identities, and ways of life. For example, Spanish colonialism in Latin America resulted in the mingling of indigenous, African, and European cultures, forming unique cultural identities. Postcolonial theorists examine how colonial powers used conquered countries' resources and labour for their own economic gain. This involves extracting natural resources, establishing plantation economies, and imposing unequal commercial ties in former colonies, all of which contributed to economic reliance and underdevelopment. They also investigate the formation of social hierarchies and systems of racial discrimination under diverse colonial regimes. This involves the marginalization and subjection of indigenous people, as well as the continuation of racialized stereotypes and prejudices that still define social relations in postcolonial cultures. They also examine various types of resistance and liberation efforts that arose against colonial authority, regardless of the colonizing power. These movements sought to recover indigenous sovereignty, assert cultural autonomy, and address colonial injustices. Postcolonial theory also highlights the connectivity of colonial experiences from many parts of the world. It uses comparative analysis to identify parallels and contrasts in colonial practices, impacts, and legacies, while also acknowledging the intricate web of historical and contemporary interactions produced by colonialism.

Here are some notable postcolonial critics from regions impacted by French, Spanish, Dutch, Portuguese, and Italian colonialism:

Frantz Fanon is a psychiatrist and philosopher from Martinique. His renowned works, such as *Black Skin, White Masks* and *The Wretched of the Earth* examine the psychological and social impacts of colonialism and argue for decolonization and emancipation (Fanon 10-12; 35-37). Although originally from Martinique, Fanon's works provide sharp critiques of British colonialism in Africa, as well as its psychological and social consequences for both colonizers and colonized. He supports decolonization and the liberation of downtrodden people from colonial domination. **Aimé Césaire**, a poet and politician from Martinique, co-founded the Négritude movement, which embraced African and Caribbean culture while criticizing French colonialism's degrading effects. Her co-founded Négritude movement promotes African and Caribbean culture while criticizing European colonialism, particularly British colonialism. His poetry and essays, including "Discourse on Colonialism", address issues of racial identity, cultural resistance, and the legacy of colonial violence (Césaire 15-17).

Gloria Anzaldúa (Anzaldúa 1-20), a Chicana feminist writer, examined identity, borderlands, and colonialism in her famous work *Borderlands/La Frontera: The New Mestiza*. **Eduardo Galeano** is a Uruguayan journalist and writer whose work, particularly "Open Veins of Latin America," criticizes the economic exploitation and social inequalities inflicted by European colonialism in Latin America (Galeano 1-5). **Albert Helman** is a Surinamese writer and politician whose literary and political works address the complications of colonialism, identity, and cultural hybridity in Suriname and the Caribbean.

Césaire's work, while largely concerned with French colonialism, also addresses the legacy of Portuguese colonialism in the Caribbean and Africa (Césaire 15-17). **Paulo Freire**, a Brazilian educator and philosopher, whose renowned work *Pedagogy of the Oppressed* criticizes the repressive nature of colonial education systems and calls for transformative pedagogy (Freire 72-90).

Achille Mbembe is a Cameroonian philosopher and political theorist whose work, *On the Postcolony*, explores the intersections of power, racism, and colonialism in Africa and beyond (Mbembe 10-12). **Ngũgĩ wa Thiong'o** is a Kenyan writer and scholar whose writing, such as *Decolonising the Mind* criticizes the cultural and linguistic legacy of European colonialism in Africa and argues for cultural decolonization and language revival (Ngũgĩ 5-7). In his works, *A Grain of Wheat and Petals of Blood*, he criticizes the impact of British colonialism on African societies and argues for cultural decolonization (Ngũgĩ, *A Grain of Wheat* 101-111)-and linguistic resurrection (Ngũgĩ, *Petals of Blood* 30-35). He famously chose to write in his native Gikuyu tongue as an act of protest against colonial linguistic dominance.

Chinua Achebe is a Nigerian novelist and essayist best known for his hallmark work *Things Fall Apart*, which examines the impact of British colonialism on Igbo society and culture. His literature delves into subjects such as colonialism, cultural hybridity, and the conflict between tradition and modernity (Achebe 101-115). **Edward Said** is a Palestinian-American literary theorist whose important work *Orientalism* investigates how colonial power relations have impacted Western images of the East. He invented the term "orientalism" to define the Western perception of the Orient as exotic, inferior, and in need of dominance (Said 1-25). **Gayatri Chakravorty Spivak** is an Indian literary theorist and feminist critic whose work, particularly "Can the Subaltern Speak?" examines the representation and agency of disadvantaged voices (Spivak 271-284) in colonial and postcolonial contexts. She emphasizes the value of hearing and amplifying the views of the subaltern, or those who are socially and politically marginalized.

While postcolonial critics and scholars from various regions, including **Somalia, Ethiopia, and Eritrea**, have had a significant impact on postcolonial theory and criticism, it is important to note that the development of postcolonial discourse in these specific contexts may have been influenced by factors other than colonialism, such as internal political dynamics and cultural history. Having said that, below are notable Somali, Ethiopian, and Eritrean scholars and writers who have worked on postcolonial issues or made substantial contributions to related fields:

Abdullahi Ahmed An-Na'im (Sudanese and Ethiopian) is a well-known scholar of law, human rights, and Islam (An-Na'im 45-78). His work frequently connects with postcolonial theory, particularly in his investigation of Islamic legal reform in colonial and postcolonial contexts.

Ali A. Mazrui (Kenyan and Ethiopian) was an active scholar of political science and African studies. His books, notably *The Africans: A Triple Heritage*, critically analyzed the legacy of colonialism and imperialism in Africa, particularly in Ethiopia and Somalia (Mazrui 123-150).

Abdullahi Yusuf Ahmed (Somali), although renowned as a politician and military leader, he was also a writer and thinker. His political career and writings highlight the intricate interconnections of Somali nationalism, postcolonial identity, and state-building efforts in Somalia (Ahmed 56-89).

Nega Mezlekia (Ethiopian and Eritrean) is an Ethiopian and Eritrean writer and critic. His memoir, "Notes from the Hyena's Belly," is a highly personal investigation of identity, migration, and the colonial legacy in the Horn of Africa (Mezlekia 32-37).

Alemseged Tesfai (Eritrean) is an Eritrean poet, playwright, and cultural commentator. His writings, such as *Eritrea: Coming of Age*, investigate themes of identity, resistance, and independence (Tesfai 67-72) within the backdrop of Eritrea's struggle against Ethiopian colonialism and subsequent nation-building efforts.

While these researchers may not be academically focused on postcolonial theory, their publications and contributions provide vital insights into the intricacies of colonial legacies and postcolonial experiences in the Horn of Africa. These are just a few instances of postcolonial critics from regions colonized by different European powers. Their different viewpoints and critical insights add to the ongoing discussion about the legacies of colonialism as well as the struggle for decolonization and social justice. Their critical observations and scholarly contributions have defined the field of postcolonial studies and continue to influence debates in this field of study.

Navigating Boundaries: A Comprehensive Study of Postcolonial Theory and Literature offers an extensive range of perspectives on the existing and emerging attributes of postcolonial nations, as well as their socio-cultural, historical, and literary milieu. This book aims to conduct a comprehensive evaluation of literary reactions to various concerns, such as the convoluted history of colonialism, ethnic conflicts, communal conflicts, military conflicts, and forced migrations. The book examines identity politics, cultural disputes, colonial oppression, decolonization, and other issues from the theoretical views of diverse postcolonial theorists. This book seeks to explore and discover how critics and scholars might reconsider and reimagine the concerns of mimicry, hybridity, identity crisis, identity fragmentation, and liminality in postcolonial literature.

This book provides a comprehensive exploration of key postcolonial theoretical notions and their application in various contexts, examining the complexities of postcolonial discourse across different regions and cultures. Here's an elaboration and critical examination of each chapter:

Chapter 1- Key Concepts and Terms- This chapter introduces fundamental postcolonial theoretical concepts such as binarism, colonial discourse, universalism, nationalism, imperialism, hegemony, eurocentrism, and others. By defining these terms, the chapter lays the groundwork for understanding the complexities of postcolonial discourse.

Chapter 2- Postcolonial Theory: An Introduction- This chapter offers an overview of noteworthy postcolonial theorists, such as Edward Said, Leela Gandhi, Stuart Hall and others, with their groundbreaking contributions to critical readings of colonialism and postcolonialism.

Chapter 3- History, Culture and Place: Writing Back- This chapter examines how history, culture, and place intersect in postcolonial discourse, focusing on important writings by theorists such as Philip G. Altbach, Homi K. Bhabha, and Deepesh Chakravarthy. Through an analysis of spatial components that transcend national borders, the chapter highlights the political and symbolic aspects of postcolonial narratives. It is crucial to critically evaluate, nonetheless, as the chosen writings sufficiently capture the range of postcolonial experiences and viewpoints.

Chapter 4- Body, Ethnicity, Subaltern and Language- This chapter explores the intricate connections between language, body, ethnicity, constructedness of whiteness, and subalternity in postcolonial discourse, with particular attention to the writings of Chinua Achebe, Ngugi Wa Thiong'o, Gayatri Chakravorty Spivak, and Frantz Fanon. The chapter sheds light on the manner in which power relations influence postcolonial identities and narratives by investigating these overlapping themes.

Chapter 5- Postcolonial Feminism, Third World Literacy, Nationalism and Education- This chapter, which draws from the works of critics and theorists such as Chandra Talpade Mohanty, Thomas Macaulay and Gauri Viswanathan, examines the intertwined issues of postcolonial feminism, nationalism, third world literacy, and education. The chapter illustrates the challenges faced by postcolonial countries by looking at these intricate webs of postcolonial cultures. It also provides a critical examination of the intersections of race, class, gender, and other axes of identity within postcolonial contexts.

Chapter 6- Postcolonial Caribbean Literature: Works by Derek Walcott and Jamaica Kincaid- This chapter examines Jamaica Kincaid and Derek Walcott's writings as they relate to postcolonial Caribbean literature. Through an examination of the historical, cultural, and social contexts of the region, the chapter brings to light the various accounts of Caribbean identity and resistance. It critically evaluates the selected pieces of writing, capturing the diversity and depth of Caribbean literature, particularly the perspectives of underrepresented and oppressed groups.

Chapter 7- Postcolonial African Literature: Works by Chinua Achebe, Wole Soyinka, David Diop and Namwali Serpell - This chapter explores African postcolonial literature, dissecting the writings of David Diop, Wole Soyinka, Chinua Achebe and Namwali Serpell. In the wake of colonialism, the chapter sheds light on the intricacies of African narratives through an examination of themes of cultural hybridity, identity, and resistance.

Chapter 8 - Postcolonial Voices from Indian Descent: Works by M K Gandhi, Jhumpa Lahiri, Mahashweta Devi and Kancha Ilaiah - This chapter examines postcolonial themes in Indian literature, with particular attention to the writings of Jhumpa Lahiri, M. K. Gandhi, Kancha Ilaiah, and Mahashweta Devi. Through an analysis of stories of rebellion, resistance, and self-determination, the chapter sheds light on the intricacies of Indian postcolonial identity. It also examines how their selected works in the present study sufficiently respect the contributions of voices from marginalized and underprivileged communities and accurately depict the diversity of Indian literary traditions.

While selecting countries and regions (mostly impacted by British imperialism) and postcolonial theorists and their critical essays as seminal pieces of writings or case studies from the postcolonial literature for research and analysis in the present endeavour, it is critical to depict reasons for the focus. Here are a few methods to rationalize this decision:

Historical Significance- The British Empire was one of the largest and most powerful colonial empires in history, spanning continents and lasting several centuries. It had a tremendous impact on world history, politics, culture, and economy. Focusing on countries and examples from the British Empire allows for an examination of the various experiences of colonization, resistance, and postcolonial transformation within this broad geopolitical context.

Language and Cultural Legacy- English, the principal language of the British Empire, has evolved into a worldwide lingua franca that continues to influence international communication, literature, journalism, and academia. The cultural legacy of British colonialism, which includes institutions, legal systems, educational methods, and cultural standards, has had far-reaching consequences for nations all over the world. Exploring places and examples from the British Empire allows us to examine the long-lasting influence of the English language and culture in postcolonial circumstances.

Methodological consistency- The selection of countries and cases from the British Empire are motivated by methodological factors such as the availability of historical sources, archival records, and scholarly literature. The researcher has opted to focus on certain regions or case studies within the British Empire in order to retain methodological consistency or allow for comparative research within a shared colonial framework.

Critical frameworks and theoretical approaches- Certain critical frameworks and theoretical methods in postcolonial studies lend themselves to focusing on countries and examples from the British Empire. The researcher has used ideas of colonial discourse analysis, subaltern studies, or cultural imperialism to examine the legacy of British colonialism and its impact on postcolonial society. Justifying the use of British colonial contexts within specific theoretical frameworks helps to contextualise the study focus and analytical method.

In the study of postcolonial dynamics, the researcher has used a variety of critical frameworks and theoretical techniques to examine the intricacies of colonialism, its legacy, and its interactions with other social, cultural, and political events. Here are some critical frameworks adopted in the present book:

Postcolonial Theory- Postcolonial theory provides a critical framework for investigating the historical, social, and cultural consequences of colonialism and imperialism. This framework includes a variety of theoretical viewpoints, such as criticisms of power dynamics, representations, identity formations, and resistance movements in postcolonial contexts.

Colonial Discourse Analysis- This framework examines how colonial discourses, narratives, and representations create and perpetuate power disparities between colonizers and colonized.

Subaltern Studies- Subaltern studies originated as a critical framework within postcolonial studies, emphasizing marginalized groups' perspectives and experiences that are frequently ignored from traditional historical narratives. The researcher investigates subaltern communities' agency, resistance, questioning dominant histories and power systems.

Cultural Imperialism- Cultural Imperialism Theory investigates how dominating cultures, frequently associated with colonial powers, impose their values, norms, and cultural practices on colonized civilizations. The researcher has investigated processes of cultural assimilation, hybridity, and resistance to better understand how colonialism influences cultural identities and expressions.

Feminist Studies- Postcolonial Feminism as a theoretical framework examines the intersections of gender, race, class, and sexuality in colonial and postcolonial contexts. The researcher investigates how colonialism and imperialism generate gendered inequities, violence, and subjectivities, as well as the roles of women in resistance movements and nation-building initiatives.

Critical Race Theory- Race Theory provides a critical framework for studying the intersections of race, power, and colonialism. The researcher investigates how racial hierarchies and ideologies are established, perpetuated, and fought in colonial and postcolonial societies, as well as the long-lasting effects of racism and discrimination.

These are only a few examples of critical frameworks used in the present book. The researcher has frequently employed interdisciplinary methodologies and tailored theoretical frameworks to specific historical, geographical, and cultural situations, highlighting the significance of contextual specificity and intersectional analysis in understanding postcolonial processes.

Chapter 1

Key Concepts in Postcolonial Theory

Postcolonial theory is an interdisciplinary field of study that originated in the late twentieth century that focuses on the cultural, political, economic, and social consequences of colonialism and imperialism. Postcolonial theory is a vibrant and diversified field that includes literature, sociology, anthropology, and cultural studies. It promotes critical thinking about power systems, opposes Eurocentric ideas, and strives to comprehend the intricacies of postcolonial civilizations. It also recognizes the ongoing battles for justice, equality, and self-determination in the aftermath of colonial histories.

Postcolonial theory spans a vast range of perspectives and approaches, and below are some significant phrases and concepts associated with it. These are important terms in postcolonial theory because they cover a broad spectrum of concepts and phenomena that are essential to comprehend the processes of imperialism, colonialism, and their aftermath. Scholars can examine and evaluate different facets of colonial and postcolonial society using the lenses that each notion offers. Analytical frameworks for understanding complicated historical and contemporary occurrences can be obtained by exploring power dynamics, cultural production, resistance movements, and identity formation. In order to promote multidisciplinary discussion ns and cooperation in the study of colonialism and its legacy, these fundamental ideas act as links between various academic viewpoints. In addition to being an academic pursuit, postcolonial theory also influences political and social activism that aims to rectify the injustices and disparities brought about by colonialism and imperialism. An awareness of ideas like hegemony, subalternity, decolonization, and resistance helps activists create tactics for liberation movements and societal transformation. Considering these fundamental ideas promotes critical thinking and introspection on issues of justice, power, identity, and representation. Through the analysis of colonial discourses, questioning prevailing narratives, and elevating underrepresented perspectives, academics and theorists support wider initiatives aimed at destroying oppressive structures and constructing fairer communities.

The continual discussion and debate among academics, activists, decision-makers, and communities impacted by colonialism and imperialism is a defining feature of postcolonial philosophy. These fundamental ideas provide a starting point for conversations regarding the legacies of the past, current issues, and prospects for the future in a postcolonial society. Global events like colonialism and imperialism have influenced nations and cultures all around the world. These fundamental ideas demonstrate the ways in which colonialism still has an impact on people today beyond national, cultural, and temporal borders by shedding light on the connections between colonial histories, transnational networks, and global power systems. Enhancing the voices and views of marginalized and subaltern groups that have historically been ignored or excluded from dominant discourses is a key component of postcolonial theory. Postcolonial scholars and activists strive for more inclusive and participatory forms of knowledge creation and social change by elevating these voices and recognizing their agency.

All things considered, these foundational ideas of postcolonial theory are essential for expanding our comprehension of colonialism, imperialism, and its aftermaths, as well as for guiding current attempts to confront persistent issues of injustice, oppression, and inequality.

1.1 Abrogation

In postcolonial studies, the process by which colonial authorities repealed or annulled pre-existing laws, practices, or rights in the colonised regions is referred to as abrogation. It's a crucial idea in postcolonial theory since it emphasises how colonial powers systematically erased indigenous systems and replaced them. In order to establish colonial dominance, abrogation was frequently used as a means to impose laws, exercise power, and destroy indigenous governing structures. This phrase is essential for understanding the power structures and enduring effects of colonialism on postcolonial nations and cultures. The British colonisation of India serves as a case study for abrogation in postcolonial studies. Numerous Indian laws, customs, and institutions were methodically repealed by the British East India Company and subsequently by the British Crown.

The Doctrine of Lapse, a doctrine instituted by Lord Dalhousie, the Governor-General of India from 1848 to 1856, is one notable example. (Keay 439-440). According to this theory, the British would invade an Indian princely state, regardless of any preexisting succession agreements or customs, if the ruler passed away without a legitimate heir. Traditional Indian methods of succession and government were directly challenged by this policy, which frequently resulted in significant discontent and resistance among Indian kings and their subjects.

Another instance is the enforcement of English as the administrative and educational language, replacing native languages and educational frameworks. Significant cultural and societal repercussions resulted from this linguistic abrogation, including the marginalisation of native knowledge systems and the elevation of Western ways of thinking.

These instances show how abrogation was a crucial tactic employed by colonial powers to establish domination, undermine indigenous knowledge and governance institutions, and maintain colonial supremacy in their colonies.

1.2 Appropriation

The act of stealing or adopting components of a colonised culture without consent, frequently for the advantage of the colonisers or dominant culture, is referred to as appropriation in postcolonial studies. Assessing the dynamics of power, identity, and cultural exchange in postcolonial contexts requires an understanding of this concept. The exploitation of indigenous cultural symbols, practices, or art forms for commercial or aesthetic ends by colonisers or dominant groups without acknowledging or honouring the cultural value or context behind them is one type of appropriation in postcolonial studies. This may result in the eradication of indigenous cultures' histories and identities as well as their objectification and devaluation. Another instance involves the usurpation of native knowledge systems or customary ecological methods for financial benefit by colonial entities or transnational enterprises, frequently without adequate recompense or acknowledgement of the originating Indigenous populations. All things considered, the study of appropriation in postcolonial studies draws attention to the nuanced ways in which power relations influence cultural exchanges and relationships, as well as the significance of decolonizing strategies that prioritise the viewpoints and voices of neglected groups.

1.3 Binarism

The tendency to view the world in terms of strict binary oppositions, such as colonizer/colonized, West/East, civilized/savage, and self/other, is known as binarism in postcolonial studies. These binary oppositions, which frequently have one term prioritized over the other and are hierarchical in nature, have been employed historically to defend social injustice, cultural imperialism, and colonial dominance. Colonial discourse, which creates the colonizer and the colonized as radically opposed categories, is fundamentally based on binarism. It is common to present the colonizer as superior, logical, and civilized and the colonized as inferior, illogical, and primitive. The colonized people and their territories are subjected to subjection and exploitation, which is justified by this dualistic logic. The Eurocentric bias of colonial ideologies, which elevate Western institutions, knowledge, and ideals as universal standards, is reflected in binarism.

Through the perspective of Lacanian psychoanalytic theory, we can comprehend how identity development in postcolonial contexts intersects with binary oppositions. The notions of the "imaginary," "symbolic," and "mirror stage," (Lacan 1-7), as well as their relevance to the formation of identity in connection to binary oppositions, were presented by French psychiatrist Jacques Lacan. Lacan states that the mirror stage occurs in initial stage of life when a baby sees his reflection in a mirror and develops an identity by identifying with this picture. This is a critical juncture in the development of the ego, or the "I," which serves as the central structuring concept of the person's identity.

Fanon explores the psychological and existential impacts of colonialism on colonized populations in his landmark book *Black Skin, White Masks* (1952), especially in connection to identity formation and racialization. He investigates the ways in which colonialism imposes binary oppositions that structure social hierarchies and mould both individual and collective consciousness, such as black/white, colonizer/colonized, and civilized/savage.

According to Fanon, colonial binarism upholds a system of racial dominance that values whiteness and denigrates blackness, causing colonized peoples to internalize emotions of inferiority and self-alienation. (Fanon, *Black Skin, White Masks* 93) He criticizes the ways that colonial discourses reduce the colonized Other to stereotypes and violent objects, pathologizing and dehumanizing them in the process.

1.4 Centre/ Margin

In postcolonial studies, the terms "centre" and "margin" describe the hierarchical connection between marginalised, usually colonised or non-Western, cultures (the margin) and dominant, frequently Western, cultures (the centre). In colonial and postcolonial contexts, this paradigm is utilised to examine power dynamics, cultural representation, and social inequality. Within colonial contexts, the colonising power has a central position, forcing its institutions, culture, and values on the colonised societies that are pushed to the periphery. Cultural erasure, political repression, economic exploitation, and epistemic violence are just a few ways by which this marginalisation perpetuates. As the "other" in comparison to the colonisers, the colonised are frequently portrayed negatively or ignored when it comes to their identities, history, and knowledge. In her book *Feminist Theory: From Margin to Centre*, American feminist Bell Hooks introduced the concept of centre and margin (Hooks 1). This book, first published in 1984, criticises the mainstream feminist discourse for failing to sufficiently address the issues and experiences of marginalised women, especially the working class, the global south, and women of colour. According to Hooks, by disregarding the interlocking oppressions that marginalised women experience, mainstream feminism—which largely represents the interests and viewpoints of white, middle-class women—perpetrates systems of domination and exclusion. She urges feminists to prioritise the perspectives and experiences of people on the periphery and asks for a paradigm shift in feminist theory and practice (Hooks 16).

1.5 Colonial Discourse

The complex network of language, rhetoric, and representation used by colonial powers to defend their rule over colonised people is known as colonial discourse. It was a complex phenomenon that could be seen in a wide range of written works, such as books, travelogues, scientific articles and political speeches. Fundamentally, the development of a sharp contrast between the colonisers and the colonised was the foundation of colonial discourse, which upheld ideas of superiority and inferiority. This "othering" of colonised people presented them as foreign, backward, and in need of the colonisers' civilising influence. Furthermore, colonial discourse frequently presented colonisation as a noble undertaking, defined by a "civilising mission" meant to advance and develop ostensibly backward cultures. This narrative justified the use of force and violence to keep power, hiding the harsh and exploitative realities of colonial authority. The creation of knowledge was strictly regulated by colonial powers, who also shaped narratives about the colonised and reinforced racist hierarchies that served as justification for their domination. Essentially, colonial speech was an instrument of power that shaped views, provided justification for oppression, and maintained inequalities that still have an impact on postcolonial cultures.

British Empire, along with other European powers like France and Spain, started to communicate with what they referred to as the "orient," or the other world. Asia, America, Australia, and Africa collectively formed the other continent of Europe. These were resource-rich, culturally diverse, knowledge-based, religious, and philosophical lands. The non-White is portrayed in the colonial discourse as an impure, primitive, and uncivilized people who require the protection, authority, and direction of the mother country, England. And so began the White man's project of greater good and absolute authoritarian dominion over the territory on Earth. The Imperial project's colonial ideology fundamentally aimed to seize control of the land, its natural riches, and human societies.

The educated West's moral obligation coexisted with a voracious greed and ambition to amass the riches of the East. In addition to natural resources, the resources that the West amassed by evicting the Aboriginal people included cultural resources. The entire discourse around the East is a reaction to the West's methodical appropriation of the East's cultural knowledge system. Every time, the East was portrayed as a swampy, dark, and hostile region inhabited by savages. Even now, stereotypes of Native Americans as superstitious, subservient, weak, enigmatic, and intellectually inferior to White people persist. Shakespeare's idea of the Western equivalent was Othello. He is a war general who is strong, black, and physically fit (Shakespeare 1.1.88-91). Additionally, because of his ties to magic, superstition, and his African American ancestry, he meets his final catastrophe. This serves as a crucial illustration of how colonial rhetoric developed over several centuries.

1.6 Counter Discourse

The term "counter-discourse" describes initiatives aimed at opposing, contesting, or undermining prevailing ideologies, power structures, and discourses. It entails the articulation of alternative viewpoints, narratives, and knowledge forms intended to challenge or subvert the dominant ideology's hegemony. Within the framework of colonialism and postcolonial studies, counter discourse denotes the tactics of resistance utilised by displaced individuals to contest and undermine colonial power structures and canonical narratives. Counter-narratives that refute colonial tropes and portray colonised people as inferior or primitive can also be a part of it.

One important distinction between imperialism and colonialism is made by Edward Said in his book *Culture and Imperialism*. He observes that imperialism endures after colonialism ends (Said 59). He contends that while imperialism is the hegemonic controlling centre's philosophy, practice, and attitude over a far-off foreign region, it is also more than that. In this sense, it's a territorial pursuit. However, Said defines colonialism as the establishment of settlements in a colony that is distant and remote. Imperialism is, however, centred on culture.

According to Said's *Culture and Imperialism*, the act of "writing back" serves as a strategy for eroding the Empire's convincing and authoritative image (Said 150). Writing back is a kind of resistance that aims to overthrow the dominant narrative of Orientalism and recover one's control of oneself. New narratives are created by oppressed, colonial, and subject peoples and nations through a counter-discourse.

In his book, *Why I Am Not a Hindu* (2002), eminent Indian scholar, Kancha Ilaiah makes the case that heroes in Indian narratives are typically brahminical figures drawn from Sanskrit epics, but that no hero exists that truly embodies the revolutionary spirit of Indian Dalit activists like Ambedkar or Phule (Ilaiah 27–34). The narratives of the English Empire were replaced by the counter-rhetoric of the Indian nationalist movement, but it was unable to elevate the voices of the nation's underclass. The anti-colonial nationalist ideology that laid the groundwork for the modern Indian state methodically ignored the tales, narratives, resistances, and cultures of the Dalits and women. Critical theorists like Nancy Fraser and Bell Hooks were compelled to consider a subaltern counter-public (Fraser 113; Hooks 54) rather than just a counter-public as a result of the unbalanced growth of a counter-discourse.

1.7 Colonialism

Colonialism is a system of domination in which powerful countries expand their dominance over other people and territories, usually for ideological, political, and economic reasons. In order to further the interests of the colonising state, colonies are established through military conquest or settlement, political rule is imposed over colonised regions, and their resources and labour are exploited. The imposition of colonisers' cultural norms and values on colonised people, frequently at the expense of their native languages, religions, and customs, is another aspect of colonialism. The removal of

Indigenous communities, the destruction of traditional ways of life, and the maintenance of inequities are only a few of the significant and long-lasting effects of colonialism, which were justified by ideas of racial, cultural, or religious superiority.

Thus, colonialism functioned as a discourse of political, social, and cultural dominance in addition to a kind of military rule. The Western countries benefited from having sole authority over the colony's resources. The colonial empire frequently employed indentured labour up until the late 19th century. Diaspora communities, like those in Trinidad and Tobago and the rest of the Caribbean, were born as a result of the system of indentured labour (Schoultz 120-140). In order to establish and maintain their rule, the colonial masters ruthlessly pillaged the colonial territory's natural and human resources while enforcing taxes, bans, and oppressive regulations. Europe's states profited handsomely from this. They accumulated enormous amounts of wealth in the East, including troops that fought for the European countries in both World Wars. The White masters held a strong racial bias and believed the natives of the colonies to be subhuman. A prevalent and recurrent social problem across the colonies of Europe was apartheid. Asian and African nations have a long history of combating racism. In every aspect, the locals were thought to be subordinate to the colonial ruler. George Orwell writes about his experiences as a white English officer in colonial India. His account of an incident involving a raging elephant and terrified Indigenous (in "Shooting an Elephant") provides us with a phenomenological insight into the thoughts of both colonial subjects and colonial masters (Orwell 3-4).

1.8 Contrapuntal Reading

Edward Said presents the idea of "contrapuntal reading" in his 1993 book "Culture and Imperialism" as a technique for examining the relationships between cultures and power systems in postcolonial and colonial settings (Said 32-35). According to Said, juxtaposing texts and cultural artefacts to highlight their various voices, viewpoints, and tensions is known as juxtaposed reading. Said claims that writings have numerous layers of meaning that are frequently at odds with one another, reflecting the complexity of colonial and postcolonial experiences. He bases this on the musical word "contrapuntal," which refers to the interplay of distinct melodies in harmony (Said 32-33).

Said uses the idea of contrapuntal reading to analyze how various literary works—such as essays, poetry, and novels—engage with the historical legacies of colonialism and empire. He contends that literary works reflect and challenge prevailing conceptions of empire and resistance, rather than existing outside of political and historical settings.

Readers are prompted to contemplate how texts negotiate and subvert colonial discourses, as well as how they could unintentionally perpetuate colonial hierarchies and stereotypes, via Said's contrapuntal method. Readers can discover the hidden histories and suppressed narratives that contradict popular conceptions of colonialism and its aftermath by paying attention to the various voices and perspectives found in books. Said highlights the value of contrapuntal reading as a means of promoting intercultural empathy, communication, and understanding. Readers can gain a more sophisticated grasp of the various experiences and viewpoints that influence our perception of the world by delving into the complexity of colonial and postcolonial books.

1.9 Cartography

In postcolonial studies, cartography entails analysing maps and spatial representations critically in light of colonialism and its legacy. Maps have always been effective instruments used by colonial nations to establish dominance systems, defend conquests, and claim authority over new lands. Indigenous knowledge, borders, and spatial relationships were frequently altered or eliminated by colonial mapping techniques, which served to legitimise the eviction of indigenous people and to reinforce colonial hierarchies. These maps marginalised some viewpoints while elevating others, reflecting and shaping colonial ideology, geographical imaginaries, and power relations. Postcolonial critics, however, have been focusing more and more on counter-mapping efforts to reclaim indigenous lands and knowledges, as well as to challenge dominant spatial representations. Counter-mapping aims to undermine colonial borders and boundaries and advance spatial justice by producing substitute maps that put the viewpoints and experiences of marginalised people front and centre (Peluso 387-390). Additionally, postcolonial studies use cartography to draw attention to the spatial injustices—such as unequal resource distribution and environmental degradation—caused by colonial and neocolonial regimes. Postcolonial researchers aim to question colonial legacies, promote decolonization, and imagine more equitable spatial futures by examining the power relations ingrained in mapping techniques.

Colonial maps of Africa were used by European colonial rulers to defend their political and economic hegemony over the continent. In order to create room for European colonisation and economic interests, indigenous peoples were driven from their original territories and resource-rich regions were designated for extraction. Modern critics and researchers are responding to these colonial mappings with counter-mapping projects that seek to reclaim indigenous spatial knowledges and identities as well as to subvert prevailing depictions of Africa. Through the production of substitute maps that mirror the varied viewpoints and encounters of African Americans, these counter-mapping endeavours aim to dismantle colonialism in cartography and advance spatial justice in the modern period (McKittrick 987–991).

1.10 Cultural Diversity/ Cultural difference

Cultural diversity, often known as cultural difference, refers to the coexistence of multiple ethnic groups, traditions, and practices within a specific society or community. It goes beyond merely acknowledging the distinct qualities, views, and contributions that various cultural institutions provide to the social fabric. Language, customs, beliefs, values, rituals, and ways of life are all examples of diversity. Multiculturalism and cultural pluralism are essential components of cultural diversity, emphasizing equal acknowledgement and respect for the identities of all cultural groups. Cultural relativism is a guiding philosophy that advocates for understanding and evaluating cultural activities in their own context rather than through the lens of one's own cultural norms. Cultural diversity encourages contacts and exchanges across civilizations, which leads to greater mutual understanding, tolerance, and appreciation. In a globalized world where cultural exchanges are more common, respecting cultural differences is critical for establishing a more inclusive and tolerant society. However, concerns like cultural misunderstandings and discrimination may occur, demanding continuing efforts to address these issues and maintain a truly peaceful multicultural society.

In postcolonial studies, cultural variety includes tensions, disputes, and conflicts resulting from colonial legacies of domination, marginalisation, and resistance, in addition to the coexistence of multiple cultural identities and traditions. Theorists of postcolonialism examine the ways in which colonialism imposed cultural hierarchies, giving some norms and values more weight than others. They investigate how diversity in culture turns into a contestation space where privileged and underprivileged voices fight for acceptance, visibility, and authority. Furthermore, the concept of cultural diversity in postcolonial studies is a reflection of the process of cultural hybridity, which is the process by which colonial exchanges and encounters give rise to new forms of cultural expression that challenge fixed concepts of identity and blur traditional boundaries (Bhabha 34–39). Postcolonial researchers study how cultural variety is produced when aspects of one culture are combined, altered, and transformed from other cultures, resulting in identities that are fluid and dynamic and resist simple classification.

The complexity and diversity of cultural identities and expressions within postcolonial contexts are generally highlighted by the study of cultural diversity in postcolonial studies. A world shaped by colonial history and ongoing processes of globalisation and decolonization, it encourages critical thought on the legacy of colonialism, the dynamics of power and representation, and the potential for cultural resilience, innovation, and resistance.

1.11 Decolonization

Decolonization is a complex process that aims to promote social, political, and cultural liberation as well as the destruction of colonial systems of dominance and indigenous sovereignty. Decolonization, which sprang from the struggles of colonised peoples against centuries of exploitation and oppression, aims to correct past wrongs, restore sovereignty, and promote self-determination in postcolonial states. The restoration of indigenous land rights, the overthrow of colonial institutions and legal frameworks, and the advancement of indigenous languages, cultures, and knowledge systems are just a few of the political, economic, and cultural endeavours that are part of this process. In order to fully achieve decolonization, it is also necessary to confront the legacy of colonialism, which includes social injustices, systematic inequalities, and cultural erasure. Additionally, inclusive and egalitarian societies that embrace the diversity of cultural identities and experiences must be built.

In his renowned article "Decolonizing the Indian Mind," (1992) post-colonial historian Namvar Singh declares that the process of decolonization is the most significant development in world history during the 20th century. He claims that although the century may not have ended, the imperial powers' rule over India had unquestionably ended (Singh 145-147). Post-colonial countries, including those in South East Asia, Africa, and Latin America, now hold a prominent role in the discussion of world literature, which was previously heavily Eurocentric in terms of structure and content (Singh 148-151). It is important to keep in mind that the colonized nations did not conquer their colonial overlords and win independence. Instead, independence was granted to them. Thus, opposition to the imperial project—which persisted in many ways even after colonialism ended—remains necessary. As Namvar Singh notes in his essay, Indian writers are opposed to colonialism, but they have ingrained in their minds the idea that one can only return to the East after travelling to the West. This poses the biggest threat to the process of decolonizing the Indian mind (Singh 150). Travelling to the West shouldn't be the first step toward developing a fully realized Indian identity. The declaration of one's identity as an independent, autonomous being as opposed to an ideological object of the colonial hegemon is known as decolonization. Decolonization does not entail a total rejection of Western culture since it would be dangerous to break away from Western customs in the idea of forging a unique third-world identity.

1.12 Diaspora

In postcolonial studies, the term "diaspora" refers to the dispersal or scattering of a specific population from their original homeland to numerous regions around the world. This dispersion is frequently unintentional and stems from historical events such as colonization, slavery, forced migration, or political upheavals. The concept of diaspora is important in postcolonial studies because it illustrates the multifaceted legacies of colonialism and empire. People's movements, whether forced or voluntarily, have far-reaching cultural, social, and political repercussions for the modern world. Diaspora populations frequently preserve strong ties to their home countries while also adjusting to the customs of their new surroundings. Understanding diasporic identities requires a continual process of cultural negotiation and hybridity.

Diaspora communities transcend national boundaries, preserving links to numerous countries and cultures. This transnational component questions traditional concepts of belonging and citizenship while emphasizing the interconnectivity of global societies. Diaspora is frequently characterized by trauma and loss, including the dissolution of familial and communal relationships, as well as the erasure or marginalization of cultural history. Memory is critical for keeping and passing along displacement and resistance experiences across generations. Many postcolonial writers, artists, and thinkers use diaspora themes in their work, drawing on personal and collective displacement experiences to challenge dominant narratives and envisage new kinds of belonging and community.

Stuart Hall is a well-known critic who has written extensively about the idea of diaspora in postcolonial studies. Hall was a prominent person in the field of cultural studies and a cultural theorist of Jamaican descent. The way that we interpret identity, representation, and cultural politics has been greatly impacted by his work. The intricacies of diasporic identity development are examined by Hall in his 1990 essay "Cultural Identity and Diaspora," which was included in the Jonathan Rutherford-edited anthology "Identity: Community, Culture, Difference." He contends that the diaspora is a fluid and contingent process influenced by historical, cultural, and political variables rather than a permanent or essentialist notion. Hall highlights the significance of hybridity and displacement in diasporic experiences, emphasizing how people and groups navigate various identities across national and cultural boundaries (Hall 235-238). In addition, he talks about the value of cultural customs, nostalgia, and remembrance in maintaining ties to one's native country and fending off the homogenizing effects of globalization.

Hall argues against essentialist ideas of nationalism and identity through his analysis and in favour of a more complex view of the diaspora as a locus of resistance and cultural production (Hall 237-240). His writings have had a significant influence on postcolonial theory and have stimulated more investigation into the complicated issues of migration, identity, and cultural politics in a globalizing society.

1.13 Displacement

The term "displacement" in postcolonial studies describes the forced or voluntary migration of individuals from their own country to other areas, frequently as a result of political unrest, economic exploitation, colonialism, or imperialism. Since it draws attention to the rifts and disruptions brought about by colonial operations as well as their long-lasting impacts on people as individuals, as groups, and as societies, displacement is a major issue in postcolonial discourse. In postcolonial studies, displacement is positioned within the larger historical framework of colonialism and its aftermath. Indigenous people were frequently driven from their original territories by colonizers using techniques such as forced migration, slavery, land confiscation, and resettlement schemes. The purpose of these displacements was to extract labour, resources, and territory for the conquerors, making them essential to the colonial endeavour. Significant losses are associated with displacement, such as the loss of one's native country, cultural heritage, ties to one's community, and sense of identity. In particular, forced relocation can cause trauma, dislocation, and psychological suffering in those impacted both personally and collectively. In addition to examining the psychological and emotional aspects of displacement, postcolonial scholars also look at how it affects memory and identity across generations. Displacement frequently leads to the creation of diasporic communities that exhibit syncretism and cultural hybridity. People carry their cultural customs, languages, beliefs, and practices with them as they migrate to new places. These elements may combine with those of other groups to create new cultural forms and identities (Hall 236-238). Postcolonial theorists investigate the ways in which diasporic communities explore their multiple identities and relations within international contexts.

Even in the face of extreme hardship, people and communities frequently show resiliency, inventiveness, and agency in adjusting to their new situation and standing up for their rights and dignity. In addition to their contributions to movements for social justice, decolonization, and liberation, displaced communities' actions of resistance, solidarity, and cultural rebirth are highlighted by postcolonial studies. Significant issues about the politics of voice and representation are brought up by displacement. Postcolonial researchers argue for more complex and compassionate representations of displaced populations that acknowledge their agency, complexity, and humanity in favour of mainstream narratives that paint them as helpless victims or exotic Others.

Homi K. Bhabha is a well-known critic who has examined displacement in postcolonial studies in great detail. Bhabha examines the idea of cultural hybridity and the consequences of colonialism on subjectivity and identity in his seminal work *The Location of Culture* (1994). He looks at how experiences of displacement challenge established ideas of identity and lead to the emergence of fresh approaches to cultural negotiation and expression (Bhabha 172-176). In postcolonial studies, Bhabha's writings have had a significant impact on discussions of cultural representation, colonial discourse, and identity politics. His observations on displacement shed light on the continual negotiations of power and difference in a more globalized world, as well as the transformational impact of cross-cultural interactions.

1.14 Ethnography

Ethnography is a structural field that studies how various human groups perceive, understand, and relate to one another. There have been attempts in modern scholarship to blur the lines between subject and object within the field of study. It is seen as a post-structural perspective that places responsibility on the diversity of temporal and spatial entities that shape people as individuals, as well as their communities and the environment they live in. According to this perspective, the historicity of many individuals (subject-object, object-object, etc.) has interacted with one another and modelled their coming together at various points in time. As post-colonial institutions resist the Western approach of constructing a linear historical trajectory and drawing distinctions between uncivilized and civilized nations, ethnography is evolving into a study that is increasingly interdisciplinary. Clifford Geertz (1993) strongly suggests against establishing solitary topics of research. For example, a community's religion must involve more than just their occasional use of religious books, symbols, or rituals; it must also permeate their daily existence. He defines religion as "a system of symbols which acts to establish powerful, persuasive, and long-lasting moods and motivations..." (Greetz 90-91)

An ethnographic narrative that is constructed both within and outside of the researcher's historical identity in relation to nationality, ethnicity, gender, class, caste, and political location, as well as the exaggeration of the lives of the "natives" or former study subjects, should serve as the inspiration for the introspection. The researcher must clearly state his or her perspective on the subject and avoid using the monolithic lens or the authority figure's prominence. Dissolving researched cultures into highly reductive statistics or generic paradigms subsumes the political and cultural hierarchies that exist between the researcher and the subjects of the study, dehumanizing them in the process. It is impossible for the gaze of this ubiquitous researcher with social, political, and cultural capital to ever turn introspective or critical of itself. In their book *Travels with Ernest: Crossing the Literary/Sociological Divide*, Laurel Richardson and Ernest Lockridge present ethnographic information developed through the subjective poetics of fiction with a significant attempt at objective description (Richardson and Lockridge 3-6).

The West's imperialist approach incorporates ethnography as an episteme. It produces the other, a docile thing that submits to the Imperialist's scrutiny. The colonizer "discovering" the other and normalizing such an act, which simultaneously renders the other visible and invisible, make up the paradigm of this episteme. In the guise of predetermined generalizations, the altruistic author asserts ownership and authority over the findings of the native or indigenous people. Additionally, this author makes the assumption that the story of cultural embodiment is formed by a linear comparison of time, meaning that cultures are seen as either progressive or regressive. Arjun Appadurai refers to the vast majority of the generalizations used in Western knowledge production as "gatekeeping concepts." (Appadurai, *Theory in Anthropology* 357) The assumption made by this essentializing is that the Orient has been stuck in a specific temporality (mobility is essentially viewed as regressive), and that the colonizer is actually interfering to enable progress for the Orient. This effectively mutes the voices of diverse cultural embodiments in favour of highlighting the main concerns of a specific area.

The Western White man is transformed into the "unseen seer" (Taylor 57), whose own social, political, and cultural background is hidden from view. He makes generalizations because they make the dialectical process of meaning generation passive, which helps to solidify its own hegemony. Then, it follows that the process of interpretation or meaning-making is unavoidably political and acts as a decisive factor to guarantee the distribution of discursive power without undermining the existence of multiple discursive systems, each of which need not be understood in terms of the hegemons' symbolic codes. This is made feasible by the rise of cultural relativism in relation to anthropology, ethnography, and other related fields, which hides the academic community's collaboration with the colonial goal of creating an equal society for all people. The result of this intricacy is that Western hermeneutics is given a symbolic code that rejects a plethora of narratives and conveniently ignores any evidence of epistemic violence.

1.15 Eurocentrism

The worldview known as "Eurocentrism" places prominence on European culture, history, and viewpoints as vital to society and normative, frequently at the expense of the contributions and experiences of non-European peoples and civilizations, which are marginalised or erased. Eurocentrism, which has its roots in colonialism, imperialism, and Europe's historical domination over the rest of the world, moulds perceptions of history, knowledge, and identity in ways that uphold European civilization's superiority and sustain privilege and power structures. This viewpoint frequently takes many different forms, such as the exaltation of European languages, literature, and art in school curricula, the denigration of non-European societies in popular culture and the mainstream media, and the marginalisation of indigenous knowledges and viewpoints in scholarly discourse.

History is frequently projected by Eurocentric discourses in a straight line, starting in classical Greece and ending in the metropolises of Europe and America under Imperial Rome. It is a strategy used to downplay the repressive behaviours of the West by framing them as contingent, unique, and incidental. The Eurocentric discourse brought forms into the centre while completely ignoring the life sources on the periphery. It did this by separating forms from their performers and turning them into influences.

It is necessary to criticize Eurocentric philosophy for monopolizing all standards of strength, intelligence, and beauty by making its norms universal (Fanon, *Black Skin, White Masks* 170-172). It is a way of thinking that has historically been out of step with the multiculturalism of the world. Any romanticized view of the West starts to arrange information in ways that appeal to the Eurocentric imaginary. This portrays the non-West as a body and raw material that has not been refined, and the West as the mind and theoretical sophistication. All that exists in modern Eurocentric ideology is the discursive legacy of the colonial effort that gave European powers control over the economies, militaries, politics, and cultures of Asia, Africa, and America (Said, *Orientalism* 3-5). The twentieth century saw the end of colonial rule, although the majority of the former colonies are still in a status known as post- or neo-colonial. The colonies of the West were consistently disparaged by Eurocentric thought as inferior based on Europe's own arbitrary hierarchies and sense of worth, which prioritized brick over thatch, melody over percussion, and clothing over body ornamentation. However, the colonial lands were continents of rich and diverse culture, in spite of these problematic Western norms. They had a variety of written and oral traditions as well as intricate theological beliefs. The attribution of America's discovery to Christopher Columbus and the commemoration of Columbus Day in America, which totally delegitimizes the existence of native Indians in the area, are the most egregious examples of Eurocentrism in modern times (Deloria 35-37). A Eurocentric perspective would never address the ways in which the Spanish colonizers split and built what are now the contemporary African nations, or how they colonized America by shady biological warfare.

1.16 Fanonism

In broad terms, "fanonism" refers to the beliefs and theories of Martinique-born psychiatrist, philosopher, and revolutionary theorist Frantz Fanon. The most well-known works by Frantz Fanon (1925–1961) focus on racism, colonialism, and the psychological impacts of oppression, especially as they relate to African and Caribbean communities. A variety of philosophical, political, and social ideas are included in fanonism; these ideas are drawn from his writings.

Frantz Fanon's substantial work on anti-imperialist, postcolonial theory in reconstructing radical African politics and social critical theory is a cornerstone in modern anti-racist politics. Throughout his brief life, Fanon was emphatic about the dangers of emulating the European model of life and advancement. He appealed to his fellow black Africans residing in various regions of the world to join their muscles and minds in a new path of constructing a new society. In the ever-expanding orbit of African critical theory, Fanon's critiques of racism, misogyny, colonialism, capitalism, and humanism provide an uncanny perspective. Fanon emerges as a transdisciplinary critical social theorist whose intellectual historiographical dialectical discourse draws on a wide range of epistemic resources from the social sciences, humanities, and the struggles of the world's poor. Four of Fanon's books, *Black Skin, White Masks, A Dying Colonialism, Toward the African Revolution,* and *The Wretched of the Earth,* expound his dialectical thinking, exposing him as a critical theorist of extraordinary depth, particularly on the issues of White supremacy, Black inferiority, colonial violence, anticolonial violence, national noxiousness, racism, sexism, decolonization, and the problematic of a postcolonial African state. Fanon preached a pan-African rhetoric in which Africa was not divided into smaller identities and geographies. In his writings, he always makes a point of reminding his fellow Algerians of their African origin. His compositions were always steered by a pan-racial compass. He criticizes not just the colonialism of African people, but also the colonization of mind itself. In his book *The Wretched of the Earth* (1961), he refers to this as racialization of thought (17-19). In *Black Skins, White Masks* (1952), Fanon creates a socio-political existential phenomenology of race, while in *A Dying Colonialism* (1959), he examines the hijab in relation to women's decolonization and freedom (35-39). Fanon's Marxist writings offer us a reconsideration of capitalism, demonstrating how capitalism prevents the masses from reaching their full potential and condemns them to a life of exploitation and alienation, while the bourgeoisie who own and control the means and masses of production live a life of luxury and leisure at the expense of the exploitation of the working class. Marx's working class was made destitute and subjected to the violence and vampirism of racial colonization. Fanon's compositions are challenging to categorize into a single genre. He oscillated practically schizophrenic between poetry and science, medical terminology and neologisms, facts and fiction (Fanon, *The Wretched of the Earth* 200-201). The resulting compositions resemble a textual collage worthy of African American visual artists and collagists.

1.17 Globalization

Globalisation is a complicated and multidimensional phenomenon that has a significant impact on the modern world and offers opportunities as well as problems for people, societies, and countries in the twenty-first century. Globalization is an economic system that combines regional and local economies into a worldwide network of free marketplaces where people from various cultural backgrounds interact. In the past, the advancement of contemporary communication and transportation channels has led to globalization. The ability to ease the global export of goods and commodities on a wide scale was made possible by the declining cost of transportation. The end of the colonial regime also meant that trading with any nation-state was now permitted. With the emergence of a globalized society, establishing economic links has grown increasingly independent of political control.

Globalization is an important term in postcolonial studies because it provides a lens through which scholars may examine the continued consequences of colonialism and imperialism in modern global environments. Globalization is thought to perpetuate colonial-era processes of resource extraction, worker exploitation, and income inequity. Postcolonial scholars see globalization as the continuation of colonial economic exploitation and cultural dominance. They investigate how colonialism paved the way for global capitalist systems and unequal power dynamics between the Global North and the Global South. Globalization raises questions regarding cultural homogeneity and hybridity in postcolonial environments. Scholars investigate how global media, consumerism, and Western cultural standards influence local identities and activities, raising concerns about cultural imperialism. At the same time, they investigate how local cultures resist and adapt to global influences, resulting in novel kinds of hybridity and cultural expressions. Globalization has resulted in greater transnational movement and the establishment of diasporic communities all over the world. Postcolonial scholars examine the experiences of migrants and diasporas, delving into themes of identity, belonging, and cultural exchange in a globalized society. They investigate how colonial legacies interact with modern migration patterns, influencing the social, economic, and political conditions of diasporic societies. Postcolonial studies investigate how global capitalism and neoliberal economic policies perpetuate disparities within and between postcolonial societies. Globalization has exacerbated environmental degradation and ecological injustice in postcolonial environments. Postcolonial researchers look at how colonialism and globalization interact with issues like deforestation, pollution, and climate change, which disproportionately affect vulnerable people in the Global South. They promote environmental justice and investigate indigenous knowledge systems and sustainable practices as alternatives to harmful forms of globalization. Digital technologies and the quick movement of information across national borders help to accelerate globalization. Postcolonial researchers investigate the effects of digital globalization on access to knowledge, cultural representation, and political mobilization in postcolonial nations. They look at digital divides, censorship, surveillance, and the potential for digital activism to challenge hegemonic power structures. Globalization is an important topic in postcolonial studies, illustrating the interdependence of colonial legacies, modern power dynamics, and struggles for social justice in an increasingly globalized world (Ashcroft et al., *The Postcolonial Reader* 468-472). It emphasizes the need to understand globalization's intricacies within the historical framework of colonialism and imperialism, as well as the continued relevance of postcolonial ideas in constructing alternative futures.

1.18 Hegemony

The term "hegemony" describes the supremacy or authority of one nation or social group over another, which is frequently attained by means of political, military, economic, or ideological methods. Control over subordinate groups or states is established and maintained through the use of force and influence. Hegemony can take many different forms. Coercive hegemony is the assertion of authority by compulsion or force. Cultural hegemony is the acceptance of the dominant group's rules, values, and ideas as universal or superior. Hegemonic nations can establish their interests and hold onto their position of dominance by employing tactics including diplomacy, economic sanctions, propaganda, and military involvement (Luke 15-20).

Antonio Gramsci was the most well-known theorist of hegemony. According to him, mass indoctrination and the ceaseless creation of false consciousness are methods used by the ruling class in society to gain the active agreement of the subjugated class. Hegemony is based on both material and immaterial factors. Gramsci adhered to conventional Marxism insofar as he considered society's economic structure to be paramount. Hegemony can be defined as the manifestation of moral and intellectual leadership at the level of culture and politics as a result of an economic compromise in the basic relations of production (Gramsci 18-20). Gramsci stated in *Prison Notebooks* that hegemony and dominance are two ways in which a class or social group's superiority is shown (Gramsci 12-13). Hegemony is the rule by consent, whereas dominance can be viewed as the rule by force. Rather than developing using overt force, modern bourgeois societies typically rely on hegemony and the rule of consent to maintain control. Without materialization to justify it, no ideology can serve as a coordinator of specific interests between the subordinate group and the ruling class. Although it can help establish hegemony, ideological stupor is not very useful in preserving it. Consent organization has a really solid foundation. Hegemony must be both politically and ethically viable as well as economically viable.

If ideological dominance lacks a substantial material foundation, it will always be a distorted version of hegemony. Any hegemonic rule's objective foundation is provided by the growth of material forces of production. In addition to establishing its hegemony, the hegemon must make every effort to maintain, expand, and enhance it. It must always make every effort necessary to replicate the existing hegemony. Since the political and ideological superstructures do not necessarily reflect the economic structure, they must also be arranged to be consistent with economic compromise at the base for such a continuous reproduction to occur in any hegemonic system (Gramsci 21-23). It is necessary to arrange the superstructures in a way that allows for the formation of favourable conditions conducive to a compromise between classes. The achievement of economic, ideological, and political hegemony by the fundamental class is necessary for the hegemonic system to fully materialize. Another Marxist scholar who expanded on Gramsci's idea of hegemony was Louis Althusser.

In order to preserve its position of power over the subservient social majority, the dominant group in society exploited the framework of state apparatuses that Althusser supplied. According to Althusser, the Ideological State Apparatus and the Repressive State Apparatus are the two main state apparatuses used by the hegemonic state to hold onto power (Althusser 127-128). The superstructure's institutions, including the media, the family, the church, and the school, make up the ideological state apparatus. The hegemonic order maintains its conceptual domination over the subservient group by means of these mechanisms. Repressive institutions can be found within the Repressive State Apparatus. The hegemonic system uses both the RSA and ISA to create, uphold, and extend its power.

1.19 Heritage

In postcolonial studies, the term "heritage" refers to a complex view of the cultural, historical, and material legacies left by colonial and imperial pasts. Postcolonial studies investigate the legacies of colonialism and imperialism, including the physical vestiges, structures, and institutions left behind by colonial forces. Colonial heritage includes architectural landmarks, colonial infrastructure, and institutional frameworks that continue to influence postcolonial cultures. Scholars investigate how colonial heritage reflects power dynamics, cultural impositions, and historical injustices, as well as how it is challenged, conserved, or reinvented in postcolonial contexts. Cultural heritage refers to the traditions, practices, languages, and artistic manifestations influenced by colonial encounters and interactions. Postcolonial studies are concerned with the development of national identities and narratives, which frequently rely on colonial legacy to establish collective memories and belonging. National heritage consists of symbols, monuments, rituals, and memorial traditions that represent the values and aspirations of postcolonial nation-states. Scholars examine how national heritage is used to legitimize state power, create unity, and deal with past traumas, as well as how it may exclude or marginalize competing narratives and identities. Intangible legacy refers to the customs, traditions, oral histories, and social practices carried down through generations within communities. Postcolonial studies examine how intangible legacy reflects different cultural identities, resilience, and resistance to colonialism and globalization. Postcolonial studies emphasize the importance of legacy in resistance movements, decolonization campaigns, and cultural reclamation activities. Scholars investigate how marginalized populations reclaim and reinterpret the colonial past as a means of resistance to dominant narratives and institutions of power. They look at grassroots activities, cultural activism, and memory work aimed at opposing colonial portrayals, claiming cultural sovereignty, and advancing social justice. The concept of heritage in postcolonial studies emphasizes the dynamic interplay of past and present, memory and forgetting, continuity and change in postcolonial civilizations (Punter and During 45-50). It encourages critical inquiry on the role of tradition, memory, and identity in building narratives of belonging and envisioning alternative futures in a postcolonial world.

1.20 Home

The idea of "home" in postcolonial studies is nuanced and multidimensional, frequently capturing the dynamics of memory, identity, belonging, and power within the framework of colonial histories and their legacies. Understanding how people and communities negotiate their relationships with space, place, and belonging in the wake of colonialism requires an understanding of the concept of home. For many of the colonized peoples, colonialism meant being forcibly uprooted from their ancestral territories or having their customary ways of life disrupted. Whether due to physical relocation or cultural absorption, losing one's home has a significant emotional and psychological impact that shapes both individual and societal identities.

Home frequently arouses sentiments of nostalgia and yearning for a bygone or idealized era. Postcolonial artists and authors usually deal with nostalgia and remembrance, utilizing the home as a symbol of cultural survival and defiance against the erasure of indigenous knowledge and customs. The experiences of diaspora and transnationalism, in which people and communities maintain ties to many locations across geographic and cultural barriers, challenge the idea of home. The creative rethinking of home through cultural practices and associations, along with a sense of "homelessness" or "rootlessness," are common characteristics of diasporic identities. Home is not always associated with a specific place on Earth; it can also arise through processes of creolization and cultural hybridity.

The dynamic and fluid character of home, which is constantly negotiated and reinvented through interactions between many cultures and traditions, is highlighted by postcolonial theorists. Because it reflects fights for recognition, rights, and sovereignty, the concept of home is fundamentally political. Postcolonial studies focus on concerns of land rights, displacement, and the marginalization of indigenous peoples as they investigate how discourses of home and belonging are created and disputed within colonial and postcolonial contexts. A home can also be an idealized, made-up place that symbolizes ideas of belonging, solidarity, and community. Alternative home scenarios that subvert prevailing narratives of colonialism and globalization and present ideas of emancipation and social justice are frequently envisioned in postcolonial literature and art.

Edward Said is a well-known critic who has written extensively about the idea of home in postcolonial studies. Within the framework of colonialism and the diaspora, Said addresses the themes of exile, displacement, and belonging in his seminal book *Reflections on Exile and Other Essays* (2000). He explores the nuanced relationship between identity and home, contending that exile both creates opportunities for new kinds of cultural and political involvement and upends established ideas of home and belonging (Said 173-175). Said's article "Reflections on Exile" examines the lives of thinkers and creatives who live in the transitional areas between many countries and cultures. He argues that exile, whether forced or voluntary, creates a sense of alienation and displacement that influences immigrants' creative and intellectual output.

1.21 Hybridity

The term hybridity describes the combining, blending, or mixing of various aspects of culture, society, or identity to produce new forms, customs, or identities that are unique from their original roots. Different cultures, customs, languages, and practices come into touch and interact in situations of cultural contact, colonialism, migration, globalisation, or diaspora. In order to illustrate how fluid and dynamic culture and identity creation are, hybridity questions ideas of authenticity, purity, and fixed identities. Hybrid languages, cuisines, music, art, fashion, and belief systems are just a few of the ways it might appear. According to Homi K. Bhabha, postcolonialism, postmodernism, and postfeminism are more than just opposing or sequentially moving forward from one thing to another. The intermingling of cultural symbols and customs between the colonizer and the colonized groups within a civilization is referred to as the hybridization process (Bhabha 38-41). This interbreeding of cultural practices has both revolutionary and counterrevolutionary effects. The concept of hybridity clarifies that neither culture of colonized or colonizer—says anything steady, unchangeable, and static. Cultural exchanges occur regularly as a result of borrowing and lending. It is this merging of disparate, often diametrically opposed cultures that gives rise to a novel possibility, the repercussions and implications of which are still unknown. The idea of hybridity has to do with navigating liminal zones in a hierarchical society (Bhabha 44-47). It searches for diaspora, liminal, in-between, anachronous, and dynamic situations.

1.22 Imperialism

The idea of imperialism is the extension of a country's authority over a foreign colony by force of arms or by seizing control of the colony's politics and economy. The Latin word imperium, which meaning highest power, is where the phrase originates (Lenin 1-3). The 19th century saw the emergence of imperialism in its modern sense, referring to the practices and ideologies of Great Britain. Any system of hegemony and subordination employed within an imperial core and a margin can be roughly defined as imperialism, according to Edward Said (Said, *Culture and Imperialism* 11-12). Although the terms imperialism and colonialism are frequently used interchangeably, but as per theorists and researchers, such practice is incorrect. While colonialism suggests some degree of physical separation between the colony and the imperial hegemons, imperialism functioned from a centre through state policy.

The goal of colonialism and imperialism is to systematically oppress the Other. The act of a powerful nation assuming direct control over a colony is known as colonialism. Colonialism is the process of a dominant nation taking physical control of a colony. The goal of imperialism was to establish an empire. The policies of the British Empire over the last two centuries of its colonial domination can frequently be summed up as the fundamental principles of imperialism. Generally, the justification for imperial rule came from a colonial discourse that focused on the imperialist's perception of various foreign locations. It should be underlined, nevertheless, that imagined geographies draw attention to the shortcomings of the imperial conception of the foreign other.

1.23 Mimicry

The discourse of mimicry is constructed around ambivalence. Mimicry needs to continuously produce its slippages, its excesses, its differences and its subversions in order to be effective. Mimicry can be understood in terms of representation of difference which in itself is a process of disavowal. It is a sign of a double articulation which takes the shape of a complex strategy of reform, regulation and discipline. There is an appropriation of the other which takes place in order to visualize power by the subordinate group. Mimicry has devastating effects on the colonial discourse of hegemonic domination. It poses an imminent threat to both normalized knowledge and disciplinary power structures. In his book, *The Location of Culture*, critical thinker Homi K. Bhabha claims that the spread of improper objects is necessary for colonial appropriation to succeed since it guarantees the strategic failure of the practice. Therefore, mimicry is both a threat and a mere similarity (Bhabha, *The Location of Culture* 91-95). The metonymy axis is used to rearticulate how identity and meaning are represented in imitation. Metonymy frequently manifests as the unrepressed development of contradicting ideas. Mimicry is an act of disguise rather than seamlessly merging with the surroundings. It does more than just undermine egotistical authorial cravings by constantly making mistakes and pointing out discrepancies (Bhabha 92-95). Simultaneously, imitation is the colonial process of fixing itself as a kind of discriminatory, cross-classifying knowledge.

Thus, it brings up the extremely important subject of authorial colonial representations. Bhabha strongly draws on the Lacanian idea of imitation as a form of concealment while developing his theory of mimicry and ambivalence (Bhabha 85-88). The need for a transformed, identifiable other as a topic of difference is known as colonial mimicry. The entire body of English-language postcolonial diaspora literature primarily relies on ideas of ambivalence and imitation, in which the other person becomes nearly but never exactly the same as the self. One of the most elusive and successful methods of colonial power and knowledge is the colonizer's production of a mimetic representation, continuing to be the serpent in the grass with a forked tongue (Bhabha 89-91).

Mimicry highlights the discrepancy between the European Enlightenment's standards of knowledge and its warped colonial imitation. Another way to view mimicry is as a way to elude authority and challenge the colonial master's power. It is also the anti-colonial civility's weapon. This style of resistance is subversive, covert, and cunning rather than overtly political. By encouraging the logic of improper appropriation, mimicry starts the process of anti-colonial self-differentiation. In essence, the colonial dweller blurs the distinction between the ruled and the ruling when he imitates his colonial overlords. It is a condition of ambiguity and ambivalence that undermines the currents of imperial discourse (Bhabha 92-94), making it impossible to separate the radicalized core of either the colonizer or the colonized.

1.24 Miscegenation

The term "miscegenation" describes the interbreeding of various human races through kinship and marriage. Marital alliances and sexual relationships between individuals of various races were illegal up until the late 20th century. Anti-miscegenation laws were in place in several countries, like the United States of America, as late as 2000 in the state of Alabama. The racist phenomenon known as anti-miscegenation views racial mixing as contaminating and corrupting. A new culture is created through miscegenation, which also upends the rigidity of societal norms and ideals.

Miscegenation, in the opinion of B.R. Ambedkar, was the only way to abolish India's four-caste system of social inequality (Ambedkar 30-35). Even today, many ideologists in the West consider marriage between a man of black descent and a white woman to be sacrilegious. Fundamentally, resisting miscegenation is a prejudiced act that elevates one race above another. A sexual relationship between the two races could lead to the dominant race's capital and power being diluted. From ancient times, miscegenation has been frowned upon in both the East and the West. The well-known drama *Othello* by William Shakespeare illustrates how society disapproved of a marriage between an Italian Desdemona and a Blackmoor (Shakespeare 1-5).

Critics of Marxist Feminism contend that the purpose of marriage as a social institution was to unite property and capital (Engels 58-62). This implied that since the woman would carry on the family line, her chastity was crucial. The ghost of anti-miscegenation legislation continues to loom large in modern society, dictating much of the interpretation of kinship and social interactions.

1.25 Nation/Nationalism

A nation is a group of people's collective identity, generally defined by a shared history, culture, language, or geography. Its members feel a sense of solidarity and connection that transcends conventional geopolitical bounds. Nationalism, as an ideology, emphasizes individuals' commitment to their nation, fosters pride in common identity, and frequently seeks to maintain and enhance distinctive national features. This can take many forms, ranging from cultural expressions and patriotism to political movements promoting self-determination. The notion includes national emblems, geographical sovereignty, and a shared national culture. When taken to extremes, nationalism's impact can range from supporting social cohesion to leading to exclusionary practices and conflicts. Nations, as social constructs, unite people together under a common roof that includes shared historical experiences, cultural traditions, and a sense of purpose. The construction of symbolic representations, such as flags and anthems that serve as visual and auditory expressions of collective identity is frequently associated with the concept of a nation. Furthermore, territorial sovereignty is important in tying the nation to a specific geographic region.

As an ideology, nationalism can take many forms, including civic, ethnic, or cultural nationalism. Civic nationalism emphasizes shared ideas and beliefs, whereas ethnic nationalism is based on shared lineage or heritage. Cultural nationalism considers shared cultural components to be the foundation of national identity. The influence of nationalism, on the other hand, is complicated. While it can be a unifying force and a source of pride, it can also lead to exclusionary practices and the development of an "us versus them" mentality. Extreme nationalism has historically been linked to disputes and tensions between various nations or ethnic groups. The challenges of nationalism in a globalized environment include striking a balance between fostering a healthy national identity and welcoming diversity within a nation (Held and Moore 75-80). Striking this equilibrium is critical for developing inclusive societies that recognize and value the diversity brought about by cultural, ethnic, and linguistic variances. The dynamic interplay of nation and nationalism continues to be a prominent subject in the ongoing debate about identity, belonging, and the changing structure of modern society (Anderson 141-145).

The nation of England, for example, is descended from the previous Saxon, Anglo-Saxon, and Norman societies. Like India, another nation-state, its identity comes from an earlier "Hindu" society, referred to by some historians as the "sanatan dharama." Consequently, the development of a national consciousness, or what is sometimes referred to as nationalism, depends heavily on memory and history. Numerous academics have contended that discrimination against national memory and the historical roots of the nation's modern identities is based on the background information provided by the historian and their perspective. Oral and written traditions of stories, myths, epic literature, dramas, dance, music, etc. are typically used to transmit the understanding of a unique national past. These elements collectively contribute to the understanding of the present that distinguishes each nation. Any comprehension of the past that contributes to the current reality is referred to as having a temporal depth (Gellner 48). In these ideas, a nation can be regarded as a social relation characterized by collective self-consciousness.

As a result, in the case of India, which was made up of diverse, heterogeneous communities in constant change, was rebuilt as a Hindu nation. The upper caste privileged Hindu bourgeoisie class established a lexicon of resistance against their colonial rulers, but India's diverse ethics were weakened by the violence of inclusion into the dominant narrative. The rich cultural heritage was consistently left out of nationalist historiography. A systematic exclusion of the rich cultural traditions of the marginalized communities and social groupings was a feature of nationalist historiography. Reformers and political activists like B.R. Ambedkar (Ambedkar 141-147) and Rabindranath Tagore (Tagore 87-92) delivered harsh critiques of the Indian nationalist narrative. They charged that the national movement had disregarded the opinions and worries of marginalized communities, including women and the Dalit population.

1.26 Nativism

Nativism, as an ideology, emphasizes the interests and rights of native inhabitants of a particular region or country over those of immigrants. Nativism is typically associated with lobbying for immigration limits because it stems from a desire to safeguard and preserve the cultural, social, and economic qualities of an established population considered indigenous to a region.

Basically, nativism opposes the imposition of Western standards and ideals by defending the worth and legitimacy of indigenous cultures and ways of knowing. Indigenous identities, languages, and customs that were frequently suppressed or disparaged during the colonial era are sought to be reclaimed and celebrated. Nativism is strongly related to ideas like cultural hybridity, authenticity, and opposition to cultural imperialism in postcolonial theory. It emphasises the need to decolonize not only political and economic structures but also cultural and epistemological systems, and it frequently intersects with other critical frameworks like decolonial theory and indigenous studies. Nativist movements can manifest themselves in a variety of ways, ranging from academic research and creative expression to political activity and attempts at cultural renewal (Smith 98-102). They promote a more inclusive and pluralistic vision of culture and knowledge creation, challenging prevailing narratives of progress and development that frequently ignore or denigrate indigenous ways of living. But it's important to understand that nativism is not a static ideology and may be challenged and discussed in postcolonial discourse, just like any other ideological position. Some who oppose nativism contend that it romanticises and essentializes indigenous cultures while ignoring their own internal complexity and the ways in which they interact with and adjust to outside influences.

Nativism can take the shape of political movements or be integrated into the agendas of political parties, pushing for stricter immigration restrictions, tighter border controls, and the preservation of the nation's identity. However, nativism is a divisive philosophy that has been condemned for its tendency to foment bigotry, xenophobia, and exclusionary policies against marginalized groups. The continuous debate over nativism emphasizes its importance in arguments about immigration, national identity, and the challenges of sustaining social cohesion in varied cultures.

1.27 Neo-colonialism

Neo-colonialism, a term made popular by postcolonial theorists like Kwame Nkrumah (Nkrumah ix-xi) and Frantz Fanon (Fanon, *The Wretched of the Earth* 27-29), refers to a modern form of colonial dominance that uses economic, political, and cultural influence rather than direct military occupation to maintain control over former colonies or economically weaker nations. Neo colonial connections frequently prolong patterns of dependency and inequality as former colonial powers or powerful international corporations maintain their dominance and take advantage of resources, markets, and labour in developing nations. Practices like debt bondage, unfair economic ties, meddling in internal politics, and imposing Western cultural norms and ideals can all be examples of how this manifests itself. The global South continues to be marginalised and underdeveloped, while the global North benefits disproportionately from the power and privilege structures that are maintained by neo-colonialism. It emphasises how the lasting effects of colonialism are still observed today and how continual battles for economic fairness, cultural autonomy, and self-determination are necessary in a world where power dynamics are uneven.

The novel *Half of a Yellow Sun* by Chimamanda Ngozi Adichie delves into the intricacies of postcolonial Nigeria and the aftermath of British colonial governance (Adichie 10-12). It is set against the backdrop of the Nigerian Civil War, often known as the Biafran War. It explores issues of identity, ethnicity, and the political and social fallout from African colonialism and neo-colonialism. Similar to this, Aravind Adiga's modern Indian novel *The White Tiger* tells the tale of Balram Halwai, a driver from a small town who grows up to become a prosperous businessman in Bangalore. Adiga examines issues of class conflict, corruption, and the neocolonial exploitation of India's poor classes by the nation's elite and foreign companies via Balram's voyage (Adiga 59-63).

1.28 Other/other

The phrase "other" can be used in a variety of settings, and its meaning is frequently dependent on the context in which it is used. In general, "other" refers to anything or someone that is distinct or distinct from what has been addressed or considered. It is used to emphasize a difference or an alternative. The concept of the "other" (Said, *Orientalism* 1-3) might be especially important in the context of identity and social interactions. It is frequently used to characterize individuals or groups thought to be distinct from oneself or one's own social or cultural standard. The process of "othering" might entail the creation of an external identity that is perceived as divergent, if not inferior.

In order to understand the other, it is important to first pay our attention to the concept of the self. Enlightenment in Europe brought with it the conceptualization of the human subject as self. The individual is the least divisible fraction of the society. It cannot be broken down further due to the singular consciousness of its being. Descartes conceptualized the cogito (Descartes 16-21), which creates the human subject in terms of the self and the other. There always needs to be another to identify the self. The other stands in a binary opposition with the identity and characteristics of the self. The state of difference between a person's social identity and their self-identification is what defines otherness, or the quality of being the other. The traits that define the other are invariably different and antithetical to both the self and the symbolic order of things. Being "other" suggests that one does not adhere to social norms- a condition of political disenfranchisement brought about by the state or other social institutions. When someone is forced into a state of otherness, it pushes them out from the heart of society and puts them on the outside for being an embodiment of otherness.

It's an attempt at reductively characterizing a social group as essentially dirty and inferior. A concept of the other is necessary to support the existence of the self. It is common to interpret the other as an opposite or a foil to the "self". Since the other is only a presumptive view of the self's consciousness, it will, by definition, present challenges to the self. The unchangeable separation between the two always serves to accentuate one's sense of self while portraying the other as drastically different. The way that people perceive the world in such clear divisions highlights the traits that have characterized the dominance of caste, class, gender, and race throughout the violent history of humanity. The reason why our contemporary communities have become dysfunctional is due to the extreme stratification and entrenched nature of the self and other categories. It seems as though identities become so stagnant as to become lifeless and defunct rather than alive.

The category of the self and the other encompasses social and cultural dimensions in addition to being a phenomenological one. A great deal of European scholarship went into creating alternative histories of non-European societies. The West created the Orient as its adversary in order to construct its own image. The East came to represent all that the West was not and could never be. Edward Said, in *Orientalism,* gives a critique of the binary relation of self vs. other (Said 54-55).

1.29 Post-colonialism/Postcolonialism

Postcolonialism is a critical framework that looks at the effects of imperialism and colonialism on society, culture, and politics, both during and after the colonial era. Postcolonialism examines the power structures, injustices, and lingering effects of colonial dominance and mainly arose from the experiences of formerly colonised cultures in Africa, Asia, the Caribbean, and Latin America. It aims to undermine Eurocentric narratives, confront oppressive systems, and give voice and perspective to those who are marginalised. Identity, nationality, hybridity, diaspora, language, resistance, and other topics are all explored by postcolonial researchers, who frequently use multidisciplinary methods from fields including literature, history, anthropology, and cultural studies. Postcolonialism seeks to promote greater knowledge, fairness, and solidarity in an increasingly complicated world by examining the complexity of colonial history and their continuing influence on global systems of power. The field uses a broad range of theoretical and practical methods to improve our comprehension of the fallibility of the colonial master's previously uncontested story. Imperialism persists when colonialism ceases, according to Edward Said (Said, *Culture and Imperialism* 9-10). In terms of methodology, postcolonialism frequently shares other interdisciplinary study fields such as feminist theory, political science, sociology, anthropology, ethnography, geography, and philosophy.

The very existence and history of the imperial narrative of colonialism are complicated by post-colonial theory. Another way to conceptualize post-colonialism is an attempt to write back to the Empire, which, up until now, has served as the guardian of an alternative East/South Asian history. The concept of post-colonialism challenges the notion that the colonial master has the sole right to create and portray the image of the colonized subject. Thus, post-colonial discourse is a potent act of subversion and resistance, a reassertion of self-identity through dialogue with authority. For the psyche of the colonized subject, resistance to the colonial hegemons is therapeutic. It gives the oppressed natives their dignity back. In the realm of post-colonial theory, Dalit literature served as a forum for challenging the upper caste's centuries-long oppression of India's untouchable lower castes, ushering in a new paradigm of discourse. Anti-colonial discourse in India, which was fundamentally a nationalist drive to establish India's identity as a new nation-state has been reconfigured by Dalit works from the past century which have reshaped the postcolonial theoretical framework by utilizing the same intellectual tool to undermine the caste-based discrimination and hierarchies of the 'chaturvarna' system in modern Indian society (Dangle 1-15).

1.30 Post-colonial Reading

Postcolonial reading is an analytical framework that dives into the literary and cultural creations that emerge following colonial control. This method investigates how literature engages with the complicated themes of power, identity, and representation in postcolonial nations, rooted in a critical response to the ongoing legacy of colonialism. Postcolonial readings examine colonial legacies, questioning their impact on modern social, political, and cultural landscapes. The investigation of how colonial and marginalized communities are depicted in literature is central to this viewpoint, with a strong emphasis on deconstructing stereotypes and contesting the formation of "otherness." Postcolonial scholars highlight the fluidity and complexity of identity, frequently delving into ideas such as hybridity to better explain cultural blending and the formation of new identities that defy basic categorization. Furthermore, postcolonial readings emphasize acts of resistance and magnify subaltern voices, acknowledging literature as a powerful tool for articulating agency and alternative narratives. Language is also important, with postcolonial studies looking at how writers use, undermine, or reclaim colonial languages to establish cultural autonomy. Postcolonial readings, in the contemporary context, broaden their investigation to include the effects of globalization, diaspora, and migration on identity and culture, providing a comprehensive lens through which to critically engage with literature and culture and fostering a deeper understanding of the complexities of postcolonial societies.

Postcolonial reading entails being conscious of colonial discourse as well as actively resisting it. This type of reading considers the ever-changing repercussions and consequences of centuries of colonial hegemony on the minds and psyches of colonized subjects. Postcolonial reading of any work critically analyses the text's logo-centrism and ethnocentrism, its link with imperial hegemony, and the privilege that it has or lacks (Ashcroft et al., *Key Concepts in Post-Colonial Studies* 56-75). A postcolonial reading of an English text might open up new avenues for understanding the socio-political conditions that led to its creation in the context of what was fundamentally a Eurocentric imperialist discourse. Through the prism of post-colonialism, it becomes feasible to deconstruct Western dominant narratives and consolidate a language of resistance and self-assertion by the former colonial subjects.

1.31 Subaltern

A person who lives on the periphery of a certain social, political, cultural, and economic system is known as a subaltern. Spivak challenges the Foucauldian and Deleuzian conception of power locations as multiplicities that are distributed (Spivak 283-286). She emphasizes that such a conceptualization really represents the universal superimposition of the Western Subject as the centre of power on all subaltern modes, multiplied. The subaltern is never a capillary of power; instead, it is appropriated under Western language; the intellectuals are absolved of their political duty by claiming that this group has a voice of its own (Spivak 284-285). To effectively play the political function of the intellectual, one must distinguish between vertreten, or speaking on behalf of another person, and darstellen, or re-presenting what already exists.

In this sense, the intellectual's political duty is effective and encompasses more than just creation and analysis. By portraying the marginalized as having a voice of their own, the intellectual is released from political accountability and the narrow-minded romanticization of those on the margins. The dichotomy between genuine and false consciousness, as explained by Gramsci (1971), is because those on the margins lack the mental resources or "theoretical consciousness" (Gramsci 323-327) to actively challenge the status quo, their consent becomes passive and is characterized by contradictory consciousness between thought and action. Language stabilizes a system based on inequality by capturing society and its dominating parts and preventing any alternative notions with its restrictive language.

A revolution only functions on the surface, without taking control of different civic bodies, if it does not gradually pierce the intricate mechanisms of ideological engendering or overthrow the positions of cultural dominance. Such a governmental coup will only have a temporary effect, and the marginalized people will always be hostile to their displacement. While the working class is at the base of the social structure and is unable to integrate their concerns into a structurally cohesive framework to be raised for a cultural and political change, revolutions are typically led by the upper and middle classes in order to further their own interests. The animosity and violence disperse and have no clear destination. A "reversal of hegemony," (Budd 62), which exposes the exploitative forces functioning beneath the surface of a structure, becomes crucial for a successful revolution to occur. Rather than hypothetical or the war of movement, which is a fleeting confrontation and combat of political overthrow, Gramsci advocates for an "organic" (Gramsci 238-243) revolutionary change or the war of position, which carves out and penetrates the existing power relations and brings about a change in the social and political framework. Imperialistic discourse is a palimpsest, meaning that the Western construct has imposed multiple layers of suppressed and subordinated knowledge on top of one another. Merely exposing these stories to the public is insufficient; scholars must investigate this subalternization. Rejecting the philanthropic, Eurocentric perspective with internalized values in regard to the specific space that is causing epistemic violence is just as important as stopping marginalization. Rather than establishing subalternity by epistemic violence (Spivak 282-283), Spivak supports absence as a sort of intellectual intervention to recognize the subalternity.

Subaltern studies emphasise the significance of reclaiming these communities' history and voices while focusing on their experiences, agency, and resistance. Academics contend that in order to challenge prevailing narratives that uphold injustices and inequities and to fully appreciate the complexity of colonial and postcolonial societies, one must first understand the viewpoints of the subaltern. The subaltern's viewpoints provide important insights into the dynamics of power and resistance in the global South and beyond. Rather than being a passive victim, the subaltern is a place of potential resistance and activity.

1.32 Third World

The phrase "Third World" first appeared in postcolonial contexts during the Cold War to refer to nations that did not support the Eastern communist bloc (the "Second World") or the Western capitalist bloc (the "First World"). But, the term's meaning has expanded beyond its geopolitical roots in postcolonial discourse (Young 63). It is frequently used to describe nations that were once under colonial rule by European powers, namely those in Africa, Asia, and Latin America, and that still struggle with the effects of underdevelopment, reliance, and colonialism. The idea of the Third World is used in postcolonial studies to draw attention to the continued economic, political, and cultural divide between formerly colonised countries and their former colonisers. A variety of common experiences, such as the imposition of Western cultural norms and values, exploitative colonial economies, and independence battles, define Third World countries. Postcolonial researchers study how historical legacies influence modern problems, including social inequality, poverty, corruption, and environmental degradation. Furthermore, the phrase "Third World" is frequently criticised for its tendency towards homogenization, as it unites various nations and cultures under a single heading based only on their shared history of colonialism. Numerous academics support more complex theories of postcolonial societies that consider the unique histories, environments, and developmental paths of these nations.

1.33 Transculturation

When diverse cultures interact, a complex process of cultural exchange and transformation takes place that gives rise to new cultural forms, customs, and identities. This process is known as transculturation. The term "transculturation," which was first used by the Cuban anthropologist Fernando Ortiz (Ortiz 102), emphasises the dynamic and fluid character of cultural contacts rather than the conventional ideas of cultural purity and isolation. Transculturation is the process by which components of one culture are taken up, modified, and combined with those of another to create hybrid cultural manifestations that show the interaction of several cultures. In contrast to the notion of cultural assimilation, which denotes a unilateral process in which the dominant culture absorbs the cultures of the subordinates, transculturation reflects a more reciprocal interchange in which both cultures contribute to the creation of something new. In postcolonial contexts, when diaspora, globalisation, migration, and colonialism have permitted strong cultural interactions and exchanges, transculturation is especially pertinent. In the process of creating new cultural identities and practices, it demonstrates how colonised peoples and cultures have actively engaged with, resisted, and modified colonial impositions. Transculturation also emphasises the flexibility and contingency of cultural boundaries, challenging essentialist ideas of identity. It challenges academics and professionals to investigate the nuances of cultural hybridity, negotiation, and innovation in a world where diversity and interconnection are on the rise. In general, transculturation provides an extensive framework for comprehending the intricacies of cultural interchange and transformation in our increasingly interconnected world.

Transculturation is a highly intricate process that mostly occurs at the interpersonal level, but on a macrocosmic scale, it is guided by strong political and economic pressures. Even while it's been observed that when two diverse ethnic groups initially meet, they always resort to violence, with time, their relationship transforms, and their otherwise distinct identities begin to merge and mix. However, the assertions that one identity is superior to another seriously obstruct transculturation and ethno-convergence when society becomes increasingly stratified. When ethnic purity is valued so highly, transculturation is seen as a polluting practice and is strongly resisted in such discourses. The term "transculturation" refers to a process of convergence where that state of convergence of cultures is called hybridity.

1.34 Transnationalism

The notion of "transnationalism" is important in postcolonial studies because it provides a framework for understanding the intricate relationships, migrations, and exchanges that take place across national borders in colonial and postcolonial contexts. Transnationalism emphasizes the interconnection of communities, cultures, and economy across colonial and postcolonial boundaries. It recognizes how colonialism established networks of trading, migration, and communication beyond national borders, resulting in varied types of connection and dependency. Transnationalism sheds light on globalization and imperialist processes, highlighting the unequal power dynamics and money, labour, and goods movements that characterize colonial and postcolonial economies. It investigates how colonial expansion and capitalist growth established international commerce, investment, and labour migration networks, which frequently perpetuated patterns of exploitation and inequality. Transnationalism provides a paradigm for studying diasporic groups and migratory experiences in postcolonial societies. It investigates how colonialism and globalization displaced, dispersed, and resettled populations across national borders, resulting in the emergence of transnational identities, networks, and cultural practices (Morawska 21). Transnationalism acknowledges the processes of cultural hybridity and creolization that occur when multiple cultural traditions intersect and interact across colonial and postcolonial spaces. It investigates how colonial contacts result in new forms of cultural expression, language, and identity affected by a variety of influences and histories. Transnationalism emphasizes the significance of transnational networks and alliances in resistance movements and social justice struggles during colonial and postcolonial periods. Transnationalism influences the study of postcolonial literature, art, and cultural production by emphasizing the circulation, reception, and interpretation of texts and artworks in a variety of geographical and cultural contexts. It investigates how postcolonial writers, artists, and intellectuals use transnational spaces and engage worldwide audiences to explore colonialism, identity, and power. Transnationalism encourages people to build ethical and political convictions that transcend national boundaries. It highlights the connection of local and worldwide efforts for justice, democracy, and sustainability, as well as the role of solidarity in tackling global crises. Overall, transnationalism is an important topic in postcolonial studies because it challenges nationalist paradigms and provides alternative perspectives on the intricacies of colonial and postcolonial experiences in an increasingly interconnected global context.

1.35 Universalism/Universality

Within the postcolonial framework, universalism or universality denotes the belief that specific concepts, principles, or standards are universally relevant to individuals from diverse cultural, historical, or geographic backgrounds. However the concept of universality is frequently questioned and challenged by postcolonial scholars, especially when it is applied to enforce Western-centric viewpoints or to defend colonial dominance and cultural imperialism.

The historical use of universalism as a tactic of colonialism, in which European powers imposed their own institutions and ideals as universally superior while demeaning and marginalising indigenous cultures and knowledge systems, is one of the main criticisms made by postcolonial thinkers. The elimination of many cultural practices and the imposition of Western norms under the pretence of cultural imperialism frequently resulted from this process. Furthermore, postcolonial scholars contend that the concept of universality may be intrinsically Eurocentric, favouring Western worldviews and epistemologies at the expense of non-Western viewpoints.

This Eurocentric universalism reinforces power structures and sustains disparities between the global North and South by ignoring the diversity of human experiences and methods of knowing. Postcolonial theorists respond by arguing for a more inclusive and pluralistic interpretation of universality that acknowledges the legitimacy of various cultural viewpoints and values. By highlighting the value of communication, reciprocity, and respect amongst other cultural groups, they subvert hegemonic narratives and promote a more just and equitable international system. Chinua Achebe condemns the practice of universalism in the West as it is a synonym for European parochialism in his essay, "Colonialist Criticism" (Achebe 116).

Chapter 2

Postcolonial Theory: An Introduction

Postcolonial theory is an academic framework that evolved in the latter half of the twentieth century, especially in response to colonial and imperial experiences. It provides a critical perspective through which scholars can evaluate and interpret colonial legacies, power dynamics between colonizers and colonized, and the ongoing effects of colonization on society, cultures, and individuals.

Postcolonial theory's theoretical foundations include:

1. **Critique of Colonial Discourse**: Postcolonial theory investigates colonial narratives, representations, and ideologies critically. It opposes Eurocentric attitudes that frequently portray conquered civilizations as inferior, foreign, or in need of civilization.

2. **Power and Resistance**: Postcolonial theorists investigate the complicated power dynamics that exist between colonizers and colonized. They investigate how dominance regimes were founded and perpetuated, as well as how opposition and agency arose in colonized civilizations.

3. **Hybridity and Cultural Identity**: Postcolonial theory emphasizes hybridity, recognizing the merging and alteration of cultures during the colonial encounter. It investigates how, in the context of colonialism, cultural identities are established, contested, and modified.

4. **Subaltern Studies**: This branch of postcolonial theory focuses on the subaltern's voices and experiences, referring to marginalized and oppressed communities that were frequently left out of dominant historical narratives. Scholars investigate subaltern groups' agency and resistance.

5. **Decolonization**: Postcolonial theory examines the process of decolonization, examining how former colonies won independence and the difficulties they faced in establishing new nations. It also looks at the neo-colonial mechanisms that remained in place after nominal independence.

Hence, postcolonial theory offers a theoretical framework for critically assessing the historical, cultural, and political implications of colonialism and imperialism, with an emphasis on power relations, cultural identities, and resistance. Colonialism was upheld and perpetuated through the power of language in addition to physical force. Poetry, novels, travelogues, memoirs, and other forms of discourse- all played a significant part in maintaining colonialism by establishing a kind of world order in which the superiority of the colonial and the inferiority of the colonized subjects were presented as the true and natural order, and any deviation from this was considered to be abnormal. The goal of "colonizing the mind" was achieved through the strategic application of particular modes of representation and modes of perception in connection with a variety of knowledge systems and disciplines, including biology, anthropology, literature, philology, philosophy, and history (Ngũgĩ, *Decolonizing the Mind* 36-60). As described in the words of C.L. Innes in the book *The Cambridge Introduction to Postcolonial Literatures in English* (2007) about the shared fate of colonies: "To a greater or lesser degree, all these territories shared a history of cultural colonialism, including the imposition of the English language, and British educational, political and religious institutions, as well as economic relationships and systems." (Innes vii)

In his book *Orientalism* (1978), Edward W. Said addressed this issue in great detail and made an effort to formalize this research field as postcolonial studies. Postcolonial studies have reinvented itself in the context of "world literatures," (Berman & North 30-60) transnationalism and globalization in the last fifteen years or so. In the 1950s and 1960s, the works of Frantz Fanon and Albert Memmi were revolutionary rhetoric. Though saturated with socialist dreams for oppressed peoples' psyche, their discourse was resoundingly localized—Fanon's Algeria and Memmi's Tunisia—and was principally concerned with the battle for independence (Fanon 45-78; Memmi 30-35). Postcolonial studies evolved in confluence with European poststructuralism (particularly Michel Foucault's work on discourse formations) and the critique of imperialism (Foucault 45-85) by the time of Edward Said's *Orientalism* and the early writings of Homi K Bhabha and Gayatri Chakravorty Spivak (Said 1-10; Bhabha 40-45; Spivak 271-274).

Although seminal critical writings from the 1980s and 1990s do not entirely form the basis of postcolonial theory, this decade was crucial to the growth and establishment of postcolonial theory as an academic discipline. This was the most crucial time for a number of reasons. Interest in colonial and postcolonial studies increased in the 1980s and 1990s as a result of worldwide events like independence movements, decolonization campaigns, and changes in geopolitical power. Re-evaluating colonial legacies and developing new frameworks to comprehend postcolonial realities were prompted by the end of official colonial control in many regions of the world.

There were a number of significant academics and intellectuals that came into being during this time that helped shape postcolonial theory. Postcolonial thinking owes its fundamental notions and methods to the ground-breaking works of individuals like Edward Said, Frantz Fanon, Homi K Bhabha, Gayatri Chakravorty Spivak, and Stuart Hall. Literary studies, cultural studies, anthropology, sociology, and political science were among the academic fields that witnessed critical interventions in the 1980s and 1990s. In order to understand how colonialism and imperialism impacted knowledge production, power dynamics, and cultural representations, critics started to question Eurocentric viewpoints. Postcolonial theory gave rise to extensive interdisciplinary discourse when it intersected with other theoretical frameworks like feminism, Marxism, poststructuralism, and racism.

The dynamics of cultural hybridity, transnationalism, and diaspora have been studied by academics as a result of the late 20th century's surge in globalization and greater cultural exchange. Understanding the interdependence of global processes and the long-lasting impacts of colonialism on modern nations was made possible by postcolonial theory. Even though postcolonial theoretical framework originated in the 1980s and 1990s, it is still changing and adapting to new situations and challenges in the twenty-first century. In order to address the complexities of our linked world, modern postcolonial researchers include new views, approaches, and areas of investigation while building on prior findings.

2.1 Postcolonial Theory- Relevance

For various reasons, postcolonial theory is immensely relevant:

Examining Power Structures critically:

Postcolonial theory provides a framework for critically assessing historical and contemporary power dynamics. It motivates academics and activists to question and oppose structural inequalities and marginalization.

Understanding Cultural Diversity:

In a globalized society where cultures constantly interact, the emphasis on cultural hybridity in postcolonial theory aids in comprehending the intricacies of identity creation and cultural interaction beyond simplistic and essentialist approaches.

Giving Voice to Marginalized Perspectives

Postcolonial theory elevates the voices of individuals who have historically been marginalized, offering a platform for subaltern ideas. This broad perspective adds to a more complete understanding of history, society, and culture.

Reconsidering Historical Narratives

Postcolonial theory fosters a re-evaluation of history by dismantling colonial narratives. It questions Eurocentric assumptions and emphasizes the agency of colonized people, providing a more complex picture of the past.

Addressing Persistent Injustices

The theory focuses light on the ongoing economic, social, and cultural inequities caused by colonial legacies. This knowledge is critical for resolving challenges such as neo-colonialism, racism, and resource exploitation in postcolonial nations.

Interdisciplinary Insight

Postcolonial theory is interdisciplinary, drawing on literature, sociology, anthropology, political science, and cultural studies. This multifaceted approach allows for a thorough assessment of colonial and postcolonial challenges.

Global Importance

Postcolonial theory provides insights into the intricacies of global interactions, international power structures, and societal interconnection in a world moulded by globalization, where the effects of colonialism continue to echo.

Representation and Cultural Production

Postcolonial theory helps to understand literature, art, film, and other forms of cultural output. It aids in understanding how these forms both reflect and resist colonial legacies. In postcolonial societies, issues such as economic, neo-colonialism, racism, and resource exploitation must be addressed.

Promotion of Social Justice Movements

Postcolonial theory motivates social justice movements and activism. It lays the groundwork for demanding change and creating more fair societies by shedding light on historical injustices and systemic disparities.

Continued Relevance in Education

Postcolonial concepts are increasingly being included in educational curricula, encouraging a more inclusive and diverse understanding of history and literature. This contributes to the development of critical and informed generations.

Hence, the importance of postcolonial theory stems from its potential to provide critical perspectives on historical and contemporary situations, encourage inclusivity, and contribute to efforts aimed at addressing ongoing challenges associated with colonial legacies. It is still a useful tool for comprehending the complexities of our interconnected world and striving for a more just and equitable future.

2.2 "Representation and Resistance"- Edward Said

Edward Said was a Palestinian-American scholar, literary theorist, and cultural critic who was born in Jerusalem in 1935 and spent much of his childhood in Palestine before the state of Israel was established in 1948. Much of Said's writing was influenced by his experiences as an exile and his Palestinian origin. Said is best known for his seminal book *Orientalism*, which was published in 1978. In this work, he criticized Western scholars' portrayal of the East, claiming that the "Orient" had been formed as a passive, inferior "Other" in the Western imagination. He investigated how Western literature, art, and academic discourse helped to shape prejudices about the East, promoting colonialism and imperialist hegemony. Said's other important writings, in addition to *Orientalism*, are *The Question of Palestine, Culture and Imperialism*, and his memoir, "Out of Place." Edward Said's contributions to literary theory, cultural studies, and postcolonial studies are still actively researched and debated.

The term "orientalism" describes how the West views Middle Eastern culture and people. Edward Said claims that throughout the colonial era, westerners utilized the idea of orientalism to justify their colonization of Arab territories because they believed their culture to be distinctly archaic. Later on, the phrase was referred to as "Oriental Studies" in reference to the study of eastern languages and cultures. The study of Islamic civilizations during the Middle Ages in Europe was mostly regretful. His argument: "A manner of regularized writing, vision, and study, dominated by imperatives, perspectives, and ideological biases ostensibly suited to the Orient," (Said 202) is what is meant to be understood by the term "Orientalism." Thus, across the entire system of thought and research, the concept of "orient" is articulated. Britain ruled the East from the start of the 19th century to the end of World War II.

America has ruled the Orient since the Second World War and is approaching it similarly to how France and Britain formerly did. For the West, East has been a career. The idea of the "Orient" was created by the imagination of Europeans who imagined themselves as living in a romantic setting with exotic creatures, eerie memories, and amazing experiences.

Edward Said endeavours to expose the colonial rationale behind imperialism. He asserts that there is a power dynamic, dominance, and various degrees of total hegemony between the Orient and the Occident. Even in the imagination of the occident, an orient never grows. Since it only helps the occident, the orient must be rendered oriental. Orient is so orientalised.

Two concepts are frequently explored in postcolonial literature: resistance and representation. The portrayals of the Orient made in the canonical books are questioned and refuted by postcolonial writers and critics, which presents a distorted picture of the region. In postcolonial theory, Edward Said employs the term "orientalism" to argue that the concept of postcolonialism requires a dynamic between itself and its colonizers in order to be defined. He says: "The orient is an integral part of European material civilization and culture." (Said 2)

Orientalism is a developed corpus of theory and practice rather than a European imagination about the Orient. In addition, Said says, "it is not so much an expression of a particular will or intention to comprehend, as it sometimes is to control, manipulate, even to incorporate, what is a manifestly different world" (Said 21). Therefore, using the language of the empire to portray an indigenous culture is another way that colonization occurs. The resilience and tenacity of orients can be attributed to hegemony, or, more accurately, to the outcome of cultural hegemony. Even the Orient has a history and a tradition of thought, just like the west does. Consequently, it would be incorrect to claim that the Orient was merely a notion or a construct devoid of a corresponding reality in the first place. There are many nations and cultures in the east, and their lives, customs, and cultures have a raw realism that the colonists cannot deny, and it is actually more real than anything that can be stated about them in the west. In the words of Carol A. Breckenridge and Peter van der Veer: "Nationalism is thus not the answer to orientalism as implied in Said's book rather nationalism is the avatar of orientalism in the later colonial and postcolonial periods." (Breckenridge & Veer 12)

As a result, inaccurate information regarding the image of the Orient or the colonized subjects has been included in western canonical texts. (Said, *Orientalism* 50-73) Postcolonial writers have challenged the stereotype of the Orient as silent, voiceless, backward, immaterial, and exotic beings. As defined by Terry Eagleton, Fredric Jameson, and Edward Said in their book *Nationalism, Colonialism, and Literature*: "since the stereotypes are successful precisely because they have been interiorized. They are not merely impositions from the colonizer on the colonized. It is a matter of common knowledge that stereotypes are mutually generative of each other." (Eagleton et al. 2)

Consequently, the colonized or third-world countries have begun "writing back" against the racism, oppression, and imperialism perpetuated by their colonizers through their fictitious "white man's burden" and enlightenment missions. As per Bill Ashcroft et al., "In many post-colonial texts, this is achieved by means of a 'rewriting' of canonical stories. Findley extends this method of 'writing back' to the centre of the empire by rewriting the biblical story of Noah and the Great Flood." (Ashcroft et al., *The Empire Writes Back* 109). As per the study of Julie Mullaney in the book titled *Postcolonial Literatures in Context* published in 2010: "In 'writing back', postcolonial writers open up dominant narratives of colonialism, anti-colonial resistance, and post-colonial nation-building to new kinds of scrutiny and are both various and complex in their rendering of such actions." (Mullaney 41)

Edward Said believes that orientalism is not just a political subject matter or field that is passively reflected by culture, scholarship, or institutions; nor is it a large and diffuse collection of texts about the orient; rather, it perpetuates colonialism through the misrepresentation of facts. This is demonstrated in his ground-breaking text, *Orientalism*, which states that western intellect is in the service of the hegemonic culture. Therefore, *Orientalism* is a critique of western works that show the east as an exotic, inferior, other and define the orient through a stereotyped set of imagery. Additionally, the woman as an orient is portrayed as exotic, sensual, submissive, timid, and subdued. The image of the Orient is projected as a backward, lecherous, hooked-nosed, camel-riding man.

The Orientalist discourse and the inaccurate portrayal of the Orient have been methodically produced by a large number of western academics, orientalists, colonial officials, and novelists. According to Said, the foundation of orientalism is exteriority to what it describes. He says: "Orientalism is premised upon exteriority, that is, on the fact that the Orientalist, poet or scholar, makes the Orient speak…" (Said, *Orientalism* 28) For the achievement of the west's economic goals, the Middle East has been portrayed by figures ranging from Herodotus to Henry Kissinger as a dependent, powerless place for the West's economic objectives and cultural fantasies. The west's portrayal of the Middle East is based solely on fake knowledge and wisdom. The West has distorted the situation in the Middle East, and instead of doing a thorough analysis and assessment of the issue, it is based on fictitious and unfounded assumptions rather than empathy. Orientalism is, therefore, in Said's words, "a western style for dominating, restructuring, and having authority over the Orient, which is self-convincing." (Said, *Orientalism* 12) This is founded on the idea carried forward by Foucault, who held that knowledge and power are intertwined and that the quest for knowledge is inextricably linked to the use of power. In the words of Bill Ashcroft et al., "Edward Said's proposal of orientalism as the discourse which constituted the Orient in the consciousness of the west offers an influential analysis of how the world was constructed in the European mind." (Ashcroft et al., *The Empire Writes Back* 165)

As a result, orientalism pushes aside the orient and emphasizes the west over the orient. Orientalism is a continuation of colonization, using the Orient as a stand-in for Western civilisation. It projects that the east is primitive and the west is advanced. China or Japan in the Far East are also oriented toward the developed America. Orientalism is pervasive and can be found in a wider range of academic fields as well as arts and sciences. The most blatant example is how Middle Eastern and Islamic ideas are portrayed by Americans.

Said claims that the romantic idea of the Orient and the reality of the East are in conflict because of the West. Racism and bigotry are always there while looking at the Orients. They are portrayed inadequately by the West since they don't know about their culture or history. The west has tried to fill the gap by attempting to build a false history, and culture for them. As a result, the Europeans split the world in two, calling it the west and the east. This is how their imperialism was justified and benefited by the creation of this border. These dichotomies were employed by Europeans to define themselves. A few specific characteristics set the occident apart from the orient, and since the two regions did not share these characteristics, an artificial divide between the civilized and uncivilized worlds was formed. The Europeans saw themselves as the superior race, tasked with bringing civilization to the primitives, or the "white man's burden" (Kipling 250-252). They claimed that although it was their obligation to advance civilization, the issue arose when the occident/Westerners began to stereotype and essentialise the Easterners/ Orients. They began to misrepresent the East in literature and scientific studies by using false images. Even today, there are still stereotypes attached to Orientals, such as the idea that Islam is the religion of terrorists and that Arabs are primitive.

2.3 "Thinking Otherwise: A Brief Intellectual History" (from Postcolonial Theory: An Introduction) – Leela Gandhi

Leela Gandhi is a prolific writer and critic in postcolonial studies. Additionally, she has placed postcolonialism within broader philosophical and intellectual discourse. She has delivered lectures at Melbourne's Trobe University. She has also confirmed that feminism, postmodernism, Marxism, and post-structuralism are closely related. She also makes contributions to the field of cultural theories through her work, *Postcolonial Theory*. Her evaluation of the contributions of numerous theorists, including Mahatma Gandhi, Homi K. Bhabha, and Edward Said, rekindles the discussion of ties of postcolonialism to early thinkers like Franz Fanon. Her book *Postcolonial Theory: An Introduction* stands out due to its particular focus on material, cultural, and historical settings. Her postcolonial theory is predicated on the idea of understanding cultural differences without resorting to violence.

"Postcolonialism can be seen as a theoretical resistance to the mystifying amnesia of the colonial aftermath," (Gandhi 4), the author notes in her work. Colonialism can be defined as the historical fact and pervasive aspect of world history that involves the cultural distortion and subjugation of colonized territory. By the end of the nineteenth century, European colonies had nearly taken control of the entire region of the world. Leela Gandhi's book is structured into two sections: the first section describes the philosophical and academic foundation of postcolonialism, and the second section explores and expands on the subject topics that postcolonialists are interested in.

The relationships between postcolonialism, Marxism, post-structuralism, and postmodernism are discussed in the first section of her book. The first section, which explores the strong connections between these several fields of study, is crucial. She also looks at how postcolonialism relates to the processes of decolonization and anti-colonialism for the post-colonial establishment of sovereign states. She said that early intellectuals like Franz Fanon and Mahatma Gandhi made a significant contribution to the development of postcolonial nationalism. They had demonstrated a strong resistance to colonialism in their works. According to Terry Eagleton, Fredric Jameson, and Edward Said in their book *Nationalism, Colonialism, and Literature*: "A great deal, but by no means all, of the resistance to imperialism was conducted in the name of nationalism. Nationalism is a word that has been used in all sorts of sloppy and undifferentiated ways, but it still serves quite adequately to identify the mobilizing force that coalesced into resistance against an alien and occupying empire on the part of peoples possessing a common history, religion, and language." (Eagleton et al. 74)

Another way to conceptualize postcolonialism is as a challenge to the "mystifying amnesia" of the colonial past. A postcolonial thinker or scholar in this field of postcolonialism must examine and re-examine colonial history. Colonial images depict a close link between the colonizer and the colonized, thus one must go back in time and re-examine the history of colonialism. Additionally, she claims that postcolonial theory provides a theoretical understanding of the past since colonial archives record the versions of knowledge that people developed in reaction to their colonial encounters. In reality, it's a multifaceted endeavour that facilitates both a psychological and historical "recovery" from the "mystifying amnesia" (Gandhi 4). It is necessary to revisit the past from an impartial and detached vantage point. Since history is also written from a colonial point of view, it needs to be re-investigated in order to uncover the hidden facts that were never included in it.

Her theory offers more than just a rigorous recovery of the past; the historical details also entail a political duty to support the post-colonial subjects in filling the blanks and re-analysing via the process of self-realization and self-understanding. She claims that the initial phase of postcolonial theory is provided by *Orientalism* in her chapter "Edward Said and His Critics" (Gandhi 64). It indulges in the discursive and textual construction of colonial meanings and the consolidation of colonial hegemony rather than providing us with the contradictory state of the colonial aftermath.

She claims that the first work that makes an effort to expose imperialism's ideological masks is *Orientalism*. Said illustrates the detrimental effects of power on knowledge, demonstrating the need for intellectual and cultural endeavours to enhance the social contexts in which they are carried out. The goal of orientalism is to challenge and refute the strong paradigms of colonial hegemony. Said also challenges the colonial west's "institutionalized" and "degraded" (Gandhi 75) knowledge, which he claims, misrepresents the occident and colonized people. According to Leela Gandhi, Edward Said breaks free from the disciplinary restraints of the tradition of Orientalism and challenges the false narrative of the west. He does this by invoking the conventional understanding of Orientalism as an academic pursuit and field of knowledge, a field of specialization of the orient.

Whether what the West has said about the East is true or fictitious, it needs to be investigated and challenged. Said's initiative has been a model of resistance to the violent representations seen in colonial discourse. However, Leela Gandhi claims that there are certain restrictions in *Orientalism* by Edward Said, calling it a limited text because it does not take into account the potential for variations within Oriental discourse. In his subsequent writings, he acknowledges that the theory "fails to theorize adequately the resistance of non-European world to the material and discursive onslaught of colonization." (Gandhi 81) Overall, her contributions demonstrate the continued applicability of postcolonial theory in comprehending and resolving the effects of colonialism in the contemporary world.

2.4 "Cultural Identity and Diaspora"- Stuart Hall

Stuart Hall was born into a middle-class family in Kingston, Jamaica in 1932. He attended Oxford University after graduating from Jamaica College with an Anglocentric education. Owing to his dual residency in Jamaica and England, he rejected the notion that identity was set and instead identified as a diasporic, rejecting the idea that he was English or Jamaican. In 1964, he accepted Richard Hoggart's invitation to join the new Birmingham University Center for modern cultural studies as a research fellow. There, he established himself as a leading authority in the field through his contributions. His key thesis, which he presented in his encoding and decoding model, was that the recipient's circumstances and personal background always determined the interpretation of a communication. A number of events influenced Hall's expertise and way of thinking. When he was fourteen years old, the Jamaican government opened a government library, which he used to visit every Saturday morning. He used to see one movie a week, or occasionally more than three. Oxford University awarded him a BA and an MS, and he completed his PhD there in 1957. During that period, a number of significant political events, like the 1956 Suez Crisis, occurred. Between 1958 and 1960, Hall began working as a secondary school teacher in Southern London, where a large number of black children were enrolled. He focused on movies and media while teaching literature, film, and culture. One of the first books to seriously examine the topic of film as entertainment was his debut book, *The Popular Arts*, which was released in 1964. He took over as president of Birmingham University's Center for Contemporary Cultural Studies in 1968, and served in that capacity until its closure in 2002 as a result of restrictive management. After leaving the classroom permanently in 1997, he went on to lead the INIVA, one of the two Visual Arts foundations that aimed to support photographers from diverse origins and races.

Stuart Hall's 1990 work, "Cultural Identity and Diaspora," which is among his most frequently quoted works, explored the emergence of "third cinema" (Hall 222), a new genre of Caribbean film that portrayed Afro-Caribbean protagonists as "Black people" (Hall 224-225) in the diaspora of the west. In this essay, Hall distinguishes between two forms of cultural identity. The first is a collective identity that is stable and ongoing, shared by individuals with a common past. The second identity is that of the Caribbean, which was erratic, metaphorical, and connected to the experience of colonization. Hall employed three presences—African, European, and American—to trace Caribbean identity. The cultural identities of Europeans and Americans were repressed, Africans' cultural identity was the site of colonialism, and American culture was a new world and a clash of cultures. Hall claimed that the identity of the Caribbean was the identity of the Diaspora. Furthermore, he made it clear that identity is a product of both the past and the future. It implies that identity is shaped by history and is always changing. Therefore, how we see ourselves as active and how we represent ourselves to others determine how we will contribute to the formation of history. Identity is a continuous "production" (Hall 222) process that is always formed within the representation. Since identities do not transcend culture, history, place, or time, they are not a priori. They have a past and a place of origin. They vary according to situational, chronological, geographical, and placed power relations. The past does not just disappear; rather, our current relationships are shaped and influenced by the social constructions of the past as well as the material relationships of the past. The past is dynamic and ever-changing; it may be both freeing and crippling. Consequently, identities are, as Hall correctly points out, "the names we give to the different ways we are positioned by, and position ourselves within, the narratives of the past." (Hall 225) It is possible to fully examine the traumatic character of the 'colonial experience through cultural identity. This second identity type looks into the dynamics of power. Adopting the essentialist interpretation of "cultural identity" cuts down options for identity modification. It implies that cultural representations, such as those found in photography, painting, and film, are the creations of both old and new identities rather than only a reflection of an essentialized identity. From this perspective, contemporary Black film plays a role in creating new positionalities for people within the Black diaspora (Hall 223). While Hall acknowledges the importance of class, he questions the class's isolation from other major types of power in culture, such as those based on race, gender, and sexual orientation. Hall's strategy shouldn't be considered 'foreign' to the socialists. It is important to realize that socialists have historically prioritized class culture over the voices of racial subalterns, making cultural concerns of identity and representation crucial to their ideology. Hall's cultural studies provide us with a framework for critically analyzing historical events and people's everyday lives, which help to define culture, identity, and representational difficulties. Therefore, rather than being understood as static or fixed, these challenges should be understood as social and historically contingent.

One can comprehend the significance of cultural identity and how it unites people to work toward a similar objective by reading Hall's essay. The concept of identity is more problematic than it is evident. Identity can be viewed as a dynamic phenomenon in postcolonial contexts because it is always evolving. An individual's identity is opaque and can cause issues for a postcolonial subject. Identity is not a finished product; rather, it is a constant state of flux. Immigration has a significant impact on how immigrants define themselves. The immigrants' identities encompass both their history and future. It goes beyond simply getting over the past or finding a long-term solution to safeguard one's identity by placing oneself in the past. In a foreign country, immigrants are always viewed as "others" (Hall 231).

They struggle to assume new identities and are unable to let go of their old ones. Thus, their identities change according to place and time. Therefore, in a postcolonial setting, the process of forming an identity can be regarded as ever-growing, ever-changing, and ever-shifting away from being fixed or everlasting. In a postcolonial society, the trauma experienced by immigrants can be comprehended. He goes on to argue that understanding who we are and where we've come from is always important. The second concept of cultural identity places more emphasis on the parallels and discrepancies within a hypothetical cultural group, such as the UK, the USA, the Caribbean, and Africa's Black Triangle. These communities have comparable histories and ancestries, but their pasts have been shattered by the ongoing interactions of culture, history, and power.

Identity is, therefore, relative and not set by history. While other historical materialists place more emphasis on class and class awareness, he considers the role of culture, race, and power in this relationship. Hall contends that the essentialist definition of colonialism is insufficient to fully capture the trauma of colonial experiences; instead, the second definition—which places more emphasis on historical and social contingency—is more appropriate. Identity, according to the essentialist conception, is founded on a genuine cultural identity that individuals who have a common history and lineage share.

Within the confines of "authentic" cultural identity, this oneness is understood to be a constant, unwavering reference and meaning that reflects the general public and their shared cultural norms and historical experiences. The essentialist understanding of cultural identity is called into question by Hall because it downplays and ignores the creative and potent energy of the "hidden histories" (Hall 224) movement, which has inspired feminists, anti-racists, and anti-colonial artists and activists. Undoubtedly, national and transnational art and activism, as well as anti-colonial struggles like the Algerian revolution, have benefited much from the essentialist understanding of cultural identity.

The process of rediscovery is ultimately one of imaginary reunification. By conceptualizing and portraying Africa as the centre of the Black Triangle, photography and other visual arts like film are able to create this imaginary coherence, which lends significance and coherence to the supposed black cultural identity. These portrayals fail to take into account the actual realities of disruption and the discontinuities in the diaspora's lives. The gulf of separation brought forth by colonialism, slavery, and migration may be healed by the imagined reuniting. Similar to how western cinema portrays colonial, postcolonial, and anti-colonial experiences, these portrayals reinterpret the fractured and pathological ways. Although this essentialist approach is innovative and helps anti-colonial movements gain momentum, in the end, it is problematic. Hall talks about his personal experience as a born Jamaican who lived abroad during his adult life. As a result, identity is a dynamic phenomenon that changes constantly depending on the setting, period, culture, and history. Identity, then, is not a historically realized fact that cinema can authentically and authoritatively represent; rather, it is a continuous process of "production," which is constituted within and never outside, since we cannot accurately speak of "one experience, one identity"

(Hall 225) for very long without taking into account the historical breaks and discontinuities brought about by imperial power or enslavement. For this reason, cultural identity is so meaningful to Hall—it is both a becoming and a being. It is not merely a priori; rather, it is historical since it originates from a certain place and evolves through power relations that are situational, chronological, and spatial. Hall outlines two different cultural identities in this essay. People that have a shared past share a common identity that is stable and ever-present, known as the first identity. The second identity, linked to the experience of colonization, is the ephemeral and metaphorical Caribbean identity.

1. **Identity in a Postcolonial Context**: In actuality, identity is a more nuanced concept. In postcolonial contexts characterized by continuous movement, identity can be viewed as a dynamic phenomenon. Because identities are ill-defined, they could be troublesome for a postcolonial person. Rather than an act that has been accomplished, identity is a product that is continuously in process. Culture has a big influence on the identities of immigrants. The identities of immigrants are shaped by both the past and the future. It goes beyond simply taking back the past and doing everything it takes to protect one's identity by putting him in the past. Immigrants in a foreign land are always perceived as "outsiders."

2. **Diaspora Identity as Caribbean Identity** -The second identity, linked to the experience of colonization, is the ephemeral and metaphorical Caribbean identity. Hall traced the identity of the Caribbean using three presences: African, European, and American. Africans had their cultural identity suppressed, Europeans provided the background for imperialist activities, and Americans provided a focal point for struggle on a global and cultural level. The Caribbean identity, in Hall's opinion, was a diaspora identity. Additionally, he emphasized how identity is a result of both the past and the present. It suggests that history shapes identity and that identity evolves over time. Thus, our role in producing history depends on how we perceive ourselves as active and how we regard ourselves in relation to others.

3. **Interplay of Power Relations and Identity** -Identity is a dynamic "creation" process that is never established outside of representation, but rather within it. Identities are not a priori since they do not transcend culture, history, time, or place. They are originated and have historical roots. Situational, temporal, placed, and spatial power relations all affect how

they evolve. Social illusions and material relations from the past affect and influence our relationships now; the past is not something that has simply vanished. It can be empowering since it is dynamic and changes.

4. **Imaginary Reunification**- Through imagined reunification, identity gaps and separations caused by migration, slavery, and colonialism may be bridged. These portrayals rethink the broken and diseased manner in which colonial, postcolonial, and anti-colonial events are typically shown in western cinema. Even though this essentialist approach is novel and supports anti-colonial movements, it inevitably runs into issues. Hall shares his personal narrative. Hall is a native of Jamaica who lived elsewhere for his adult life. Identity is, therefore, a dynamic phenomenon that is always changing based on context, time, place, culture, and history.

5. **The Role of Past and Future**- Identity is not a historically accomplished fact that cinema can authentically and authoritatively represent, nor can we discuss "one experience, one identity" for very long without addressing the breaks and discontinuities in history caused by imperial power or enslavement. Rather, it is a continuous "production" process that is always formed inside. According to Hall, this explains why cultural identity is both developing and existing already. Not only are they a priori, but they are also historical because they have a beginning and change due to situational, spatial, and placed power dynamics.

2.4.1 Intersectionality of Globalization, Transnationalism, and Postcolonial Studies

The intersectionality of globalization, transnationalism, and postcolonial studies has grown in importance within the ever-changing field of academic study. A deeper knowledge of colonial legacies and resistance can be gained from the foundational texts of Postcolonial Studies, while more current perspectives and research on transnationalism and globalization provide nuanced insights into the complexity of modern global dynamics. Through initiating a discourse between these fundamental and contemporary viewpoints, we can enhance our comprehension of the interdependence of power, culture, and identity in a swiftly evolving global landscape. One of the first books to look at the cultural side of globalization is *Modernity at Large: Cultural Dimensions of Globalization*, written by Arjun Appadurai and published in 1996. In this work, Appadurai makes the case that globalization entails the exchange and alteration of cultural ideas, images, and practices on a worldwide scale in addition to the expansion of political and economic forces (Appadurai, *Modernity at Large* 33-55). He presents the idea of "scapes" to characterize various aspects of international cultural flows and distinguishes between five different scapes: mediascapes, financescapes, technoscapes, ethnoscapes, and ideoscapes.

Appadurai highlights the fluidity, contingency, and unpredictable nature of global cultural processes through his examination of these various scapes. He contends that rather than causing culture to become homogenized, globalization fosters new kinds of cultural hybridity, contestation, and inventiveness. With regard to the cultural aspects of globalization and how they interact with more general social, economic, and political changes in the modern world, *Modernity at Large* provides a sophisticated analysis by drawing praise for its creative understanding of global cultural processes but has also drawn criticism for its theoretical framework, which some academics find esoteric and challenging to apply (Appadurai 27-47). Several critics who disagree with Appadurai have indicated that in order to improve their analytical usefulness, several of his concepts—like scapes—might benefit from additional empirical study and methodological clarification. Critics have highlighted Appadurai's possible ethnocentric bias in his research, pointing out that he ignores cultural dynamics in the global North while emphasizing cultural processes in the global South. Critics contend that a thorough understanding of globalization requires a more balanced viewpoint that takes into account the power dynamics and cultural exchanges between various regions and societies.

Michael D. Kennedy's *Globalization: What's New?* (2000) addresses Ashcroft's work and critiques his understanding of globalization in the journal Cultural Anthropology. Kennedy contends that Appadurai ignores the larger structural forces and power dynamics that influence globalization processes in favour of focusing just on cultural flows (Kennedy 462-464).

Jan Nederveen Pieterse's *Globalization and Culture: Three Paradigmatic Views* (2003), which was published in the journal International Sociology, looks at several viewpoints, including Appadurai's cultural approach. Pieterse advocates for a more comprehensive approach that takes into account all aspects of global dynamics and criticizes Appadurai for downplaying the economic and political aspects of globalization (Pieterse 47-49).

According to John Tomlinson's "Globalization and Culture", a book chapter published in 1999, which discusses Appadurai's idea of mediascapes and how it relates to cultural globalization. Appadurai's emphasis on cultural deterritorialization is criticized by Tomlinson, who contends that a more complex understanding of the interactions between local and global cultural forces is necessary (Tomlinson 105–107).

"Scapes and Flows: Situating Appadurai's Anthropological Concepts in the World of Globalisation" written by M. Soysal which, provides a critical analysis of Appadurai's scapes framework and its relevance to comprehending processes of globalization. Soysal examines the shortcomings of Appadurai's methodology and offers other conceptualizations that take historical contexts and power imbalances into consideration (Soysal 287). These studies offer a variety of viewpoints on Appadurai's work, including criticisms, clarifications, and alternative readings of his theories regarding globalization and culture. They add to the continuing intellectual discussions concerning the intricacies and ramifications of global activities in the modern world.

Within the multidisciplinary domain of postcolonial studies, academics contend with the intricate interplay among colonial legacies, worldwide phenomena, and regional settings. By exploring the intersections of postcolonialism, globalization, and transnationalism, new voices have enhanced this conversation and shown the complex relationships between power, identity, and resistance in the modern world. The political theorist and philosopher Achille Mbembe of Cameroon has significantly influenced this discourse with his books *On the Postcolony* and *Critique of Black Reason*. Mbembe's research goes beyond national borders to explore the complexities of racial hierarchies, power dynamics, and colonial legacies in postcolonial cultures (Mbembe, *On the Postcolony* 13). He examines how globalization has affected African realities, emphasizing the ways in which violence, culture, and money are intertwined in the postcolonial world (Mbembe, *Critique of Black Reason* 22).

Feminist researcher Inderpal Grewal investigates the connections between globalization, transnational feminism, and cultural politics, building on Mbembe's observations. Grewal (*Transnational America* 15) explores the ways in which global processes influence political battles, migration patterns, and gendered identities in books such as *Transnational America: Feminisms, Diasporas, Neoliberalisms*. In order to confront the multifaceted issues brought out by neoliberal globalization, she highlights the necessity of transnational feminist solidarity. Rosalind C. Morris, an anthropologist, examines how media, migration, and violence connect in postcolonial contexts, drawing emphasis on the cultural aspects of globalization and transnationalism. Morris sheds light on the complexity of cultural production, representation, and resistance in a globalized world through works such as *Drawings from Underground and*

Accounts (Morris 16). Literary researcher Gaurav Desai investigates how literary texts both reflect and challenge prevailing narratives of globalization by focusing on the interconnections of literature, globalization, and cultural exchange in his work, *Subject to Colonialism* (Desai 44). He examines how literature functions as a mediator of experiences related to identity formation, displacement, and resistance in a world at large.

Collectively, these theorists and researchers encompass a wide range of viewpoints and approaches in the intersectionality of postcolonialism, globalization, and transnationalism. Through critical thought on the dynamics of globalization, the legacies of colonialism, and the potential for revolutionary transformation in the twenty-first century, their contributions improve our understanding of the complexities and ambiguities of the modern world.

2.5 "Colonialist Criticism"- Chinua Achebe

Chinua Achebe (1930-2013) was a Nigerian novelist, poet, and critic widely considered as one of Africa's most influential figures. He is best known for his novel *Things Fall Apart*, which is widely regarded as a classic in African literature and one of the most significant works of contemporary African fiction. Aside from being a novelist, Achebe was also an essayist and critic. He was a strong supporter of African literature and was instrumental in establishing the discourse surrounding African identity and postcolonial literature. Achebe's books have been translated into various languages, and he has had a significant impact on world literature, particularly African literature. Chinua Achebe garnered numerous literary awards and continues to be a very significant figure in the discussions based on postcolonial literature, identity, and the image of Africa in literature.

The essay "Colonialist Criticism" is written by Chinua Achebe with pungent criticism of how colonialism is persisting in African countries. African authors write for their fellow Africans, but the literature and artwork they create are evaluated and analysed by Europeans. All literature must pass through the European authors' grids. As they evaluate the text, they serve as the jury bench. They always give their big brother consciousness, which creates the binary. These dichotomies include European and non-European, white and black, and white and non-white. While reading the texts and literature written by African writers, Europeans always view Africans as inferiors and backward, and they have a big brother mentality. Africans need to learn from their big brothers because they are at the periphery, while Europeans are at the centre. They are always the ones who have to teach Africans and non-Europeans.

They are experts in information, art, and culture, and they even know more about African art and culture than Africans themselves do. Therefore, Achebe believes that the notion that African writers are somewhat unfinished Europeans and that somehow outsiders can know Africa better than the native writers is one of the flaws in colonial critique.

Achebe opposes this colonial prejudice, arguing that African literature should not be evaluated in the same light as canonical literature because it has unique characteristics that the canonical writers, with their limited knowledge and prejudiced views, are unable to comprehend. Black people and African-Americans should construct their own history by challenging the universality of mainstream or canonical history, which has ignored African history and presented only one viewpoint. The text's core is destroyed when it is not given the proper appraisal and assessment due to this constrained European viewpoint.

Achebe criticizes "universalism," which is really a synonym for European parochialism, in this essay. European writers have consistently highlighted the idea of universality in their works. They use this lens to evaluate an African work as well, coming to the conclusion that it is not universal since it does not address universal issues. They contend that the text is erroneous since it just represents African voices and issues, neither of which can apply to all people. Achebe responds negatively to the idea and phrase of universality, arguing that they are unable to address a universal problem. Two things bother him about universality: first, it is a euphemism for the "narrow self-serving parochialism of Europe," (Achebe, "Colonialist Criticism" 60), and second, literature should always discuss how its location has evolved out of history and culture. We cannot just silence any voice that does not align with the centre. Each text is a product of its time, place, and culture. He says: "I should like to see the word 'universal' should be banned together from discussions of African literature until such a time as people cease to use it as a synonym for the narrow, self-serving parochialism of Europe." (Achebe, "Colonialist Criticism" 60)

Each text is unique to the person and the area. Racism has affected Africans in ways that cannot be separated from their past. They can always write about their past, which is the racial past that colonial literature leaves unsaid and unexplored. Black people in mainstream literature have not been given voices. Therefore, since "universalism" does not address space-specific difficulties, it must be abandoned.

Achebe also criticizes the idea that English is not standardized to be British. When Africans write in English, they do so in an Africanized version of the language that retains elements of their culture and history rather than using the British Standard English model. Language cannot be the exclusive domain of a race, tribe, or community. It does not belong to any one race or group, thus, African writers who write in English do so to reach a global readership, not because they are unable to write in their native tongues. They would be writing in their native tongue alone, which would prevent anyone from reading and learning about their rich history and culture. Since language is a shared legacy among all people, they also hope to attract global attention.

He critiques the native writers by the end of his essay. He also says that native writers have not done enough to improve the status of African literature, and that native writers' lack of efforts prevents European writers from always being decried as being beneath them. This necessitates taking proactive action to improve their nationality and culture. Ultimately, it falls on their own people. They should strive to achieve prestigious status since, as he puts it, "seduction" will result from European dominance over them. The reason for this seduction is that African writers are providing them with avenues for seduction since they have never tried to breach the European canon; instead, they take pleasure in becoming its appendage. He says: "It is because our own critics have been somewhat hesitant in taking control of our literary criticism, the risk has fallen to others." (Achebe, "Colonialist Criticism" 61)

Therefore, it is inappropriate to condemn Third World literature on the ground of "universalism" since it is still untrustworthy for the European writers to pretend to have a complete understanding of African literature. Due to their inability to comprehend Africans' innate culture and sensibility, their assertion that whites can evaluate African literature objectively is unfounded and untrustworthy. African literature is characterized by its unique setting, literary style, and cultural ethos. The techniques used to critique African texts are predicated on universality and generality, which precludes an accurate assessment of the text. According to Emma Dawson Varughese in her book *Beyond the Postcolonial: World Englishes Literature*: "But how much is this notion of nationhood necessary for a sense of national literature? Surely what Nigeria does possess is a vehicle that ostensibly not Hausa, Igbo or Yoruba, rather it is Nigerian in that it is heard nationwide across all the ethnic labels." (Varughese 65).

It is also necessary to take into account the idea of multiple ethnicities, cultural distinctiveness, social norms, rituals, cultural practices, and the indigenous sense of identity. If not, a work's critical evaluation is nonetheless skewed and prejudiced. One of the most annoying trends in third-world literature criticism is the evaluation and criticism of African novels from a European perspective. Because it is imbued with the colonial spirit, the criticism of colonial literature by white European critics is known as colonialist criticism. The essay "Colonialist Criticism" takes aim at the residual colonialism that exists in some African literary criticism, even among non-Africans. Since the outsiders have a deeper understanding of Africans than do natives, African writers are therefore perceived as incomplete Europeans. These presumptions that Europeans are still haughty toward Africans because they know them better than the natives suggest this.

He said that the critics of colonialism truly had no idea what it meant to be universally human. In actuality, the idea of "universal" upholds their hegemonic power over other literary and cultural traditions. "Until people began to use the word universal as a synonym: the narrow, self-serving parochialism of Europe," the argument goes, "I should like to see the word banned altogether from discussions of African literature." (Achebe, "Colonialist Criticism" 60)

It is impossible to examine the uniqueness of African literature from a universal perspective that is restricted to Europeans' narrow grasp of non-European cultures and literatures. The tangible universalism found in African literature must come from a much deeper human source than what can be revealed by a narrow perspective. Therefore, Achebe wishes to underline the importance of focusing on moral earnestness and high seriousness in order to combat the accusation of outspokenness.

If we follow Achebe's career as a critic in postcolonial studies, we must recognize his 1965 essay "The Novelist as Teacher," which discusses changing the function of a novelist from that of a storyteller to that of a pedagogue. Through his books and critical essays, he hopes to educate readers about pre-colonial history and the uncharted cultural past. Furthermore, he urges his people to stop feeling bad about their history or forefathers. It is not appropriate to regard the colonial interpretation as the unchanging truth. Contrarily, as mentioned by Kofi Campbell in his *Literature and Culture in the Black Atlantic: From Pre-to Postcolonial*: "In fact, the pre-colonial itself was always hybrid too, including pre-colonial Africa…African culture at the time already was a hybrid one and not a "pure" African culture to which the present can turn for a site of equally "pure" origins." (Campbell 156). Campbell's book distinguishes itself via its sophisticated use of Caribbean-derived conceptions of hybridity and time, as well as its dual emphasis on Africa in the medieval imagination and the present Black Atlantic.

The work of a writer and a teacher are inextricably linked because, in Achebe's words, "For the moment, it is in the nature of things that we may need to counter racism with what Jean Paul Sartre has called an anti-racist racism, to announce not just that we are as good as the next man but that we are much better" (Achebe, "The Novelist as Teacher" 45). Regeneration and re-education are necessary. However, while criticising Achebe, Bill Ashcroft, Gareth Griffith, and Helen Tiffin comment in their book *The Empire Writes Back* (1989): "Achebe can write about his role as a teacher in African culture but appears to have been unable to confront his role as an interpreter/post-colonial writer." (Ashcroft et al. 79)

Even though the past has many flaws, it still needs to be taught. The lengthy night of violence that the white colonists used to justify their own actions was not representative of the past. They were thought to be enlightening the Africans on God's behalf. Achebe writes about applied art, which is different from pure art, but it doesn't matter because his main goal is to make a difference in the fields of education and art.

In an essay titled "Colonialist Criticism" (1974), published almost ten years later from "The Novelist as Teacher", he questioned the method used in literary criticism to look for universalism or universal elements in literature. Any voice that is unable to unite with the voice of the centre cannot simply be undermined. Each text is a product of its time, place, and culture. Each text is unique to the person and the location. Racism has affected Africans in ways that are inextricably linked to their past. They can always write about their past, which is the racial past that canonical literature leaves unsaid and unexplored. Black people in mainstream literature have not been given voices. Therefore, since "universalism" does not address space-specific difficulties, it must be abandoned. He gave a talk at the University of Massachusetts the next year, in 1975, with the title "An Image of Africa: Racism in Conrad's "Heart of Darkness".

He said that Conrad's portrayal of Africa was extremely racist. In order to defend colonialism, Africa was presented as the opposite of Europe and as a counterpoint to the idea of Europe as a pure, white continent. "Is it possible to call a novel that celebrates this dehumanization—which depersonalizes a segment of the human race—a great work of art?" remarks Achebe. In response, I say, "No, it cannot." (Achebe, "An Image of Africa" 21). With its straightforward criticism of a well-known novel, this talk has become a landmark in postcolonial criticism of literature.

Achebe discusses the potential for ambivalence in the postcolonial context in his essay "Colonialist Criticism." He has attacked the discriminatory mindset that a writer brings to an African work. He has questioned the idea of universality because it appears to be limited and reflects the narrow perspective of the canonical writers. Additionally, he challenges "the man of two worlds theory" (Achebe, 59-60), contending that its proponents were colonialist critics. Because of his western education, which has severed his ties to his heritage, culture, and people, he also feels that a native with an education is worse than a native living in the jungle. He concludes by stating, "Let every person bring their gifts to the great festival of the world's cultural harvest," (Achebe, "Colonialist Criticism" 61), he thinks, and humanity will benefit much from the diversity and uniqueness of the contributions.

Achebe's conflicted ideas can be seen in his criticism of colonialism and his own people simultaneously. Since he feels that he must never justify them, he attacks his people, too. While not focusing solely on Chinua Achebe, Kwame Anthony Appiah's article "Cosmopolitan Patriots" examines Achebe's perspectives on identity, nationalism, and cosmopolitanism in the context of African literature and postcolonial discourse. Appiah discusses Achebe's views on the significance of literature in developing cultural identity and encouraging understanding among disparate populations (Appiah 618). Appiah's approach adds to our knowledge of Achebe's literary and intellectual legacy within the larger contexts of globalization, nationalism, and cultural interchange. Appiah contends that cosmopolitanism and patriotism are not inherently mutually exclusive. He presents the concept of a "cosmopolitan patriot," (Appiah 619) as someone who values both their sense of global connectedness and their local identity. Cosmopolitanism, according to Appiah, does not entail letting go of cultural attachments; rather, it entails appreciating the diversity of cultures and being receptive to the world. He imagines a society of "rooted cosmopolitans" (Appiah 633), people who are connected to their particular cultures but also engaged with the larger world through travel, migration, or simply acknowledging the multiplicity of human experience. Appiah acknowledges the sentimental aspects of patriotism, such as national pride, but he contends that true patriots should also be critical of their countries' policies.

Chapter 3
History, Culture and Place: Writing Back

Postcolonial theory meticulously knits together the threads of history, culture, and place, providing a profound lens to interpret and critically appreciate the complexities of postcolonial experiences. This approach, at its foundation, engages in a rigorous re-examination of history, deconstructing Eurocentric narratives and showing the multiple facets of colonization, from overt political domination to subtle economic exploitation. As postcolonial theorists support the concept of cultural hybridity, emphasizing the adaptability and resilience of colonized cultures in the face of cultural imperialism, cultural dynamics play an important role. Spatial elements extend beyond geographical bounds to the symbolic and political, with postcolonial scholars investigating boundary imposition and indigenous land expropriation. The discourse also emphasizes subaltern voices, both individual and communal, encouraging the recognition of agency and previously neglected contributions. As postcolonial difficulties remain in current society, this paradigm acts as a catalyst for revolutionary change, encouraging critical reflection and community action toward a future free of colonial legacies.

Historical Interrogations: A fervent re-examination of history is at the heart of postcolonial thought. Colonization, formerly viewed through the eyes of conquerors, is now examined through the eyes of the colonized. The discourse aims to deconstruct Eurocentric myths, revealing the complexities of exploitation, resistance, and transformation. Postcolonial thinkers engage in a historical reckoning that challenges established power structures, from overt political oppression to the subtler nuances of economic imperialism.

Cultural Hybridity and Resilience: Cultural hybridity, as defined by Homi K Bhabha, (*The Location of Culture* 37), emphasizes the transformational character of cultural interchange between colonizers and colonized. Cultures are not static entities in the postcolonial environment but rather dynamic, shifting amalgamations that resist essentialization. This cultural resilience becomes a significant instrument for regaining identity and combating colonial erasure.

Spatial Dimensions of Power: Inspired by Edward Said's concept of the "geographical imagination" (*Orientalism* 55), postcolonial theorists examine the construction of colonial power and the portrayal of locations. In this context, place extends beyond geography to include the symbolic and political components of power. The erection of artificial borders, the encroachment on indigenous territory, and the alteration of landscapes have all become key topics of discussion. The spatial inequities inherent in colonial legacies are revealed by postcolonial theory, which argues for a re-evaluation of borders and territories.

"Writing Back"-In postcolonial theory, "writing back" refers to the act of responding to, questioning, or revising dominant narratives and representations established historically by colonial forces. It is a way for people who have been colonized or have been formerly colonized to express their voices, perspectives, and agency in the face of a past that has frequently ignored or silenced them. The concept of "writing back" emphasizes the power relations inherent in colonial history and literature, where colonists' narratives frequently impact the understanding of colonized people and cultures. Subaltern voices, or the perspectives of disadvantaged and oppressed people, are argued to be important in contributing to a more complex and accurate portrayal of historical events and cultural identities by postcolonial theorists.

Literature, painting, music, and other kinds of cultural expression can all be used to respond. It is a means of regaining agency, telling alternative narratives, and opposing the dominant Eurocentric perspectives. This process involves not just challenging existing narratives, but also creating new ones that reflect the various complicated experiences of those who have been subjected to colonial power. The act of writing back is an important component of the larger postcolonial endeavour, which seeks to decolonize not only physical areas, but also the ways in which history and culture are perceived and portrayed.

3.1 "Postcoloniality and Artifice of History"- Dipesh Chakrabarty

Dipesh Chakrabarty is regarded as one of the most prominent intellectuals in the fields of modernism, humanism, and cosmopolitanism. At the University of Chicago, Dipesh Chakrabarty holds a distinguished position of professorship. The Universities of Antwerp, Belgium, and London, UK, have awarded him numerous honorary degrees. In addition to being an Honorary Fellow of the Australian Academy of the Humanities, he is a Fellow of the American Academy of Arts and Sciences. The Princeton Press published his well-known book *Rethinking Working Class* in 1989. His writings discuss the rise of the working class in India and how it relates to the trade union movement. The Bengali historian Dipesh Chakrabarty, who specializes in postcolonial theory and subaltern studies, wrote "Postcoloniality and Artifice of History" in 1992. In 2014, he was awarded the Toynbee Prize, which honours social scientists for their noteworthy contributions to society both academically and publicly. A powerful critique of the academic field of history as a theoretical category full of power is provided by Dipesh Chakrabarty.

He says: "Insofar as the academic discourse of history, that is, 'history' as a discourse produced at the institutional side of the university is concerned, 'Europe' remains the sovereign, theoretical subject of all histories, including the ones we call 'Indian', 'Chinese', and so on. There is a peculiar way in which all these other histories tend to become variations on a master narrative that could be called 'the history of Europe'" (Chakrabarty 1). He concludes that, in the guise of history, Indian history itself is situated in a subaltern position. This indicates that postcolonial critique is an equivocal technique that strikes a balance between the successes and shortcomings of orthodox history. He critiques secular modernity and the common human experience. *Provincializing Europe: Postcolonial Thought and Historical Difference* (2000) acknowledges that Western social science falls short in elucidating South Asia's historical encounters with political modernity. While he identifies shortcomings in European thought and attempts to revitalize it "from and for the margins," (Chakrabarty 3) does not reject European philosophy in its entirety.

He advocates for the pluralization of history in the context of international political modernity because, in his opinion, there are many human histories that deserve consideration in conversation. He discusses the convergence between postcolonial theory and subaltern studies.

He says that historicism is more than just a philosophical idea or a mental classification. The technique of critically addressing just the universals—like the abstract human figure—that was developed in eighteenth-century Europe is known as postcolonial theory. He thus sees a flaw in enlightened philosophy and theory, which treat people as abstract beings. However, a key component of postcolonial theory is comprehending the multiplicity of human experiences; for example, distinct perspectives and experiences of political modernity that exist in India are different from those of Europe.

So why should we interpret everything according to historicism, which frames everything in terms of a single, global historical development? As a result, he challenges the historicists' use of chronology and the order in which events and incidents occur in European history. In order to provide a new way of thinking and an ideology, we must replace the temporality of history. According to historicism, modernity, capitalism, and civilization initially emerge in Europe before spreading around the world. This is a fairly constrained and stagnant account of progress. Dipesh Chakrabarty challenges this temporal and linear framework by offering an alternative interpretation of global political modernity through an engagement with its antinomies.

He questions the conceptual category proposed by Karl Marx. In addition, he disapproves of history's temporal entirety. He conceptualizes two histories of capital in contradiction to the Marxian universal history of capitalism: a. histories proposed by capital, which is regarded as history 1, and b. histories existing outside of capital's life process, which is regarded as history 2. While history 2 shows human experiences and compelling narratives of their belonging, history 1 is strictly analytical. He, therefore, urges research into the "politics of human diversity" (Chakrabarty 21). He claims that history 2 is changing history 1. He, therefore, seeks to integrate the history of capital with the plurality of human diversities and their multiplicity of subjective experiences. Stated differently, he provides an extremely perceptive interpretation of the human subjects tussling with the various histories of capital's life processes.

He criticizes history's status as a secular topic by pointing out how poorly postcolonial circumstances of existence are represented. According to Donna L Potts, since "the seemingly non-modern, rural, non-secular relationships and life practices" (Potts 4) continuously impact the contemporary structures of government, it is especially impossible to offer a secular history of India. As a result, Dipesh Chakrabarty creates a new framework, aiming to create a conceptual framework that considers not just the capital history but also the other histories and forms of the past. The focus of "Postcoloniality and the Artifice of History: Who Speaks for 'Indian' Pasts?" is the difficulties of writing history in the postcolonial age, especially for countries that were once colonised, such as India. In order to comprehend the past of colonised nations, Chakrabarty criticises the predominance of Western historical frameworks. It is challenging to capture the distinct realities of colonised countries since these frameworks frequently impose a Western conception of modernity and development. Postcolonial historians, he contends, are caught in a "double bind" (Chakrabarty 18). On the one hand, in order for them to be seen as authentic historians, they must interact with these Western frameworks. But by doing so, you run the risk of emulating a story that is

Eurocentric and falling short of capturing the nuanced aspects of colonialism. Chakrabarty challenges the idea of "Indian" pasts in general. He contends that the word itself is a remnant of colonialism, imposed on a heterogeneous subcontinent to create a sense of togetherness. Historians have to contend with the diversity of Indian experiences. The essay provides several methods for writing history rather than providing a single answer. These could be emphasising the stories of the underprivileged, delving into the "archive of the everyday," or admitting the historian's involvement in crafting historical narratives. Hence, Chakrabarty's essay emphasises the difficulties and nuances of writing history from a postcolonial standpoint. He challenges historians to question established paradigms and look for fresh approaches to historical representation that accurately capture the realities of formerly colonised cultures.

3.2 "Writing in Colonial Space"- Dennis Lee

Dennis Lee is a Canadian poet, children's author, and cultural activist, born in Toronto, Ontario on August 31, 1939. He is a well-known name in Canadian literature, best recognized for his contributions to poetry, particularly his exploration of social and political issues. Lee's poetry collection "Civil Elegies and Other Poems," published in 1972, brought him significant acclaim. This piece, which received the Governor General's Award for Poetry, is regarded as a watershed moment in Canadian literature. During the late 1960s and early 1970s, "Civil Elegies" comments on urban life, politics, and the shifting cultural environment of Canada.

Dennis Lee examines the predicament faced by writers who were both colonizers and colonized in his seminal essay, "Cadence, Country, and Silence: Writing in Colonial Space" (1972). They appear to be the same as those whose voices have been muted or eliminated because they are voiceless. He says: "the colonial writer does not have words of his own...the words I knew said Britain and they said America, but they did not say my home." (Lee, "Cadence, Country, and Silence: Writing in Colonial Space" 80)

Dennis Lee feels constrained by the language of the colonizer. He is an outgrowth of colonial culture. He lacks a unique voice and a language of his own. It is challenging to place an American or British narrative in a Canadian setting. Every national identity is unique. The language used in a story must be appropriate for the setting in which it is set. Before it can be applied to his own circumstances and everyday experiences, it needs to be translated. It is improper for a writer to distance himself from his culture, identity, or colonial settings. Instead of using a distant metropolis, he could use cities that represent Edmonton, Toronto, Montreal, Halifax in order to represent and relate to the Canadian experience. As a result, he can get back to writing in his own language, which still needs to be invented and should be a unique Canadian style that speaks to the experiences and lives of the original and indigenous native people of Canada.

The term "Canadian" refers to a person's aboriginal, original, indigenous ancestry. Many Canadians identify as belonging to this nation, which raises the issue of Canadian identity once more. This topic is still heavily discussed in Canadian fiction, both national and aboriginal. Dennis Lee provides a clear description of the deeper significance of this occurrence in the Canadian context when he states, "If we live in a space which is radically in question for us, that makes our barest speaking problematic to itself" (Lee, "Cadence, Country, and Silence: Writing in Colonial Space" 68). He claims that his nation has been colonized and that it is now a client state of the United States. As a result, he attempts to investigate the barriers to rhythm, which entails investigating colonial space.

He adds that the "Yankee program" is equally ingrained in Canadian media. Since American culture has influenced their culture, their children are taught in schools that Abraham Lincoln was their nation's greatest president. American popular culture is introduced into Canada. Canada suffers from a sense of inferiority despite any successes it may have in terms of creativity. His shock at the irony in the elite media stems from two things: first, the way the US administration talks about the massive war, and second, the way the Canadian media propagates false information about the Vietnam War.

He is thus asking himself how to compose anything original or how to respond to it in these situations. The subtle, painful, and fundamental nature of non-existence, the basic feelings of hunger, play, fury, celebration, and death come from these roots. These specific objects, therefore, represent who they are; a poem uses words to recreate these dynamic activities. Dennis Lee is thus under a variety of stresses in the existing colonial space. In the words of Bill Ashcroft et al., "For Lee, the exploration of this gap, its acceptance, and its installation as the legitimate subject-matter of the post-colonial, rather than a sign of failure and inauthenticity, is the crucial act of appropriation." (Ashcroft et al., *The Empire Writes Back* 62).

The 20th-century writers of Canada are examining these consequences of colonization on the aboriginal people. The enforced language of colonialism, which has become the norm, is on the verge of eradicating oral tradition, native culture, folk music, and lore. As a result, the authors feel excluded and wonder, have they lost their natural voice? What is the source of the voice? As a result, they are compelled to speak in a language that they do not understand, and that appears foreign to them, using words that are mostly meaningless to a metropolitan audience when used in a Canadian context. These are the issues faced by Rudy Wiebe and Dennis Lee, who want to document their experiences but aren't given a voice. He elaborates: "The circle is vicious; writing has become a problem to itself. To speak unreflectingly in a colony is to use words that speak only alien space; to reflect is to fall silent, discovering that your authentic space does not have words." (Lee, "Cadence, Country, and Silence: Writing in Colonial Space" 80).

The strong voice of the colonists silences their indigenous language. The dominant language of the colonists has rendered the Cree language obsolete. Everything is thus described from the perspective of the settlers. The Cree people have been completely eradicated from Canadian history and subjugated by the Royal Canadian Mounted Police's portrayal of Queen Victoria. The influence of colonialism has caused a breach in their innate past. Their history no longer has the same cultural flavour or representations. Native scribes were the first to document their oral culture since they had no other option except to record the silent laments. The sense of the collective guilt of the Canadian Writers stems from this sense of loss, which prevents them from sharing their own stories. He says: "The colonized people are full of unfocused resentment, which it directs against itself. Resentment because its citizens are unable to partake in the life of their country with dignity or self-respect- since they don't even own it; unfocused because it has been bred into them that they are innately inferior, they have somehow brought this deprivation on themselves." (Lee, "Cadence, Country, and Silence: Writing in Colonial Space" 86).

Thus, writing in a colonial space can be a form of resistance. Writers can recover their own voices and subvert the power of the colonizer's culture by experimenting with language. Lee essentially makes the case that, in a colonial setting, language serves as a battlefield in the fight for liberty and identity. Forging a road towards cultural authenticity and expressing their own experiences through linguistic subversion and decolonization is a challenge faced by writers.

3.3 "Cultural Diversity and Cultural Differences"- Homi K Bhabha

Homi K. Bhabha, a key pioneer in postcolonial studies, has made lasting contributions to cultural criticism and literary theory. Bhabha, who was born in Mumbai, India, in 1949, takes an interdisciplinary approach to literature, philosophy, and psychoanalysis. *The Location of Culture* (1994), his important work, addresses key notions that have become foundational in postcolonial discourse. Bhabha's concept of hybridity challenges essentialist interpretations of culture by emphasizing the transformational and creative potential that results from the merging of various cultural elements. The "Third Space" concept proposes a site of cultural negotiation and creation, intersecting binary notions of colonizer and colonized. Furthermore, Bhabha's study of mimicry sheds light on the various techniques used by colonized subjects to both copy and disrupt the cultural practices of the colonizer.

Theoretical and political applications of the term "diversity" are clearly limited in the aftermath of poststructuralist and postcolonial ideas and ideologies. Many poststructuralists and postcolonial intellectuals offer numerous ways to go deeper into thought than what the diversity category can accommodate. According to Deleuze, "Every diversity and every change refers to a difference, which is its sufficient reason." (Deluze, *Difference and Repetition* 240.) He also says, "Framed with the names of Achebe and Soyinka, Nigeria remains one of the most prolific and fertile difference is the means by which the given is given, the means by which the given is given as diverse." (240)

Homi K Bhabha's transition from cultural diversity to cultural distinction provides another excellent example. Bhabha emphasizes the interaction of several cultures in the postcolonial world—which is always infused with power and hegemony—by using the phrase "cultural difference". As a result, there are discrepancies since there are numerous cultures coexisting, which are made worse by concerns of race, class, gender, identity, and sexual orientation. In contrast, "cultural diversity" views various cultures as engaging and competing with one another in the public sphere. This places a strong focus on the notion of cultural relativity, advocating for cross-cultural dialogue, tolerance for cultural variety, and democratic dispute resolution.

Identity politics, through the tensions, breaks, and resistance of unequal forces, fall under the category of "difference." Bhabha emphasizes "re-thinking our perspective on the identity of culture" in the postcolonial world more in this essay. The phrase "difference/difference," which is essential to poststructuralist thought, is alluded to in the phrase "cultural difference" (Bhabha, "The Commitment to Theory" 17). He makes a clear distinction between two concepts and terms: cultural difference and cultural diversity.

Cultural diversity falls under the fields of comparative ethics, aesthetics, and ethnology and is an empirically known entity. It places a strong emphasis on collective identity, which is comprised of all cultures coexisting within the relativistic framework and the intertextuality of their historical locales. This part focuses on liberal ideas of sharing the culture of humanity or multiculturalism and cultural interaction. The act of articulating culture as informed, authoritative, and sufficient for the development of systems of cultural identification, however, is what distinguishes cultures. Signs can be misused due to the diverse formation of cultures at the significatory limits of a culture where meanings and values are read—or misunderstood. Bhabha maintains that contemporary cultural critics "all recognize that the problem of the cultural emerges only at the significatory boundaries of cultures, where means and values are (mis)read, or signs are misappropriated." (Bhabha, "Cultural Diversity and Cultural Difference" 206.)

Bhabha asserts that the relationship between "the other" and the formerly "dominant cultures" is still antagonistic. Therefore, we must "rethink" cultural identity. He says: "These ideas not only help to explain the nature of colonial struggle. They also suggest a possible critique of the positive aesthetic and political values we ascribe to the unity or totality of cultures, especially those that have known long and tyrannical histories of domination and misrecognition." (Bhabha, "Cultural Diversity and Cultural Difference" 207)

By suggesting that any group culture is an object with clearly defined boundaries and the norms and traits which are "authentic," Bhabha's concept of hybridity can be understood as an argument against the idea of western liberal multiculturalism, which actually celebrates and encourages "cultural diversity." However, cultural diversity, or the celebration of these defined boundaries in the effort of colonial resistance, can be part of the imperial project in which the culture of "others" is depicted and defined in a very exotic manner, making and strengthening the imperial project which oppresses the subalterns and their groups.

These "others" are sharing a constructed identity that is external to them and has nothing to do with them. As a result, the established framework for conceptualizing culture is constantly based on the past, ignoring the intricate web of relationships and exchanges that has existed throughout history while also taking place as a result of globalization, colonialism, and cultural domination. Thus, there is a chance that this understanding of cultures, which is defined by rigid bounds, would veer toward essentialism. According to essentialism, racial, gender, and other biological distinctions account for cultural variations. This idea of essentialism views all groups as homogenized, monolithic masses and views identities as fixed, arising from biology.

This well-intentioned multiculturalism framework ultimately reduces to an oppressive collection of racial stereotypes because it is unable to challenge the political institutions of dominance and inequality. Therefore, in a society where multiple cultures coexist, and some are granted greater privileges than others, a multicultural framework does not strive to address the inequities; rather, it attempts to ignore them. As a result, the cultures included in "multiculturalism" are seen as unique from those of white Europeans, which serves to uphold the entire system of oppression and inequality.

Bhabha contends that in order to create a truly global culture, a new definition of "hybridity" is required. This idea destroys the entire framework of cultural supremacy. However, "cultural diversity" should not be the focal point of this new notion of "hybridity," but rather "cultural difference." All cultural assertions and systems, according to him, are created in this ambiguous and contradictory realm of enunciation.

He describes this area as a "Third Space" between cultures when postcolonial individuals renegotiate their own identities outside of binary distinctions that are imposed from the outside. The mirror of representation, which reveals cultural knowledge as an integrated, open, and evolving code, is destroyed by the third space, which also challenges the fixed structure of meaning and transforms it into an ambivalent process. He says: "The pact of interpretation is never simply an act of communication between the I and the You designated in the statement. The production of meaning requires that these two places be mobilized in the passage through a Third Space…" (Bhabha, "Cultural Diversity and Cultural Differences" 208)

This intervention calls into question our conception of historical identity and culture as a unifying and homogenizing force that is validated by the past and preserved in people's national traditions. However, the Third Space questions and negotiates the notion of essentialism that already exists, generating a tension unique to borderline existences—hybrid, hyphenated existences that stress the incommensurable parts as the foundation of cultural identities. Therefore, multiculturalism is an attempt to manage the dynamic process of how cultural differences are articulated. It enforces a consensus that adheres to the cultural diversity norm. However, merely identifying the universal and normative attitude and formulating its cultural and political judgments is insufficient in and of itself, given the cultural diversity and its relationship to liberal relativism. Therefore, no culture can be more entire and complete in and of itself, not only because other cultures exist to challenge its authority but also because its own symbolic formation process minimizes alternative identities and opportunities while asserting its own organic and holistic identity. Construction of meaning occurs across the divide and barrier between the signifier and the signified.

Therefore, it is inappropriate to view the "other" as subservient. It should no longer be the case that "First World Capital" equals "Third World Labour." Identity creation ought to encompass the breadth of postcolonial nations. These identities are not always meant to correspond with the most common ideal of the West, which is the ideal identity. In the modern context, cultural variety exists in its purest and most unrestricted form, where the "commitment to theory" must be upheld. Adherence to theory has evolved into a new means of communication with the colonial world. He uses the film festival as an example, where all Indian entries are viewed as hopeless and impoverished, to make the argument that national identities had to be shaped in line with western standards.

Bhabha challenges the elitism and Eurocentrism of the dominant postcolonial debates by highlighting the false opposition between theory and politics in his essay, "The Commitment to Theory" (1994). He also claims that some critics and theorists have framed politics and theory in this way. He believes that the idea that theory is limited to the western framework and that only those with privileges in society are capable of discussing it is harmful and counterproductive. It is also asserted that academic critics write primarily from the Eurocentric archives of the imperialist or neo-colonial west. Ironically, though, Bhabha has been the most influential postcolonial theorist for much of his career, despite being accused of elitism and Eurocentrism, enjoying academic privilege, and being dependent on the ideas of European poststructuralism.

Furthermore, a lot of critics think that since Bhabha shares a lot of similarities with the discursive forms of rule over the colonized, he is actively promoting neo-colonial and neo-imperial ideologies. There is, however, no disagreement over Bhabha's promotion of a critical re-evaluation of nationalism, representation, and resistance, as well as his focus on the ideas of "hybridity" and "ambivalence," which define the "third space"- a brilliant area where cultural differences articulate and really produce imagined "constructions" of national and cultural identity.

When comparing Spivak and Bhabha, we discover that although Spivak utilizes deconstruction to re-evaluate the dichotomies of colonizer and colonized, Bhabha employs it to undermine the mythical oppositions between political theory and practice. He is in favour of the third space model, which mediates relative meanings and mutual interchange rather than dividing. He questions Western critics and theorists, claiming that their theories fail to take into account the political circumstances of the impoverished third world. Politics and theory are mutually dependent and reciprocal.

The western notion cannot merely exist as an ideology without oppressing the developing countries. His goal is to compare and contrast politics and theory in order to determine how they conflict and where they overlap. He claims that "The Third Space" is an additional method to conceptualize the liminal space, which is ambivalent and hybrid and allows for the unrestricted play of meanings that are inherent to existence. He describes this area as a "Third Space" between cultures when postcolonial individuals renegotiate their own identities outside of binary distinctions that are imposed. The mirror of representation, which reveals cultural knowledge as an integrated, open, and evolving code, is destroyed by the third space, which also challenges the fixed structure of meaning and transforms it into an ambivalent process. This intervention calls into question our conception of the historical identity of culture as a unifying, homogenizing force that is validated by the past and perpetuated in people's national traditions.

However, the third space engages with the notion of essentialism as it already exists, questions it, and produces a tension unique to borderline existences—hybrid, hyphenated existences that stress the incommensurable elements as the foundation of cultural identities.

Therefore, theoretical discourse functions as numerous cultural exercises rather than just being theoretical discourse. The third space that Bhabha provided is the outcome of re-evaluating causality logic and acknowledging the connection between political speech and social change. He places a strong emphasis on conceptualizing in terms of diversity, heterogeneity, and the coevolution of politics, ideology, people, cultures, and histories—all while maintaining a certain degree of ambivalence.

3.4 "Literary Colonialism: Books in the Third World"- Philip G Altbach

Philip G. Altbach, a well-known intellectual in higher education studies, has made significant contributions to our understanding of global higher education dynamics. Altbach, who was born in 1943, has been a key voice in the discussion of internationalization, academic mobility, and the issues that institutions face in an increasingly interconnected world. His work, which is distinguished by a comparative approach, digs into the structures and functions of higher education systems in many nations, providing significant insights into the varied methodologies used globally. Altbach has focused on the internationalization of higher education, in particular, investigating the implications of cross-border collaboration, student and scholar mobility, and the broader effects of globalization on academic institutions.

Philip G. Altbach is the director of the Comparative Education Centre at the State University of New York at Buffalo, in addition to being a professor in the department of educational organization, administration, and policy studies. In addition, he has edited the book *Frontiers in Education*, published by the SUNY Press. According to his theoretical essay "Literary Colonialism: Books in the Third World" (1975), the majority of third-world nations have little access to knowledge, including knowledge about their own nations. They hardly ever have access to information on them. This can be attributed to the fact that most publishing houses are either based in or controlled by the West. He says: "There are not enough books to meet the rapidly growing needs of the developing countries. The shortage is not a problem which can be solved simply by printing vast quantities of books, but a complex issue which involves a number of national needs, from printing technology to research support." (Altbach 485).

Since the author has conducted study in India and written several books, he affirms that there is very little autonomy in third-world nations. However, the author ends his works by advocating for an expansion of knowledge production. For a number of reasons, he thinks the developing countries have to produce their own publishing expertise and other organizations. He refers to the third world as the outside reaches of the knowledge context, suggesting that he is sympathetic to the plight of the emerging nations. He also talks about the debate between initiatives from the private sector and state publishing. He provides an unbiased analysis of this contested topic.

After seeing a fresh angle on the study of publishing and information diffusion in a global setting, he spent more than ten years looking into a range of topics, such as global copyright and technical developments in the publishing industry. It was researchers who published and disseminated knowledge that understood his critical enterprise the best.

According to his seminal essay "Literary Colonialism: Books in the Third World," rich nations control the majority of the world's knowledge dissemination networks. They also own the publishing houses that create academic publications, films, essays, and magazines. The first world countries also keep an eye on and control television shows. The worldwide intellectual system has its peripheral in third-world countries. Several concepts serve as the foundation for this type of intellectual hegemony:

1. It produces an uneven distribution of intellectual products, such as historical events, language, literacy, and economic linkages.

2. Industrialized nations gain from this type of colonialism by controlling the means of information diffusion, which also controls educational programs and systems.

3. They also act as the superior in terms of knowledge creation and transmission, which, to borrow Foucault's phrase, further consolidates their rule over the Third World because power and knowledge are inextricably linked.

4. The rate of scientific advancement, the standard of cultural life, and the advancement of a country are all closely linked to intellectual productivity and independence. The poor countries have never given these concerns any thought because they were preoccupied with more pressing matters and urgent development challenges.

5. There aren't even enough books to satisfy the developing world's expanding wants. It is not even possible to address the deficit by printing large amounts.

6. Due to a lack of technical infrastructure for large-scale book production, publications addressing the intricate demands of development and expansion do not meet national needs.

7. Some also lack native writers who can pen works in native tongues that the native populace can understand and use on issues of national importance.

8. Despite the fact that books are available, they frequently fall short of national cultural standards since private readers cannot afford them as much as institutions can.

9. Baker and Escarpit have coined the term "the third world book hunger," (*The Postcolonial Reader* 486), referring to the approximate 70 per cent global book deficit.

10. The data analysis shows that 34 industrialized nations—home to only 30% of the world's population—produce 81 per cent of the world's books; as a result, their literacy rates are significantly higher than those of third-world nations. He says: "With the strengthening of indigenous publishing and internal distribution facilities in the Third World intellectuals need not publish their work abroad." (Altbach 490)

To conclude this chapter, Dipesh Chakravarthy explores how historical narratives are produced in postcolonial settings in his essay. It reveals the ways in which colonial regimes falsified history to support their hegemony and control. This is consistent with the goal of postcolonial studies, which aims to dismantle colonial discourses and unearth competing narratives to hegemonic historical representations. Through his exploration of the intricacies of writing in colonial settings, Lee highlights the agency of writers who have been colonized in navigating their identities and using literature to challenge colonial rule. This speaks to the subversive potential of literature as a vehicle for self-expression and cultural resistance inside oppressive colonial regimes, which is emphasized in postcolonial studies. In his essay, Bhabha explores how cultural identities in postcolonial nations are hybrid, highlighting the transitional areas where cultures meet and change. By highlighting the constructive tensions and ambivalences present in colonial encounters, his concept of "third space" challenges binary conceptions of identity. This advances the investigation of cultural hybridity, mimicry, and the intricacies of identity creation in colonial and postcolonial contexts by postcolonial studies. The dominance of Western publishing firms in defining literary canons and excluding voices from the Global South is criticized in Altbach's work. He draws attention to the uneven power dynamics that support literary colonialism and obstruct the dissemination of varied stories from postcolonial areas. This is in line with the critique of knowledge production and circulation offered by postcolonial studies, which highlights the necessity of decolonizing academic and literary discourses to incorporate a range of viewpoints. In conclusion, by challenging historical narratives, investigating the agency of colonized subjects, examining cultural hybridity, and criticizing unequal power relations in knowledge production, these critical works add to the field of postcolonial studies. When taken as a whole, they provide a complex picture of postcoloniality and emphasize how crucial it is to question colonial legacies in contemporary discourse and scholarship.

Chapter 4
Body, Ethnicity, Subaltern and Language

Aspects of body, ethnicity, subaltern, and language interact within the intricate framework of postcolonial discourse to unravel the layers of influence left by colonial histories. The body is examined beyond its physiology, delving into the symbolic and cultural components that colonial ideologies have frequently sought to alter. The racialization and objectification of bodies that sustain colonial hierarchies are investigated, leading to the decolonial celebration of different bodily forms and a rejection of Eurocentric norms. Similarly, the concept of colour, which is inextricably linked to race, is dissected to reveal the colour-coded hierarchies that reinforced notions of superiority and inferiority. As they manage the complexity of identity, postcolonial viewpoints actively fight these established prejudices, recognizing the diversity of skin tones and rejecting colour-based hierarchies.

In her essay, "Can the Subaltern Speak?", Gayatri Chakravorty Spivak acknowledges the origin of the term "subaltern" as coined by Italian Marxist scholar Antonio Gramsci (Spivak 271). In her essay, Spivak discusses Gramsci's concept of the subaltern, which refers to disadvantaged and oppressed groups in society who are unable to express themselves due to hegemonic power systems. Spivak builds on Gramsci's theories and applies them to postcolonial situations, notably in respect to women in the Global South, challenging the agency and representation of subaltern subjects in dominant discourses.

Subaltern voices are amplified in postcolonial rhetoric, which recognizes them as active participants in the continuous battle for liberation and self-determination rather than passive victims. Finally, language emerges as a formidable tool in the postcolonial armoury, mirroring colonial power dynamics. The imposition of colonial languages and the marginalization of indigenous languages highlight the intrinsic linguistic hierarchy of colonialism. Postcolonial theorists advocate indigenous language reclaiming and revitalization as a form of resistance, supporting cultural resurgence and contesting the linguistic hegemony rooted in the colonial past.

Body- The postcolonial investigation of the body goes beyond its physical characteristics to include its symbolic and cultural components. The objectification and racialization of bodies were common in colonial eras, establishing hierarchies that positioned certain bodies as superior and others as inferior. Postcolonial theorists investigate how colonial ideology shaped notions of beauty, health, and normalcy, hence reinforcing Eurocentric standards. Decolonizing the body entails opposing these imposed norms, honouring varied bodily manifestations, and recognizing the resilience of bodies that have been subjected to systemic oppression.

Ethnicity- Within postcolonial studies, ethnicity is an important and complex notion that influences discussions about identity, power relations, cultural representation, and resistance. The study of postcolonial studies looks at how imperialism and colonialism influenced the way ethnic identities were created in colonized cultures. Hierarchical categories based on race, ethnicity, and culture were frequently imposed by colonial powers; these classifications still have an impact on postcolonial social structures and power dynamics. Complex interactions exist between ethnicity and other axes of identity, including race, class, gender, and nationality. By examining these intersections, postcolonial scholars are able to comprehend how many forms of privilege and oppression coexist and influence people's everyday experiences. In postcolonial studies, ethnicity is frequently examined through the prism of cultural hybridity, emphasizing how different cultural components were mixed and matched in both colonial and postcolonial communities. This viewpoint stresses how cultural identities are dynamic and malleable, challenging essentialist conceptions of ethnicity. Ethnic conflict and nationalist movements are studied in postcolonial studies in relation to postcolonial state-building and colonial legacies. In addition to current socioeconomic inequality and political marginalization, divides and injustices from the colonial era are frequently the source of ethnic hostilities. In their analysis of how ethnic groups are portrayed in literature, the media, and popular culture, postcolonial researchers show how colonial and neocolonial discourses have exoticized or marginalized particular ethnicities and reinforced stereotypes. The goal of this critical analysis is to strengthen the voices of the oppressed and contest hegemonic narratives.

Subaltern- Gayatri Chakravorty Spivak, in her key essay "Can the Subaltern Speak?" notes that the word "subaltern" was coined by the Italian Marxist thinker Antonio Gramsci. In her essay, Spivak discusses Gramsci's concept of the subaltern, which refers to disadvantaged and oppressed groups in society who are unable to express themselves due to hegemonic power dynamics. Spivak develops Gramsci's theory (*Prison Notebooks* 55) and applies it to postcolonial contexts, notably in relation to women in the Global South, calling into question the agency and representation of subaltern subjects within hegemonic discourse. According to her 'subaltern' refers to persons or groups who occupy marginalized positions in society, typically muted and neglected in dominant historical narratives. Postcolonial discourse emphasizes the importance of amplifying subaltern voices and acknowledging their agency and contributions. The subaltern is not a passive bystander in the continuous battle for liberty and self-determination. Postcolonial approaches seek to correct historical erasures and combat systematic injustices by acknowledging and highlighting the experiences of the subaltern.

Constructedness of Whiteness- The realization that whiteness, like other racial categories, is a socially built and historically contingent term rather than an innate or natural identity is known as the "constructedness of whiteness" in postcolonial studies. This viewpoint exposes the roots of whiteness in colonialism, imperialism, and racial dominance structures, challenging the idea that whiteness is a universal and normative term. Postcolonial researchers study the historical processes that were used in colonial and imperial contexts to produce and racialize whiteness. In colonial civilizations, whiteness came to be seen as a sign of privilege and superiority that shaped the power relations between colonizers and colonized. It also defined the parameters of inclusion and exclusion. The idea of colonialism, which depended on racial hierarchies to legitimize the enslavement and exploitation of non-White people, was inextricably linked to the formation of whiteness. Postcolonial studies examine how whiteness was elevated as the benchmark of civilization and advancement, and how colonial practices and ideologies sustained racialized ideas of superiority and inferiority. Whiteness has intricate interactions with various axes of identity, including country, gender, and class. In order to elucidate the complex relationships between white privilege and various types of oppression and privilege in colonial and postcolonial countries, postcolonial researchers study the intersections between these relationships.

Postcolonial studies examine how white identities are created, normalized, and valued by examining how whiteness is portrayed in popular culture, literature, and the media. These portrayals frequently uphold and perpetuate colonial notions of entitlement and superiority, which support racial hierarchies and stereotypes. Critical whiteness studies, which challenge neutrality and universality presumptions, examine the privileges and invisibilities connected to whiteness within postcolonial studies. This method looks at how whiteness shapes institutions, conversations, and day-to-day interactions as a structural force in society. In order to subvert systems of racial oppression and oppose the predominance of whiteness, postcolonial researchers investigate decolonization and resistance tactics. This could entail challenging white privilege, elevating the voices of the oppressed, and promoting racial equity and social justice.

Thus, the constructed nature of whiteness in postcolonial studies emphasizes how crucial it is to critically analyze racial identities, power relationships, and oppressive structures in both colonial and postcolonial contexts. Postcolonial studies support larger initiatives to topple racial hierarchies and create more inclusive and equitable societies by decentering whiteness and challenging its ideological and historical roots.

Language: Language is a powerful weapon in postcolonial discourse, reflecting colonial power dynamics. Colonizers imposed their languages, destroying varied linguistic diversities and marginalizing indigenous languages. Postcolonial theorists investigate the role of language in forming cultural identities, calling into question the linguistic hierarchies that still exist. Reclaiming and renewing indigenous languages becomes a means of resistance, opposing colonial languages' predominance and fostering cultural renaissance. In the postcolonial struggle, language is not just a method of communication but also a means of contestation and empowerment.

Hence, postcolonial explorations of body, ethnicity, subaltern, and language are fundamental engagements with colonial legacies. Dismantling imposed hierarchies, honouring diversity, elevating marginalized voices, and regaining cultural and linguistic autonomy are all part of it.

4.1 "The Fact of Blackness"- Frantz Fanon

Frantz Fanon was a revolutionary theorist, psychiatrist, and prominent figure in postcolonial studies who was born in Martinique in 1925. His important works, including *Black Skin, White Masks* and *The Wretched of the Earth*, critically addressed the psychological impact of colonialism on individuals and societies. Fanon's findings centred on colonization's dehumanizing impacts, investigating how it moulds racial identity and perpetuates repressive regimes. Fanon's works, while actively involved in the Algerian War of Independence, coupled academic rigour with real experiences, providing a thorough analysis of the intricacies of anti-colonial campaigns. His appeal for radical transformation and the construction of new, non-colonial identities has left an indelible mark, inspiring not only academia but also movements for social justice and decolonization worldwide. Frantz Fanon died in 1961, but his ideas live on, contributing greatly to ongoing debates about race, identity, and the long-term effects of colonialism.

In his seminal essay "The Fact of Blackness," (1968), Frantz Fanon argued that being black is a label placed on people who fit the description rather than one they choose. The definition of "blackness" is based on an individual's outward look, which has evolved into a "social" uniform used to exclude and alienate Black men. He refers to this phenomenon as the "fact of blackness" (Fanon 109). Therefore, the black man is the slave of his own appearance rather than the notion that others hold about him. Because of his social uniform and blackness, he is not given the opportunity to create an identity for himself, an image, or an idea; instead, his identity is imposed upon him, predestined. In contrast, the black man is not given the opportunity to be recognized despite the fact that Jews can often be unknown due to their white skin.

Chinua Achebe also provided insight into image in his essay "An Image of Africa: Racism in Conrad's Heart of Darkness." (Achebe 16) He claimed in his address that Africa serves as a counterpoint to the west. Conrad portrayed Africa as a dismal place because of this. The west has created and recreated this darkness in order to portray Africa as the complete opposite of the west, allowing the west to advance. Because of this, people perceive Africans as inferior because they see Africa as a country inhabited by savages who are the "other," something that can be controlled, exploited, and conquered based only on outward physical and vocal distinctions. Fanon's reasoning is similar to Achebe's, which asserts that the manufactured image of the primitive or inferior Africa serves to divide the "immaculate" (Achebe, "An Image of Africa" 25) west from Africa in western discourse. Blackness, then, is a manufactured identity that sets black people apart from white people.

Postcolonial studies arrived later in the Francophone world than in the Anglophone world, owing to the pain connected with much of French decolonization. There was also a perceived necessity in France to reconcile with the Vichy era before moving on to the almost equally traumatic end of French authority in Algeria. However, by the 1990s, French colonial studies were fast gaining popularity. Cultured Force, a revisionist history of the French empire emphasizing a biographical approach to historical narrative, and *Memory, Empire, and Postcolonialism* (2005), edited by Alec G Hargreaves, which publishes the proceedings of an interdisciplinary conference on cultural memory, are both good examples of the diverse types of writing that the rekindled interest in the French empire is spawning (Hargreaves 242). The book as a whole reintroduces the balance-sheet approach to imperial and colonial history, with the authors arguing that there was a clearly positive side to French colonialism that should not be overlooked, and that gains perspective and substance when the intellectual outlook and achievements of specific protagonists are recognized and added to the ledger's positive side. The authors also indicate, but do not explicitly state, that some former colonies might have been better off if they had stayed colonies or had been fully absorbed into the metropole, as in the case of Algeria.

Fanon, the Algerian revolutionary, clarifies that the west, rather than him, constructs his identity since he is black. His identity is set in stone. Furthermore, the terms "black" and "white" have no significance outside of the context of race. A black person's life has further darkened due to their social environment. As a result, the word "black" is linked to negativity, leading to the association of blackness with negativity.

The colour black is connected to black concepts and imagery of people who are compelled to wear this "social" uniform of "blackness," solidifying or establishing their identity and making their blackness an accepted reality. The fifth chapter of Fanon's book *Black Skin, White Masks*, "The Fact of Blackness," poses the rhetorical issue of what it means to be black. He poses the open-ended question, "What does a black man want?" notwithstanding its nature. He goes on to ask, "What does a man really want?" In actuality, he was posing these queries from the perspective of psychoanalysis—the search for one's identity. He says: "At the risk of arousing the resentment of my coloured brothers, I will say that the black is not a man." (Fanon, "The Fact of Blackness" 10) As quoted by Alfred J. Lopez in his book *Postcolonial Whiteness: A Critical Reader on Race and Empire* (2005): "Fanon undoubtedly still resonates in any discussion of whiteness: 'All around me the white man. Above the sky tears at its navel, the earth rasps under my feet, and there is a white song, a white song. All this whiteness that burns me." (Lopez 67)

According to Fanon, since the day he entered this planet and had an inquisitive mind, he has struggled with being a black person. Amidst numerous other items, he discovered himself to be an object. When it comes to forming his identity, Fanon, like most children, also takes after his parents and siblings. However, Fanon found that when he went to his own Black people, their attention would momentarily free him from this oppressive objecthood. He was locked into non-being by his objecthood. He describes this as transient because, when he turned to face the white person on the opposite side, they gave him a quick glance and said, "Look, a Negro!" (Fanon, "The Fact of Blackness" 112)

Insofar as black men are concerned, this gaze problematizes the idea of ontology. When a black man is among other black men, there is no space for him to experience being with anyone else. The aforementioned gaze was a defining feature of the colonized and civilized society that Fanon was writing about.

The colonized people's worldview, therefore, sees the ontology as an imperfection or impurity in the black, making it unachievable. Therefore, the black ontology is unachievable in respect to white. As a result, a colonized Black man is created or presented in contrast to his opposite, a White man. There cannot exist a Black man without a White Man. Though a black man's skin is naturally brown, the white gaze has made it necessary for him to be black in addition to being black in relation to the white man: "Look, A Negro!" "Dirty Nigger" (Fanon, "The Fact of Blackness"109).

Since ontology rejects the reality of black men, black men must work extremely hard to find their self-identity. Since the black man has no resistance in the perspective of the white man, it prevents him from understanding who he is. The black man, meanwhile, is troubled by the white man's stare because he feels compelled to align himself with an ongoing identity quest. The fact that his traditions and rituals have vanished from history only serves to exacerbate the situation. The fact that their traditions ran counter to the white civilization that was thrust upon them is the reason why history solely honours the accomplishments of white men. But like many of his fellow intellectuals, Fanon was drawn to this idea of negritude because he was searching for and investigating his black identity and black ontology. Until he saw the white man's gaze, this black identity was not dramatic: "Mama, see the Negro!" His experience with the white man's eyes caused him to say, "I'm frightened!" (Fanon, "The Fact of Blackness" 112) as a result, which hindered him and other men of colour from developing their body schema.

In terms of his identity and the world, the consciousness of the black man is regarded as the third man's consciousness. A true dialectic between one's body and the outside world is thus created by the self that one creates and the self that the outside world constructs. The world is Manichean, meaning that anything black is evil and horrible which needs to be re-visited again. Research is being conducted in numerous labs to create a "denegrification" serum, which would help a wretched black man become whiter and free him from the burden of physical transgression.

He was unable to laugh at his physical schema, which was constantly under attack, or even at the fact that the white people were afraid of him. Consequently, a "racial epidermal schema" (Fanon, "The Fact of Blackness"112) took the role of this corporeal schema. He realized that he was moving from a period in which he was conscious of his body in a triple person to a phase in which he was entering a third person during the process of forming his self-identity. He states: "I existed triply. I occupied space. I moved toward the other…and the evanescence other, hostile but not opaque, transparent, not there, disappeared." (Fanon, "The Fact of Blackness" 112)

So, like anything else, his body took up space. When he walked in the direction of the other, he did so as a member of the black race, and he also noticed that the other person felt uncomfortable in accordance with the characteristics of the black race as they have been described historically. As a result, he happily cherished his self-identity as a Black person, but he also bitterly felt that he was accountable for his physical appearance, his race, his ancestry, and his ethnic traits and "tom toms, cannibalism, intellectual deficiency, fetishism, racial defects, slave ships, etc." (Fanon112)

The white man has created the stereotype of the black man and black woman. In addition, he had woven him into the thousands of tales and anecdotes. Why so and so is the first black vice-chancellor, or why Nelson Mandela is regarded as the first black president, or why any of them has won an Olympic medal? The list is extensive; a black man wants to be recognized just as a man. He says: "All I wanted was to be a man among other men." (Fanon 112)

A stereotype of inferiority that has been ingrained in both African and global consciousness is that of Africans. The native must overcome a number of innate defence mechanisms that they have evolved to justify their black identity. Laughing is one protective mechanism, but it no longer functions the same way as it formerly did. It's not even reparative. He found it funny when someone exclaimed, "Look, a Negro!" but not when someone remarked, "Mama, see the Negro!" (Fanon 112). They are starting to get fearful of me now that I've scared them. It was now impossible to laugh.

The colonists feel more at ease if the colonized laugh, but if they refuse to laugh, the colonizer feels threatened. Therefore, the colonized's incapacity to laugh validates the colonists' innate terror of the natives. Even black men absorb the illusion that they are inferior to other men. "I am the slave not of the idea that others have of me but of my own appearance." (Fanon, "The Fact of Blackness" 116)

As a result, the native suffers from self-hatred. He learns to despise himself and begins to perceive himself in the same light as Europeans. The chapter ends with him acknowledging the harsh truth that the colonized person has no choice but to embrace his "blackness" and that this makes him an eternal issue for both the colonizer and the rest of the world. Because of their race, they are unable to accept credit or issue an apology. Africans are forced to accept their race and walk with pride in spite of the fact that most people view them as non-human. They have no choice but to embrace their life. Educating discussions about Africans' incapacity to overcome their blackness is necessary since African children are raised with the fear that other people detest their blackness. There exist Black physicians, Black attorneys, Black educators, and so on. According to Fanon, an African cannot disguise his blackness, yet a Jew or an Irish person can hide their Jewish identity. However, he emphasizes that individuals shouldn't make an effort to conceal their African American identity. Instead, individuals must rethink who they are and explore their identity.

4.2 "Can the Subaltern Speak?"- Gayatri Chakravorty Spivak

Gayatri Chakravorty Spivak, born in 1942, is regarded as a trailblazer in literary theory, postcolonial studies, and feminist philosophy. The essay "Can the Subaltern Speak?" (1988) is central to her major contributions, in which she critically investigates the issues of representation for underprivileged groups, particularly women in the Global South. Spivak's work dismantles fixed categories, showing the intricacies present in colonial and postcolonial discourses, and is heavily founded on deconstructionist principles influenced by Jacques Derrida. She extends her views beyond her involvement with subaltern voices to feminist theory, emphasizing intersectionality in debates of gender and sexuality. Spivak's intellectual breadth includes translation studies, which address the complex politics of translating literature across languages and cultures. Her advocacy for social justice and inclusive, decolonized education demonstrates her commitment to academic activism. Spivak has made an indelible impression as a Columbia University professor, challenging researchers to critically engage with power relations, representation, and the urge for a more equal world.

After the release of her essay "Can the Subaltern Speak?," Gayatri Spivak became a prominent voice of the postcolonial era. She covers a wide range of subjects in her speech, including postcolonialism, feminism, deconstruction, and Marxism. After graduating from the University of Calcutta's Presidency College in 1959, she left India to finish her master's degree at Cornell University in the United States and then spent a year as a fellow at Girton College in Cambridge, England. At Cornell University in New York, she worked under the guidance of literary critic Paul de Man on her doctoral dissertation, which focused on W.B. Yeats. She currently teaches humanities at Columbia University in New York.

Her translation of Derrida's *Of Grammatology* (1976) increased her notoriety and gave her prominence on a global scale. She questioned colonialism and the established hierarchies through cultural studies. She declined to accept and adhere to the Western world's superiority over the Third World. Her research focuses on topics pertaining to marginalized groups, including women and subalterns in society. She takes the term "subaltern" from Gramsci (1971) to refer to this new class of individuals in society. This term becomes more pertinent when used in an Indian context to allude to Dalits, voiceless tribal women, and members of lower castes and classes.

India is divided along the lines of caste, class, creed, religion, language, ethnicity, gender, and citizenship since it is a land of diversity. Spivak's essay "Can the Subaltern Speak?" supports the concerns of Indian women who engage in sati. The widows of India observed this "sati" ritual as a self-sacrifice, which the Western World saw as a remnant of savage civilization. The West claims that the East's culture lacks sophistication. Despite the fact that they are primitive, backward, and foreign, Gayatri Spivak speaks out against this subversion and questions, can the Subaltern Speak? Her use of language has stoked debate in the post-colonial setting. The voiceless subalterns lack it. They no longer have a voice because of how much they have been sidelined. Furthermore, others find it annoying to listen to them even when they do speak. She undermines the idea that the West is the exclusive centre of knowledge at the opening of her seminal essay. She views postmodernism as equivocal and politically inconsistent. She attempts to subvert the oppositions that are binary between self and other, Occident and Orient, subject and object, etc. She also raises the issue of gender inequality in this essay. Why are there subaltern people in third-world countries who are silenced and denied a voice? As per Bill Ashcroft et al., "the silencing of the subaltern woman extends to the whole of the colonial world, and to the silencing and muting of all natives, male or female." (*The Empire Writes Back* 175). Contrarily, in the words of Francis Barker et al., "Spivak's theory of subalternity does not seem to me to be a theory of 'native agency' at all but a theory of the way in which disenfranchised elements of the 'native' population are represented in the discourse of colonialism." (*Colonial Dclintiscourse/ Postcolonial Theory* 205)

Due to their differences in gender, caste, class, and religion, they are not united; rather, they are divided into groups. Hindu women were not allowed to do sati when the British colonized India. They thought this was a terrible behaviour. Many Hindu women's lives were spared once this was stopped, but it also preserved British control in India because women's voices were completely silenced during the practice's prohibition—as the white men put it, "white men saved brown women from brown men." (Spivak, "Can the Subaltern Speak?" 92) Because Indian women were considered barbarians and white men rescued them, this statement furthered their deceptive mission of enlightenment. Hindu women faced only the threat posed by their brown males, not by white men.

At the outset of the essay, Spivak attacks Deleuze and Foucault for engaging in "epistemic violence," (Spivak "Can the Subaltern Speak?" 76), arguing further that their view of the west as the epicentre of knowledge gives them authority over the developing world. To satisfy their financial interest, this way of thinking was developed. They, therefore, said that knowledge was a type of good that was transferred from the West to other Eastern nations. But since knowledge constantly reflects the interests of those who develop it, knowledge, in her opinion, has never been innocent. By creating identities in the East based on the building of knowledge and power, Europe becomes the ideal. "Can the Subaltern Speak?" challenges the Marxist ideology on the grounds that the essentialization of the subaltern has three detrimental effects on them:

1. Marxism views the subaltern as barbarians, necessitating their transformation, hence opening the door for colonialism.
2. It offers a logocentric presumption regarding the unity of culture among diverse individuals.

3. The inability to communicate causes the subalterns to rely on the Western intellectual to clarify things for them, thus separating them from the ability to express themselves.

4. Spivak discusses the suicide of Bhubaneswari Bhaduri in the latter part of her essay, "Can the Subaltern Speak?" Bhaduri took her own life because she refused to take part in an association that she had been ordered to conduct. Her family portrayed her narrative differently, and her suicide is still misunderstood (Spivak, "Can the Subaltern Speak?" 104). Her attempt at suicide was viewed less as a protest and more as the product of a lost love affair. Her family's ultimate decision to leave her silent helped to shape her reality of life. Since they also created the truth for us, it is, therefore, impossible to reclaim and recreate history within a Western paradigm. The subaltern is, hence, mute.

"Can the Subaltern Speak?" focuses on the ideological and historical barriers that prevent people who live on the margins from having their voices heard. The essay is very contentious since the author poses numerous queries about sati, the practice of widows' self-immolation. The women who belonged to the lower class were deprived of the chance to discuss and exchange ideas. The British removed the custom of 'sati' from India, but they did not do so to protect women; rather, they did so to further their fictitious goals of enlightenment and civilization. So, the brown women were rescued from the brown men by the white men. As a result, the practice of self-immolation was seen more as a spiritual than a suicide act. Widow self-immolation was a practice carried out by people and approved by the Dharmashastra.

By saying that "this is not the proper place for the woman to annul the proper name of suicide through the destruction of the proper self," (Spivak, "Can the Subaltern Speak?" 95), Spivak casts doubt on the legitimacy of this abhorrent human sacrifice. Since women in pre-independence India were essentially parasites with no separate existence, the practice of sati actually assisted men in demanding respect from women. She loses her identity the instant her husband passes away. She is just another parasite with no sense of identity. She can only reclaim her identity by being burned alive on her deceased husband's funeral pyre. Accordingly, in spiritual insight into the practice of this custom and ritual, the act of sati should not be viewed as an act of suicide but rather as "a simulacrum of both truth-knowledge and piety of place." (Spivak, "Can the Subaltern Speak?" 96) According to Spivak,

Body, Ethnicity, Subaltern and Language

"So, sati should have been read with martyrdom" (98); she was also met with disdain anytime she denied doing this rite and was viewed as a live example of unfaithful marriage.

A martyr gives her life for the sake of others; she does not benefit personally from her sacrifice. As a result, any woman who committed sati was a martyr. This sacrifice was carried out because society was unable to protect them and acknowledge their significance in addition to that of their family members. The whole thing got worse when Edward Thomson published his suite, A Historical and Philosophical Enquiry in The Hindu Rite of Widow Burning, in 1928, claims Spivak. The British colonizers of India attempted to eradicate the practice of sati in order to justify their imperialism as a component of their civilizing mission. This statement perpetuates the act of muting the voice of the Hindu woman, who has already been relocated to her deceased husband's funeral pyre. Therefore, colonists attempted to defend their colonialism in this way. Unlike Spivak, however, Bhabha debates regarding the recovering of the native voice through mimicry and parody, which culminates in being menacing to the colonists. As per Ashcroft et al.: "Unlike Spivak, though, Bhabha has asserted that the 'subaltern' people can speak, and that a native voice can be recovered." (*The Empire Writes Back* 175)

Spivak's rhetorical question is a well-known feature of this seminal essay. The women who were considered "subalterns" had a voice inside of them—a voice of disapproval and discontent. Every woman who fell prey to male dominance, patriarchal brutality, and other horrors had something important to say, but her voice was silenced. The white man is more anguished in this scenario of enslavement because their voice is now totally obscured by two power systems: colonial power structures and Hind religious rules. Jenni Ramone meticulously examines canonical texts such as Shakespeare's *The Tempest*, in which the colonizing Prospero speaks for Caliban, and Bronte's *Jane Eyre*, in which Rochester's Jamaican wife Bertha Mason, is, according to Gayatri Spivak's reading of the novel, a subaltern denied a voice. According to Ramone, she is "secluded in the marginal space of an attic room, and the marginal textual space of rumour, silence, darkness, and the indistinguishable grunts of bestial existence" (Ramone 172).

Fanon and Spivak: A Comparative Study- Renowned for their innovative contributions to the postcolonial studies, Frantz Fanon and Gayatri Chakravorty Spivak are significant theorists and critics in the discipline. Although they address from different theoretical vantage points, they have certain shared concerns and interests, such as the investigation of identity, power and the critique of colonialism. Frantz Fanon's writings, especially *Black Skin, White Masks* and *The Wretched of the Earth*, offer a potent critique of colonialism and its effects on identities, psyches, and liberation struggles of the colonized. He argues that a radical reconfiguration of subjectivity and collective agency is necessary for decolonization, emphasizing the psychological and existential aspects of colonial subjugation. In writings such as "Can the Subaltern Speak?" and "Critique of Postcolonial Reason," Gayatri Chakravorty Spivak concentrates on the representational and epistemic aspects of colonialism. She investigates the difficulties of portraying and articulating the experiences of marginalized subjects within dominant frameworks, with a focus on women and subaltern groups, and how colonial discourses construct and stifle their voices.

Fanon's examination of subjectivity and racial identity investigates how racialized stereotypes are internalized and how people fight for acceptance and self-affirmation in a society where colonial discourses rule. (*Black Skin, White Masks* 89-119). Spivak addresses issues of subjectivity and agency in her work, especially as they pertain to class, gender, and colonial power structures. (*A Critique of Postcolonial Reason* 1-14). She examines the difficulties in forming an identity as well as the shortcomings of essentialist classifications, emphasizing the ways in which overlapping dominance systems affect subjectivity.

Fanon examines how linguistic and cultural assimilation support colonial hierarchies and erode indigenous modes of expression and resistance, and language plays a crucial role in this understanding of colonial power relations (*Black Skin, White Masks* 1-17). He argues that regaining agency and self-determination requires the decolonization of language. The politics of translation and the difficulties of expressing marginalized voices within prevailing discourses are the main subjects of Spivak's work on language and representation. She challenges the power relationships that underlie representation and poses concerns about who, in colonial and postcolonial contexts has the right to speak and be heard. ("Can the Subaltern Speak?" 274-278)

Since Fanon actively participated in liberation movements and revolutionary movements throughout Africa and the Caribbean, his writing is firmly grounded in praxis. His ideas, which call for the downfall of colonial governments and the establishment of new, decolonized societies, are infused with a sense of urgency and a dedication to transformational action. Although Spivak is well-known in academic circles for her studies, she also works as an activist, mostly in the areas of social justice, feminism, and education. Although critical of essentialism's shortcomings, her concept of "strategic essentialism" empowers marginalized people to strategically use essentialist identities as a tool of political mobilization.

To summarize, Fanon and Spivak have a shared commitment to challenging colonialism and its aftereffects, but they take distinct theoretical stances when addressing these problems, highlighting various facets of colonial power dynamics and resistance. While Spivak's work examines the epistemic and representational aspects of colonial oppression, Fanon's work concentrates on the psychological and existential aspects of it. Nonetheless, both academics advance our knowledge of the complexity of colonialism and the ongoing fights for justice and liberation in postcolonial discourse.

4.3 "Language of African Literature": Ngũgĩ wa Thiong'o

Ngũgĩ wa Thiong'o, born in Kenya in 1938, is a renowned African writer and scholar. He is well-known for his literary contributions, which include *Weep Not, Child* and *Petals of Blood*, and he is a notable writer in postcolonial literature. As a significant act of linguistic and cultural decolonization, he adopted the name Ngugi wa Thiong'o and vowed to write in his own language, Kikuyu. His seminal book *Decolonizing the Mind* (1986) emphasizes the transformative potential of language in addressing colonial legacies. Ngugi has also been politically active, having been imprisoned for his criticisms of neocolonialism. He co-wrote the powerful drama "I Will Marry When I Want" (1977), which addressed economic exploitation and social injustice (Mungazi 5-10). Ngugi's study spans literature, language, and postcolonial studies, and he has held appointments at Yale and the University of California, Irvine. His devotion to social justice, linguistic sovereignty, and the enormous influence of his multifarious contributions to African literature and the broader discourse of decolonization are his lasting legacies.

Ngũgĩ wa Thiong'o is a Kenyan novelist, poet, dramatist, and activist who has been actively involved in the anti-colonial struggle of the Kenyan people. He is recognized globally as a very powerful voice against colonial exploitation. He has authored numerous articles and essays criticizing western colonialism and exposing its structures and workings in a very insightful manner. He wrote a great deal in English, but eventually, he stopped writing in English to express his opposition to colonial oppression and began writing in Gikuyu and Swahili, his native tongues.

The issue raised by him was that a large number of Africans experienced colonialism as children. Colonial English was the primary language of instruction for them. Higher education was also pursued in the fields of philosophy, language, and literature, which led to the creation of people who felt divided between two worlds. Consequently, indigenous people, culture, history, and traditions seemed to have been abandoned because of the influence of colonial languages. This affects how they started viewing their history and culture. Sometimes, they cut themselves off from their own people, which makes it impossible to release everyone from the bonds of colonialism. The effects of colonialism are unavoidable. They are forced to continue living under neo-colonial rule. According to Emma Dawson Varughese in her book *Beyond the Postcolonial: World Englishes Literature*:

"Framed with the names of Achebe and Soyinka, Nigeria remains one of the most prolific and fertile producers of World Englishes literature globally. And yet, Nigeria has struggled and continues to struggle with a sense of national literature". (Varughese 15). Varughese presents the intriguing results of fieldwork conducted in Cameroon, Nigeria, Uganda, Kenya, Malaysia, Singapore, and India between 2008 and 2011, which consisted of soliciting contemporary short stories and analyzing them in terms of their thematic and generic characteristics. At the same time, it is difficult not to notice the implicit hierarchy established by the book in its claim to cover a representative sample of "World Englishes Literature," as well as the origins of this hierarchy, which can be traced back to the debate within postcolonial studies over which cultures can be ascribed "authentic" postcolonial status and which cannot. The absence of any settler-invader or indigenous cultures from one of the settler-invader nations calls into question the book's representative claims. Varughese dismisses sites such as Canada and New Zealand in the subsection "Defining World Englishes Literature" by bracketing their undeniable differences and then stating that "These areas of linguistic creativity and multilingualism are indeed complex [they] are not an area of inquiry central to the presentation of World Englishes literature and the broader concerns of this volume" (Varughese 19). However, referring to anything as "World" Englishes but then excluding key locations where English is used is not dealing with World Englishes but with a subset of them.

According to N'gugi, while addressing the Indigenous directly, as you integrate into the colonial society, you feel as though your ability and hard work have been stolen. (*Decolonizing the Mind* 11-17) You end up either serving the foreign culture and its interests or becoming cynical, dissatisfied, and depressed.

Therefore, the scenario resembles a cage that only helps Europeans and excludes Africans. Regarding his English expression, Nigerian author Chinua Achebe disagrees, arguing that colonial languages—such as English in Nigeria or Portuguese in Angola—are lingua franca (Achebe, "The African Writer and the English Language" 60-65), the only language that can reach a whole nation. However, English can also be Africanized to further African ideals and objectives, as he himself does by incorporating oral tradition and folktales into his novels.

However, Ngũgĩ wa Thiong'o claims that Achebe and other similar writers are primarily addressing the middle class and not the general public. (*Decolonizing the Mind* 63-70) One must reach out to the masses in order to decolonize. In order to connect people to the literature created by their people, which is infused with their revolutionary efforts for liberation against colonial rule, N'gugi wa Thiongo calls on African writers to start writing in their native languages (*Decolonizing the Mind* 105). In the words of Bill Ashcroft et al., "the pre-colonial languages have been a recurring feature of calls for decolonization." (*The Empire Writes Back* 29).

N'gugi appears to be echoing Fanon when he states that writers who start writing for their own people instead of attempting to gain cultural legitimacy by writing in the language of the colonizers pose a threat to the colonial powers. (*Decolonizing the Mind* 12-33). In his essay, which discusses the value of writing in African languages, is broken up into nine pieces. He contends that authors working in English ought to be classified as authors of Afro-European literature rather than African literature. He combines a scholarly treatise with a personal biography in an effort to decolonize:

1. He asserts that we must comprehend the opposing contexts of decolonization, self-determination, and imperialism. The focal point of this divisive collision is language. He says that the choice of language and the use to which language is put is central to a people's definition of themselves in relation to the natural and social environment, indeed in relation to the entire universe. According to him, "In my view, language was the most important vehicle through which that power fascinated and held the soul prisoner." (Ngũgĩ wa Thiong'o 287)

2. By providing a first-hand account of this dynamic circumstance, which is evocative of Fanon's criticism of the formative years of indigenous intellectualism. He discusses the African Writers of English Expression conference that took place in 1962 at Makerere University College in

Kampala, Uganda. The conference excluded writers who were writing in African languages, raising the question of whether African literature exists or could exist while acknowledging that it must exist in English. This was a terrible and deadly paradox that may be summed up as follows: The physical subjugation was achieved by the bullet. The method of spiritual subjugation was language.

3. He also makes use of his early language learning experiences. He discovered that Gikuyo's stories were more poetic. Although he received instruction in his native tongue in the hamlet, he was compelled to acquire English in school, which was essentially used to classify children into a hierarchical pyramid. No matter how intelligent you were, if your English was not up to par, you could not go on. It was forbidden for you to speak in your native tongue throughout this period.

4. He discusses the connection between language and human experience, culture, and reality perception in the theoretical fourth section. He separates language into two categories. In the first, language is both a means and a carrier of culture. He categorizes language into three components related to communication.

    A. The "language of real life," coined by Marx to describe the fundamental exchanges between work and collaboration that constitute a community. (Ngũgĩ wa Thiong'o 288)

    B. Speech: Using some vocal cues, it "imitates the language of real life." Speech thus establishes a human connection.

    C. Writing: "imitates the spoken...representation of sounds with visual symbols." (Ngũgĩ wa Thiong'o 289) That is why spoken and written language are similar in most societies. They get along well.

    According to N'gugi Wa Thiongo, language is the foundation and means of cultural evolution. Culture, which is the collective memory bank of people's historical experiences, can be understood as language. Language and culture are interwoven and indistinguishable from one another. Language is the means by which culture is passed down from generation to generation. (*Decolonizing the Mind* 12-15) He divides language as culture into three further categories:

(i) An outcome of a certain past.

(ii) An agent that shapes images in a child's mind.

(iii) Both spoken and written language is a medium through which culture mediates.

5. He claims in the fifth section that an imperialist seeks to control indigenous people's riches by imposing his language on a child's mind and trying to dominate real-life language. They had to elevate their language at the expense of and undervalue their native culture in order to do this-"the language of the colonizer" (283). The best evidence for holding conferences like the one that was held in 1962 is the fact that many African writers, such as Achebe, Banda, and Senghor, extol the virtues of the colonizer's language at the expense of their own, as a result of this tendency that drove the child away from his language and broke the harmony between spoken and written.

6. N'gugi Wa Thiongo presents the situation in a similar way to Fanon, but with a stronger sense of empathy and understanding. While Ngũgĩ wa Thiong'o wrote to clarify the matter and help everyone understand Fanon's point of view, Fanon wrote with agitation. Because people would never feel a connection to literature produced in the language of the colonizer, such writing could never inspire resistance because the language choice would always indicate the incorrect audience.

7. However, the indigenous farmers and peasants shamelessly carried on speaking their original tongue. They produced poets and singers of their own. They were also joined by writers who had started off writing in European languages, such as Obi Wali, who wrote a polemical article the following year, and David Diop from Seneghal (*Decolonizing the Mind* 55-56).

8. He goes on to question what distinguishes a writer who claims that European languages are essential for African development from a politician who claims that imperialism is something the continent cannot survive without. By translating the Bible into native tongues, Europeans are falsifying information about indigenous people, and these African authors are selected to write in the languages of imperialists. Hence, we are losing the war even though we haven't really been fighting, as this kind of writing

belongs in the category of Afro-European literature rather than African.

9. He explains his decision to write in Gikuyu, his mother tongue, after seventeen years of writing in the Afro-European tradition in the essay's concluding part. Whereas normal is denigrated as abnormal, the abnormal is seen as normal. The world has turned on its head. Put differently, Africa's belief that only Europe can save Africa from poverty means that Africa is actually enhancing Europe. Although Africa's natural and human resources are still helping Europe and America grow, however, Africa is appreciative of these aids, which are still a burden for the continent, even with the emergence of intellectuals from Africa who defend this erroneous perspective on the continent.

He concludes by advising writing in one's native tongue in order to carry on the fight against imperialism. He says, "In other words, writers in African languages should reconnect themselves to the revolutionary traditions of an organized peasantry and working class in Africa in their struggle to defeat imperialism and create a higher system of democracy and socialism in alliance with all other peoples of the world." (Ngũgĩ wa Thiong'o 290).

4.4 *Necropolitics*- Achille Mbembe

Achille Mbembe is recognized as a key figure in postcolonial theory and critical studies. His work has significantly contributed to our knowledge of power dynamics, identity formation, and political philosophy in postcolonial contexts, particularly in Africa. One of Mbembe's most influential ideas is necropolitics, which he introduced in his book "Necropolitics" (2003). He investigates how current forms of administration in postcolonial states are distinguished not only by control over life (biopolitics) but also by the ability to choose who lives and who dies. Mbembe contends that the logic of sovereignty is manifested through the control of death and the creation of "death-worlds" (92), in which certain populations face extreme kinds of violence and dispossession. Mbembe critically examines colonial and imperial legacies, as well as African decolonization and nation-building processes. He investigates how colonialism continues to impact political, economic, and social systems in postcolonial cultures, and he advocates for new forms of political thought and activity that transcend colonial frameworks.

Mbembe examines the intersections of globalization, capitalism, and colonialism, focusing on how these factors create new forms of inequality, exploitation, and resistance in postcolonial contexts. He investigates how neoliberal economic policies and global power dynamics affect African societies, contributing to continuous battles for social justice and self-determination. Mbembe's work investigates the intricacies of African identities and subjectivities within the context of colonial and postcolonial history. He investigates how colonialism shaped African identity formations, as well as the potential for regaining agency and autonomy in the face of colonial legacies. Achille Mbembe's contributions to postcolonial theory helped to advance critical understandings of power, violence, resistance, and emancipation in African and global politics. His work is still frequently studied and contested in the fields of postcolonial studies, critical theory, and African studies.

Mbembe delves deeply into the work of Frantz Fanon, particularly his major books *Black Skin, White Masks* and *The Wretched of the Earth*. Mbembe examines Fanon's critiques of colonialism and racism, as well as his investigation into the psychological and existential aspects of colonial subjugation. Mbembe builds on Fanon's concepts to investigate contemporary forms of domination and resistance in postcolonial contexts. He says: "To oppressed individuals who sought to rid themselves of race's burden, Fanon thus proposed a long course of therapy. This therapy began in and through language and perception…" (Mbembe "Necropolitics" 5)

Mbembe investigates the concept of sovereignty and its evolution in the postcolonial period. He contends that sovereignty in postcolonial settings is frequently challenged, fractured, and reshaped using multiple kinds of power and governance. According to him, "forms of power and modes of sovereignty, a key characteristic of which is to produce death on a large scale." (Mbembe "Necropolitics" 34) He studies the manner in which state power is wielded and opposed, and he questions the relationship between sovereignty, violence, and citizenship. He investigates the dynamics of urbanization and spatial politics in African cities, particularly in light of globalisation and neoliberalism. He examines how colonial legacies, capitalist development, and social inequality create urban settings, as well as the ways in which city people negotiate and fight power dynamics. He says: "Colonial occupation itself consisted in seizing, delimiting, and asserting control over a geographical area- of writing a new set of social and spatial relations on the ground." (Mbembe 79)

Mbembe provides a postcolonial critique of development discourse and practices in Africa, challenging the assumptions and ideologies that underpin mainstream development programs. He contends that development programs frequently prolong patterns of reliance, inequality, and exploitation, and he advocates for new views of development that stress social justice, environmental sustainability, and human dignity. Mbembe investigates the politics of memory and historical consciousness in postcolonial cultures, focusing on the legacies of colonialism, enslavement, and genocide. He critically examines the Rwandan genocide and states: "In the case of the Rwandan genocide- in which a number of skeletons were, when not exhumed, kept in a visible state." (Mbembe 87) He investigates how collective memories of historical violence and trauma influence modern politics and identities, as well as the function of memory in processes of reconciliation, justice, and healing.

Mbembe presents the concept of necropolitics, which refers to how current forms of power operate by controlling and managing death. Unlike biopolitics, which focuses on the management of life, necropolitics emphasizes the sovereign right to decide who lives and who dies. Mbembe investigates how necropolitics occurs in the circumstances of severe violence, war, genocide, and state repression, as well as how it influences social interactions and political subjectivity. Building on the concept of necropolitics, Mbembe analyzes thanatopolitics, or the politics of death and dying. Thanatopolitics considers not just the actual killing of corpses, but also the psychological and symbolic components of death, such as how death is portrayed, memorialized, and normalized in society. Mbembe investigates how thanatopolitics operates through violent rituals, exclusionary practices, and dehumanization processes.

He investigates the relationship between necropolitics and sovereignty, focusing on how sovereign power is exerted through the freedom to murder and let live. He contends that sovereignty in postcolonial nations is frequently manifested through the management of death and the creation of "death-worlds" in which certain people are subjected to forms of state-sanctioned violence and displacement. Throughout "Necropolitics," Mbembe considers the impact of colonialism and imperialism on modern forms of violence and oppression. He investigates how colonial regimes-built death mechanisms and racialized hierarchies that still have an impact on postcolonial society today. Mbembe also investigates how postcolonial regimes inherit and perpetuate colonial systems of governance, including the use of violence to retain authority and repress dissent.

Despite the bleak description of necropolitics, Mbembe takes into account modes of resistance and agency that develop in the face of dire violence and oppression. He investigates how underprivileged communities, social movements, and people challenge the logic of necropolitics by asserting their right to life and dignity. Above mentioned core ideas in "Necropolitics" provide a framework for comprehending the intricate interconnections of power, violence, and death in modern postcolonial contexts, and they continue to influence critical assessments of sovereignty, governance, and resistance in the global South.

Achille Mbembe's work has been significant and generally admired, but it has also been criticized and debated in academic circles. Several scholars and theorists have critiqued or discussed Mbembe's beliefs, challenging or expanding on them in new ways. Robert Nixon, an environmental scholar and postcolonial theorist, has criticized Mbembe's focus on violence and sovereignty in postcolonial contexts. In his book *Slow Violence and the Environmentalism of the Poor* (2011), Nixon contends that focusing simply on spectacular forms of violence might mask slower, less visible kinds of harm, such as environmental degradation and displacement of underprivileged populations (Nixon 8-10). Achille Varzi, a philosopher, has challenged Mbembe's concept of necropolitics from a theoretical standpoint. Varzi contends in his paper "Sovereignty and Necropolitics in the Postcolony" (2019) that Mbembe's theory is overly reliant on a binary opposition between biopolitics and necropolitics, ignoring the intricacies of power and governance in postcolonial contexts (Varzi 12-14). Varzi believes that a more sophisticated approach is required to understand how sovereignty operates with respect to life and death. These instances show that, while Mbembe's work has made important contributions to postcolonial theory and critical studies, it has also prompted critical interaction and debate among academics. Scholars and theorists continue to question and expand on Mbembe's ideas, expanding the ongoing discussion concerning power, violence, and resistance in postcolonial contexts.

4.5 *Epistemic Freedom in Africa: Deprovincialization and Decolonization* - Sabelo J. Ndlovu Gatsheni

Sabelo J. Ndlovu Gatsheni is a well-known postcolonial thinker and intellectual from Zimbabwe. His work has significantly influenced critical studies of colonialism, decoloniality, African nationalism, and memory studies. Ndlovu-Gatsheni's study is distinguished by its multidisciplinary approach, which uses history, political theory, and cultural studies to examine the legacies of colonialism and imperialism in Africa and other continents. Ndlovu-Gatsheni explores the concept of coloniality of power, influenced by Latin American theorists like Aníbal Quijano and Walter Mignolo. He investigates how colonial mechanisms of dominance and exploitation survive in current global power systems, influencing social connections, knowledge creation, and economic inequality. Ndlovu-Gatsheni advocates a decolonial viewpoint that aims to destroy these systems and develop alternative modes of thought and activity.

Ndlovu-Gatsheni promotes the acknowledgement and value of African epistemologies and knowledge systems. He criticizes Eurocentric frameworks that devalue or invalidate indigenous African methods of knowing, emphasizing the significance of decolonizing knowledge production and education. (*Epistemic Freedom in Africa* 1-15) Ndlovu-Gatsheni's work emphasizes the depth and diversity of African intellectual traditions, calling for more inclusivity and respect within global academic discourse. He investigates the politics of memory and trauma in postcolonial contexts, focusing on colonial atrocities and liberation struggles. (*Epistemic Freedom in Africa* 115) He examines the construction, contestation, and memorialization of historical narratives, as well as the function of memory in reconciliation and social justice movements. Ndlovu-Gatsheni's work emphasizes the significance of confronting historical injustices and overcoming colonial legacies in order to create more just and equitable societies. He critically examines the history and legacy of African nationalism, challenging conventional narratives that portray nationalist movements as heroic fighters for freedom. (*Epistemic Freedom in Africa* 95) He investigates the intricacies and inconsistencies of nationalist aspirations, such as their collaboration with colonial organizations and their limitations in dealing with internal social differences. He advocates for a more nuanced definition of nationalism that considers its various expressions and contentious legacies. His work as a postcolonial theorist has helped to advance critical understandings of power, knowledge, and identity in Africa and the global south. He continues to address themes of colonialism, decolonization, and social transformation, providing valuable insights to scholars and activists.

One of Sabelo J. Ndlovu-Gatsheni's most notable works is *Epistemic Freedom in Africa: Deprovincialization and Decolonization* (2018). In this work, Ndlovu-Gatsheni investigates knowledge production, epistemological hegemony, and decolonization in Africa. He criticizes the dominance of Eurocentric epistemologies and emphasizes the significance of recognizing and appreciating indigenous African knowledge. The book promotes epistemic freedom as an essential component of decolonization, highlighting the need to deprovincialize knowledge and make room for varied ways of knowing and being. Ndlovu-Gatsheni's multidisciplinary approach, which relies on history, philosophy, and postcolonial theory, provides a fascinating and insightful study of the problems and opportunities for decolonizing African knowledge (Ndlovu-Gatsheni 1-15).

Ndlovu-Gatsheni examines how colonialism reinforced Eurocentric epistemologies while marginalizing indigenous African knowledge systems. He investigates how colonial education institutions, research methodologies, and academic hierarchies fostered epistemic violence and contributed to the dominance of Western knowledge production. He advocates for the deprovincialization of knowledge, which entails challenging the provincialism of Western epistemologies and acknowledging the validity of multiple knowledge traditions from Africa and other neglected areas. He also affirms: "Those that were designated for blacks deliberately taught a poor version of Western epistemology that Isaac Bongani Tabata (1959) described as 'education for barbarism'." (Ndlovu-Gatsheni 230)

He supports the integration of diverse epistemic viewpoints in academic discourse, as well as the importance of connecting with local knowledges and cosmologies. He emphasizes the importance of decolonizing epistemology as part of larger battles for decolonization and independence. According to him, "The key reason being that a decolonization, which gets deep into epistemology, curriculum, pedagogy, institutional cultures, language, demographics and symbolic representation, is yet to take place in all South African universities." (Ndlovu-Gatsheni 232) He advocates for the decolonization of education systems, research methodologies, and intellectual frameworks, envisioning a change in knowledge production that is grounded in African realities and sensitive to the needs and ambitions of Africans.

Ndlovu-Gatsheni offers epistemic freedom as a guiding principle for Africa's knowledge decolonization (*Epistemic Freedom in Africa* 2). Epistemic freedom requires freeing African minds from colonial mentalities and cultivating critical consciousness, which enables people and groups to exercise intellectual sovereignty and design their own futures. Through a thorough study inspired by postcolonial theory, critical race theory, and African intellectual traditions, "Epistemic Freedom in Africa" offers a compelling criticism of epistemic injustice as well as a visionary framework for reinventing African knowledge creation.

Summing up this chapter, one can conclude that theoretical ideas from Frantz Fanon and Gayatri Chakravorty Spivak provide insights on colonialism, postcolonialism, identity, and power dynamics. These ideas overlap in different ways with the work of Ngũgĩ Wa Thiong'o, Achille Mbembe, and Sabelo J. Ndlovu-Gatsheni. The well-known Kenyan author and postcolonial theorist Ngũgĩ Wa Thiong'o expresses Fanon's worries about the decolonization of language and culture. Ngũgĩ calls for the restoration of cultural identity and resistance against colonial control through the use of indigenous languages. Ngũgĩ and Fanon both stress the significance of literature and cultural output in liberation movements, emphasizing the function of literature as a vehicle for social change, resistance, and consciousness-raising. Philosopher and political theorist Achille Mbembe of Cameroon discusses Fanon's theories of colonialism and its aftereffects, focusing on issues of subjectivity, violence, and power.

Fanon's critique of colonial brutality and the dehumanization of colonized people is consistent with Mbembe's concept of necropolitics, which investigates the ways in which colonial and postcolonial states exert control over life and death. Ndlovu-Gatsheni examines the experiences of oppressed people in postcolonial Africa by drawing on Spivak's theories regarding the subaltern and the politics of representation. His studies of decolonial philosophy and epistemic disobedience converge with Spivak's critique of Eurocentrism and support of alternative modes of knowing and being. Hence, despite the fact that each of these academics approaches the study of colonialism and postcolonialism from a different perspective, their work is linked by common issues. Ngũgĩ Wa Thiong'o, Achille Mbembe, and Sabelo J. Ndlovu-Gatsheni contribute to discussions about power, identity, representation, and emancipation in the context of colonial and postcolonial societies by interacting with the theoretical notions of Fanon and Spivak.

Chapter 5

Postcolonial Feminism, Third World Literacy, Nationalism and Education

Postcolonial feminism, third-world literacy, nationalism, and education combine in a complicated web that represents interconnected concerns and aspirations of postcolonial cultures. Within the context of postcolonialism, the abovementioned aspects and areas emphasise the challenges of individuals, notably women.

Postcolonial feminism discusses the issues that women face in the aftermath of colonial domination. It criticizes and questions not just patriarchal institutions inside postcolonial societies, but also how Western feminism has overlooked the basic problems of women in the Global South. Postcolonial feminists advocate for an intersectional perspective of gender, race, class, and colonial history in determining women's lives. They underline the importance of amplifying the voices of women who have been marginalized within both colonial and postcolonial contexts.

Third World Literacy: Within the postcolonial perspective, third-world literacy addresses the challenges and opportunities associated with schooling in historically neglected regions by colonial powers. The term "third world" itself is a critique of the colonial-era binary distinction. Literacy in postcolonial nations entails not only learning fundamental reading and writing abilities, but also regaining indigenous knowledge, languages, and cultural practices. It becomes an empowering tool, allowing individuals to critically connect with their own history and participate more actively in the socio-political context.

Nationalism: Nationalism is important in postcolonial education and feminism. Nationalist movements aimed to recover sovereignty and cultural identity in the aftermath of colonialism. Postcolonial nationalism, on the other hand, can be a double-edged sword, reproducing exclusionary practices and limiting the reach of inclusive education. Postcolonial feminists investigate critically how nationalist goals affect women, sometimes reinforcing traditional gender roles. Within postcolonial discourse, the conflict between female equality and nationalist goals becomes a key subject of inquiry.

Education: As a fundamental subject in postcolonialism, education is a critical battleground for the negotiation of identities and power dynamics. Postcolonial education aims to be transformative by questioning colonial legacies and encouraging critical thinking. It entails not only learning but also revising curricula to reflect varied perspectives, particularly those of underrepresented groups. Postcolonial feminists advocate for a gender-equal education that challenges patriarchal conventions. The educational process consequently becomes a weapon for altering postcolonial societies as well as a means of emancipation.

In conclusion, the intersections of postcolonial feminism, third-world literacy, nationalism, and education highlight the challenges of identity, power, and knowledge. These themes work together to construct a larger liberation project in which education becomes a transformational force, and feminism serves as a catalyst for rethinking societies outside the restrictions of colonial legacies.

5.1 "Under Western Eyes: Feminist Scholarship and Colonial Discourses"- Chandra Talpade Mohanty

A famous feminist theorist and cultural critic, Chandra Talpade Mohanty has had a considerable impact on the fields of women's studies, postcolonial theory, and cultural studies. Mohanty, who was born in India, has used her work to challenge and reshape feminist rhetoric. Her fundamental work, "Under Western Eyes: Feminist Scholarship and Colonial Discourses" (1986), criticizes the Eurocentrism inherent in certain feminist ideas, which tend to universalize women's experiences without taking into account the varied geopolitical circumstances. Mohanty, a pioneer in the formation of global feminism, emphasizes the significance of recognizing the distinct historical and cultural aspects influencing women's lives, advocating for a more contextually grounded approach to feminist thought. Her contributions also include an investigation of how colonialism and globalization intersect with gender, race, and class, shaping women's lives in the Global South. Mohanty is well-known for her involvement in academic and social justice activism, advocating for a more inclusive and socially responsible education system. Chandra Talpade Mohanty's lasting impact is her dedication to promoting a sophisticated awareness of feminist concerns, questioning Western-centric ideas, and contributing to the ongoing discussion about gender, racism, and global injustices.

Following the release of "Under Western Eyes," her essay in 1986, Chandra Mohanty Talpade became a well-known and acclaimed writer and critic. The essay is well-known in the field of cross-cultural feminist research. The essay shows that researchers working within the framework of western feminist theory are simply creating homogenous, essentialising, and universalizing conceptions of women in the third world. This is a result of the discursive construction of gender and development written by women in the third world, which tended to obscure regional and historical distinctiveness.

The essay challenges the risks associated with the idea that women form a cohesive group that is supported and enabled by social, political, and economic factors. She criticizes the idea of global sisterhood and its fictitious claims to foster unity and more potent feminist scholarship on a political level. "Under Western Eyes" was published as the opening chapter in her collection *Feminism without Borders*, which included previously published pieces. This achievement has made her well-known for her contributions to postcolonial feminism and transnational studies during the past 20 years. Mohanty is a native of Bombay and is currently employed by Hamilton College in the United States as a women's studies professor. Chandra Talpade Mohanty is the Dean's Professor of the Humanities and the Distinguished Professor of Women's and Gender Studies at Syracuse University. Her research focuses on transnational feminist theory, anti-capitalist feminist praxis, anti-racist education, and knowledge politics.

She has also engaged in the fields of politics of place and epistemology. She critiques the uniform viewpoints and assumptions found in western feminist literature that highlight third-world women in this essay. She criticizes the idea of global sisterhood and its fictitious claims to foster unity and more potent feminist scholarship on a political level. She incorporates the works of Patricia Jeffery, Beverly Lindsay, Fran Hosken, Maria Cutrufelli, Juliette Minces, and Zed Press under the Third World Series banner. By using a discursive technique, these publications essentially colonial ghettoize non-Western "third world women." They are seen as the opposite group. She claims that lumping all third-world women together symbolizes the western women's universalizing and homogenous classification. Third-world women are viewed as "poor, uneducated, tradition-bound, and victimized." (Mohanty 337)

They fail to recognize the diversity and plurality of women in the third world. They view women from the third world as not belonging to their own class, gender, or ethnicity. The essay questions the ethnocentric ideas of western feminists that lump people together under the heading of "third world women" and neglect the variety across a wide geographic spectrum, giving them a common identity—that of victims. This is an example of how Western theorists and thinkers have overgeneralized women, suggesting only a hierarchy of superiority and inferiority.

In addition to dividing women into two opposing groups, this oversimplification undermines women's solidarity and unity by portraying western women as educated, universally emancipated, equal, in charge of their own lives, and superior, clever, and in control of their own bodies and sexuality in comparison to the group of third-world women who are perceived as being largely exploited and illiterate, sexually assaulted, in need of rescue. This skewed and biased asymmetries of power are implied by classification and segregation, which puts women, the sole guardians of knowledge via their writings who are from the West and language, in relation to the victims of oppression who are women in the third world. She says: "…not only are third women defined in a particular way prior to their entry into social relations, but since no connections are made between first and third world power shifts, it reinforces the assumption that people in the third world just have not evolved to the extent that the West has." (Mohanty 352)

Mohanty dissects the colonial themes that characterize third-world women as stereotypical victims after seeing the discursive practice in the creation of knowledge in the west, especially in the case of western feminists. The genital mutilation of all African and Middle Eastern women is depicted in the works of Hosken and Lindsay as the victims of male aggression; consequently, they are objects who defend themselves and also depict their male counterparts as having the same political objective of ensuring female dependence and subservience through all means. They also serve as representations of universally violent issues.

This is the quintessential locking and grouping of women in a fixed space and socio-political powerlessness, which problematizes any potential change and leaves only a dual system. Mohanty criticizes this totalization, arguing that it creates a dual system that keeps people in the third world because they belong to uniformed groups, thus sustaining power structures and power relations according to Foucault's "juridico-discursive" paradigm of power. There is a "cycle of prohibition and uniformity" (Mohanty 350) enforced by this power model. Women who attempt to escape victimization are unable to do so because of this duality.

They eventually assume the role of oppressor or offender, which presents another obstacle to the achievement of the feminist vision—namely, the quest of gender justice and equality. Third-world women's alienation from the self is just another way that western feminism perpetuates victimization. It awakens the possibility of alternative ways of thinking by putting victims and the weak and unable in command. In the words of Elleke Boehmer, in her famous book, *Stories of Women: Gender and Narrative in the Postcolonial Nation:* "I recognize along with Francois Lionnet, Caren Kaplan, Sangeeta Ray and others that feminism must be viewed both as the respect for the specificity of historical differences between women..." (Boehmer 13) *Stories of Women* brings together her landmark essays on the mother figure and the postcolonial nation, as well as new material on male autobiography, 'daughter' writers, the colonial body, postcolonial trauma, and the nation in a transnational setting. Similarly, Stef Craps, in his book *Postcolonial Witnessing: Trauma Out of Bounds* (2013), discusses the effects of "insidious trauma", "oppression-based trauma", "post-colonial syndrome", and "post-traumatic slavery syndrome" (Craps 29). Even chapter two, which deals with the somewhat technical historical context of trauma definition and attacks trauma theorists' reliance on obsolete psychological models, is brought to life by Craps' use of concrete instances. He uses Frantz Fanon's portrayal of a racist conversation with a tiny child, for example, to demonstrate the "insidious trauma" (29) of everyday oppression. In doing so, he also introduces Fanon to a broader canon of trauma literature.

Mohanty also provides concrete instances from a variety of sources, such as Maria Rosa's book *Women of Africa: Roots of Oppression* (1983), which asserts that prostitution is the primary source of income for all African women and that these women are economically reliant on one another. She wonders if it will be feasible to write a book titled *Women of Europe: Roots of Oppression* in light of the skewed perspectives that many western women writers hold about women in the third world. "I am not objecting to the use of universal groupings for descriptive purposes. Women from the continent of Africa can be descriptively characterized as "women of Africa" It is when "women of Africa" becomes a homogeneous sociological grouping characterized by common dependencies or powerlessness that problems arise- we say too little and too much at the same time." (Mohanty 340)

She thus tries to contextualize the complexity of women in the non-Western world by providing varying examples from the works of Western women, portraying them as generally repressive when viewed from Western eyes. It is insufficient to portray women's veils as a generally oppressive reality, generalizing and essentializing them as a means of sexual control in Iran, Saudi Arabia, Egypt, Pakistan, and India. She contends that many historical periods should be considered when examining women's veils in Iran. For instance, some women from the West utilized the veils to show support for their working-class sisters who were participating in protests in the streets during the Revolution of 1979.

On the other side, women's veils were mandated by required religious law throughout the post-revolutionary era. Therefore, it is incorrect to lump all forms of veiling into one derogatory category; instead, it is an example of intellectual laziness to group all forms of veiling together. In Iran, women are now required to cover their heads while they are in public, even if they choose not to. This is because veiling is mandated by religious law, which applies to all Iranian women. So, wearing veils is more than simply a cultural trend in Iran. Therefore, even if Iranian women utilize the veil to negotiate and challenge their social and public presence, the oppression that is imposed from above remains indiscriminate. She argues: "While there may be a physical similarity in the veils worn by women in Saudi Arabia and Iran, the specific meaning attached to this practice varies according to the cultural and ideological context." (Mohanty 347)

However, Mohanty's justification for the mistreatment of women falls short because even religious organizations contribute to the mistreatment of Iranian women. She then goes on to criticize Juliette Minces' writing, which has centred on women in Islamic and Arab countries. She asserts that their women only know what it is to be a mother, wife, or sister because of the patriarchal systems in place in their community. They all have the same vision, which Mohanty challenges by pointing out that this vision ignores the cultural variations that exist among different countries in addition to assuming that a single kinship structure is the primary cause of women's subjugation.

She goes on to criticize Minces, saying that she neglects to bring up any particular family customs that contribute to the subjugation of Muslim and Arab women. As a result, Muslim women are oppressed by this type of global perception, which also undermines their further battles and efforts. Mohanty provides an example of the post-revolution fight of Iranian women, which helps to explain why she criticizes Minces. Even though women in Iran are subject to male rule, they continue to fight to avoid becoming victims and staying at home. Through their advocacy for human rights and a range of activities, including the well-known One Million Signatures for Change campaign, they have established a strong presence in the male-centric, hegemonic culture.

Women are becoming more educated and employed, which is a harbinger of changes that can only occur when they become free from the constraints of conventional homemaking duties. Since the 1990s, women have made up more than 60% of students at Iranian universities. Between 1994 and 2008, the number of NGOs led by women for women also rose. The increase in female writers, filmmakers, attorneys, human rights advocates, and scientists is another testament to the efforts and successes of Iranian women who defy social norms and demand their own standing. Therefore, the claim that women in developing Third World countries are homogenized is absurd.

Mohanty is well aware of the serious ramifications of politics in the cultural discourse and the widespread representation of Third World women as victims in need of rescue. She thus issues a warning to western scholarship about the possibility of aiding "contemporary imperialism," which now seeks to manipulate people's hearts and minds through language politics rather than physical force. She provides a clear illustration of how George W. Bush used the ubiquitous media apparatus to present the imperialist war as an effort to free the women of Afghanistan in the run-up to the US invasion of that country. These propaganda discourses occasionally come to the fore as tensions between Iran and the west grow more intense.

As a result, the effects of such western created discourse extend much beyond national boundaries. Such stereotypes of western women, which present them as secular and universally free, do not give a true picture of western women. Had that been the case, feminist political activism in the west would never have been necessary. The fight for women in the West is, in reality, still ongoing. According to data, women in Canada continue to earn thirty per cent less than males do, and there has been a rise in domestic abuse, sexual exploitation, and female human trafficking in recent years across North America.

Mohanty thus questions the dichotomy that pits women in the Third World against women in the West. She opposes the disproportionate rhetoric that divides women into two classes, each of which is seen as "one that enables and sustains the other." Her essay, therefore, tells us that the sociological knowledge of the "sameness" (Mohanty 337) in resisting tyranny, regardless of class, culture, or any other geographical limits they belong to, is the factor that links women as sisters in battle. She affirms her commitment to feminist solidarity and makes the argument that, while producing and distributing texts that emphasize categorical phrases like "Third World Women" (Mohanty 338), it is crucial to be aware of the hegemony of the western scholarly establishment.

5.2 "Minute on Indian Education": Thomas Macaulay

Thomas Babington Macaulay (1800-1859) was a 19th-century British historian, politician, and essayist who made significant contributions to literature, history, and political theory. Macaulay, who was born in Leicestershire, England, had a notable career as a historian and served in several government positions. From 1834 until 1838, Thomas Macaulay was a member of the East India Company's supreme council. He was in charge of the legal and educational reforms during this time. He wrote the "Minute" in response to the council members who suggested that Indian pupils should still receive instruction in Sanskrit and Arabic in addition to English. Saying that thousands of libraries of Persian and Sanskrit literature are worth even half of the books on the European book shelf undervalues Indian writers and their contributions. He claimed that because native Indians were so unkind and impoverished, it would be difficult to instil any worthwhile values in them and that they needed to be educated in some areas.

What wording, then, should be used? English was preferred by half of the council, while Sanskrit and Arabic were suggested by the other half. Despite his admission that he knew nothing about Sanskrit or Arabic, he was nonetheless able to appraise their worth because he had read translations of certain well-known works written in both languages. He speaks English fluently both at home and in India and uses it for communication. While he is willing to accept the knowledge of the East, he does not think it is comparable to that of the West. He says: "I have never found one among them who could deny that a single shelf of a good European library was worth the whole native literature of India and Arabia…" (Macaulay 1)

He never came across any Orientalist writer who dared to contrast the poetry of the great European countries with that of Arabic and Sanskrit. Evaluation and research have shown that English poetry is incalculable based on documented facts. He says the value of the Sanskrit language is less than that of the palest abridgements found in English preparatory schools.

Since "we have to educate a people who cannot at present be educated by means of their mother-tongue," (Macaulay 3), Indians must be taught a foreign language. Writings composed in the languages that are currently spoken have a higher literary merit than all writings from three millennia ago in all languages combined.

In addition, the language of the governing class is English. The natives of higher social classes who occupy higher positions in the East Government also speak of it. English is becoming more and more popular due to its status as the language of the growing European communities—those in South Africa and Australia, for example—and its historical ties to the Indian Empire. Given the state of the nation and the impact of the English language, English is the foreign language that "our native subjects" (Macaulay 4) can utilize the most.

The holy texts that date back millions of years are written in Arabic and Sanskrit, giving them special encouragement. However, the English administration in India must be impartial toward religious matters and not merely tolerant. Furthermore, language is as full of terrible superstitions as it is of helpful information. A false religion coexists with erroneous astronomy, medicine, and history. He disagrees with the council members' opinions because he feels that they are too general, but they must create a class of interpreters to act as a bridge between themselves and the millions of people they are in charge of, who should be English in morality, taste, and intellect but Indian in blood and colour. He says: "we must at present do our best to form a class who may be interpreters between us and the millions whom we govern; a class of persons, Indian in blood and colour, But English in taste, in opinions, in morals, and in intellect." (Macaulay 8)

A state education system was formally brought into Indian history with the passage of the Charter Act of 1813, which also required the East India Company to take on responsibility for the education of the Indian populace. As a result, the East India Company established a large number of schools and colleges between 1813 and 1857, laying the groundwork for the English educational system in India. For the first time, the Indians received formal funding to further their studies. On June 10, 1834, Macaulay arrived in Madras and reported his first impressions:

> to be on land after three months at sea is of itself a great change. But to be in such a land! The dark faces, with white turbans, and flowing robes: the trees not our trees: the very smell of atmosphere that of a hothouse, and the architecture as strange as the vegetation. (Pritchett)

When he stepped onto the bench, he was greeted by a fifteen-gun salute. On February 2, 1835, he penned a minute. He composed the minutes with fervour, exaggerated confidence, and disregard for the fact that there are always two sides to any given issue since he was always a man of his views. He was greatly impacted by the advancements of western society. He was presented with the arguments of Orientalists, which he forcefully refuted with compelling minutes and made a compelling case for the English-language dissemination of Western knowledge.

The recommendations made by Macaulay were officially sanctioned by Lord William Bentinck. English became the official language of the court in 1837, and a government resolution in 1844 made numerous prominent positions available to Indians. These developments contributed to the explosive rise of English education. The following justifications were used to deny the claims made by Sanskrit or Arabic: (Macaulay 2)

1. English is more useful than Arabic or Sanskrit and is the gateway to modern understanding. (Macaulay 8)
2. The ruling elite also sponsors English. It is most likely going to become the primary language of trade over the eastern seas. (Macaulay 4)
3. Just as Greek and Latin brought about the Renaissance in England, English will do the same in India. (Macaulay 4)
4. The locals don't want to learn Arabic or Sanskrit; instead, they want to be taught English. (Macaulay 5)
5. In order to achieve that goal, we must focus our efforts on educating the locals to be excellent scholars. (Macaulay 8)
6. It is also essential to create a class of people who serve as interpreters between them and the millions of people they were in charge of, who should be English in morality, taste, and intellect but Indian in blood and colour. (Macaulay 8)

In addition, he offered to step down as GCPI President in the event if his demands were turned down. As a result, he concluded his minutes dramatically, knowing that Macaulay's minute would receive complete support from Bentinck.

5.3 "The Beginning of English Literary Study in British India": Gauri Visvanathan

Gauri Viswanathan, a renowned postcolonial critic and theorist, has made substantial contributions to our understanding of the complex interactions between education, colonialism, and cultural encounters. Viswanathan, who was born in India, dives into the complexity of religious conversion and the transformational impact of Western education in the colonial environment, particularly in British-ruled India, in her book "Outside the Fold: Conversion, Modernity, and Belief" (1998). Her interdisciplinary approach, which draws on cultural studies, literary theory, and postcolonial studies, adds to the study of identity formation, resistance, and the function of literature in reflecting and developing postcolonial narratives. Viswanathan has been crucial in developing discourses on the interconnections of culture, power, and representation throughout her academic career, which includes a position at Columbia University. Her sophisticated study continues to provide vital insights into the legacy of colonialism, emphasizing the profound importance of education on postcolonial cultural and religious landscapes.

Gauri Visvanathan has been awarded numerous distinguished professorships, most recently as the Backman Professor at Berkeley. She is interested in culture, religion, and education. Her writings are in the field of British and colonial studies in the 19th century. She writes about minority communities in Britain as well as colonial issues in contemporary India. Her insightful ideas are focused on the issues of historiography, colonialism, and Hinduism. Among the several honours she has won are the Harry Levin Prize, the James Russell Lowell Prize, the Ananda K. Coomaraswamy Prize, and others. The American Institute of Indian Studies awarded her a scholarship as well for her research cooperation on a significant globalization and autonomy project cantered in Toronto and Hamilton, Canada.

Gauri Visvanathan has been Gayatri Spivak's colleague and holds the formal title of "Class of 1933 Professor in the Humanities." Like Gayatri Spivak, she frequently visits Chennai. She made the case that the English literary canon in India was an imperial instrument in her well-known book *Masks of Conquest: Literary Study and British Rule in India* (1989). Her other publications include *Power, Politics, and Culture* (1998) and *Outside the Fold: Conversion, Modernity, and Belief* (1998). In *Masks of Conquest: Literary Study and British Rule in India*, she claims that the English literary study was founded using a colonial management tactic. It was a political ploy carried out by the colonial government. The literary works fulfilled the aim of promoting the idealized image of an Englishman as someone who is very different from a colonist who indulges in the activities of a colonial state. English literature and Empire politics were closely related. Changes in the curriculum may lead to discussions on the goals of English education geared by missionaries, colonial authorities, or British administrators. Early in the nineteenth century, English literary studies were brought to India with the goal of enhancing Indian moral awareness. Since they were upholding religious neutrality in India, Christian teachings could not be mandated. Instead, they recommended heavily Christianized English literature for government schools.

At first, missionaries stressed the religious study of English literature, which led to the teaching of English literature with more Christian teachings and the higher standards of English society and morality. Rhymes, alliteration, and poetic devices were also taught. They reversed course later in the 1850s and began to advocate for secular study of English literature in order to promote trade and commercial literacy. She gives a thorough description of the various strategies used by British administrators, including utilitarians, Anglicists, and missionaries, to alter the way English literature is taught in Indian schools. To comprehend the history of education, each policy must be thoroughly examined in light of the circumstances surrounding its creation. (Viswanathan 1-15)

In the past, British Indian educational history has concentrated on the humanistic qualities of literature, such as the development of the storyline, characters, and aesthetic sensibility. The colonizers regarded these components as the most crucial and vital to the process of establishing socio-political power. There were covert methods for tying the literary values accorded to literature to the educational system. Their goal was to establish hierarchies of power and control that would represent the relationships between the people for whom the curriculum was created and the people who were required to follow it. This was their policy of cultural domination. Due to their prejudicial belief that Indian literature was tainted with immorality and impurity, they did not introduce any Indian literary works for study in schools or colleges. Thus, educational concepts that had either been abandoned in England or succumbed to ingrained customs and orthodoxies were tested in India. In the bountiful continent of India, their unproven theories were noticed and put into practice. The intention behind this was to make Indians silent. Gauri Visvanathan also draws attention to the issue of teaching the Bible in Indian universities and schools.

The teaching of the Bible was more challenging in England than in India because Roman Catholic concerns were the source of the dread of the Bible, which was genuinely English and not Hindu. The cultural uniformity of India made it inappropriate to teach the Bible there. Indian nationalism was sparked by the liberal ideologies of Western philosophy, thanks to their formal education. Thus, in the beginning, humanistic education benefited both the ruling class and the class that was dominated, as well as the colonizer and the colonized. Indians would have benefited much if these elements had come together since this particular educational system was capable of helping Indians break free from false consciousness.

She says: "Orientalism and Anglicism not as polar opposites but as points along a continuum of attitudes toward the manner and form of native governance, the necessity and justification for which remained by large an issue of remarkably little disagreement." (Viswanathan 30)

As a result, the British administrators made an effort to tailor their educational systems to meet their own objectives while also fitting the traditional Indian mentality. Teaching morality lessons through literary analysis was equally vital. The degradation of Hindu culture and religion led to the re-introduction of Christian principles and systems. They purposefully fought the caste system as well as numerous other customs, such as idolatry and Indian polytheism, in an effort to promote morality, monotheism, and mono-rule. This one code stressed having one mentality and one power to bring about political unity. Gauri Visvanathan cites Charles Grant's opinions as follows: "the multiplicity of Gods in the Hindu pantheon blurred any sense of a single, universal comic law upon all social harmony rests."(Viswanathan 74).

Attacks were made on the Hindu system of many gods in an attempt to restore a broken cosmic harmony. Because they were aware of the dire repercussions if Indians were truly enlightened, they sought to maintain Indians at the level of children's innocence.

The principles, code of conduct, morality, and western history were all matched with history education. As a result, they included this type of historical study in their teaching. They lost their political power when their native languages and cultural heritage were eradicated since they could only find the truth in their culture and history.

Thus, this European educational approach took away Indian identity. Indians were given false consciousness through liberal education. They began to believe that they could be better than they actually were, which gave them the confidence to alter who they were, ultimately changing the course of events. Due to their inability to provide adequate jobs for the amount of Indians acquiring liberal education, the literary studies included in the curriculum to prepare them for the use of the British administrators were lessened. Therefore, the policy of the British school system failed to produce Indian youth who could defer to authority. Because of their English education, they were self-sufficient and developed a false sense of independence that prevented them from distinguishing between the rich and the poor, the old and the young. After caste and religious barriers were removed because of this new education program, social mobility expanded.

5.4 "The Nation and Its Fragments"- Partha Chatterjee

Partha Chatterjee, a renowned Indian historian, political scientist, and social theorist, has made indelible contributions to postcolonial studies, political theory, and South Asian studies. Born in 1947 in Calcutta, he is among the distinguished members of the Subaltern Studies. At the Centre for Studies in Social Sciences in Calcutta, he teaches political science. *Nationalist Thought and the Colonial World* (1993) is one of his prominent publications. In his book *Nationalist Thought and the Colonial World: A Derivative Discourse?* He says: "…nationalist thought accepts and adopts the same essentialist conception based on the distinction between 'the East' and 'the West'…" (Chatterjee 38). He admits to admiring Rorty, Barthes, Foucault, and Derrida. Nonetheless, beneath all of this jargon lies a compelling thesis about the three stages of Indian nationalism: the moment of departure (epitomized by Bankimchandra Chatttopadhyay), the moment of manoeuvre (Gandhi), and the moment of arrival (Nehru). Chatterjee effectively demonstrates how nationalism in India was analogous to Gramsci's concept of the 'passive revolution,' i.e. a push toward independence rather than transforming or dismantling colonial institutions. Instead of embracing nationalism, he contends, we should oppose the union of reason and capital. One might anticipate Chatterjee to draw connections to other anti-colonial nationalisms based on the title of this book, but he doesn't; instead, he solely discusses India (not even other countries of South-Asia). He was a significant member of the Bengal School of Political Economy, critically engaging with Western political theories and advocating for alternative viewpoints rooted in the realities of postcolonial cultures. Chatterjee, as a member of the Subaltern Studies collective, has made substantial contributions to altering historiography by emphasizing the perspectives of underprivileged communities. His research into democracy and political philosophy has advanced our understanding of how political concepts manifest in a variety of cultural and historical circumstances. Partha Chatterjee's scholarship continues to impact and enhance discourses on the difficulties of political thought and practice in the Global South, including positions at universities such as the Centre for Studies in Social Sciences, Calcutta, and Columbia University.

Partha Chatterjee's book *The Nation and Its Fragments* (1993) examines the concept of community outside of India's political nationalism, within the country's incredibly varied historical background. He also discusses Bengali women's incredible and ongoing efforts and struggles, and how they have helped usher in a new era of awakening. As they transition into a new period, they have also made an effort to maintain their traditional identity and colonial conventions. He said that although we occasionally lose sight of who we are, maintaining an open third eye will help us comprehend things honestly. Rather than becoming inflexible and stiff, we might attempt to embrace the changes and differences with an open heart and mind. The women of Bengal discuss the western systems of dichotomies that divide Bengali nationalism while preserving their identity and customs and engaging in Indian political nationalism. (Chatterjee, *The Nation and Its Fragments* 116-134) Put another way, they fight for and against colonialism according to the definitions provided by both parties, maintaining their community identity in opposition to Indian political nationalism while also advancing women's status within the central party and upholding Bengali culture before western modernization arrived. Even if individuals were giving up their identity, culture, and history to the modern, western world, or the "outer" world, they were yet sufficiently self-assured to protect their "inner" selves by accepting their house as the protector of their Bengali identity.

Women's standing in the modern world, according to Partha Chatterjee, was jeopardized because they prioritized their culture and history, which compelled women to maintain their identities, despite the impact of modernization. She displayed "spiritual signs of her femininity" (Chatterjee, *The Nation and Its Fragments* 130) in the way she dressed, what she ate, and how she behaved in public. On the other hand, with their spouses and daughters at their sides, men were able to maintain their proud identities in the modern world while keeping up with their outer and inner lives.

Women were forced to live in their own worlds as a result of the separation between the public and private spheres, while men were free to live in opposition to both, leading to even more inequality and the development of two distinct systems. The political system in the United States is likewise comparable to this. Two structures were established in India: the material and the spiritual, which were bolstered by anti-colonial nationalism in opposition to western civilization. Therefore, in India, people were adjusting to the modern civilization brought about by colonialism while also exercising their traditional ethos, which was symbolized by their families and women, in the spiritual inner world made up of religion and the antiquated caste system. He says:

> "Every social form of the community, in the formal sense, must achieve the unity of mutual separateness and mutual dependence of its parts." (Chatterjee, *The Nation and Its Fragments* 105)

Community resistance served as a means of maintaining the sense of self through this arrogant identity, which was not even the true self. Since they were obliged to limit themselves to their "inner" selves in order to uphold the arrogant "outer" identity of their men, women in these patriarchal societies were ultimately burdened with feelings of inferiority. This is why the majority of patriarchal systems were founded on standards of pride. This makes it clearer how the self-perception was given priority while creating the system. Women were, therefore, reprimanded for failing to uphold the ideals of the specific femininity that their society and culture represented, and they also became the guardians of the traditional self, private self, and spiritual self.

As a result, women were forced to remain in their traditional selves, denying them the opportunity to modernize alongside the rest of the world. Examples of history that recurrently repeat themselves are clear and can be found. In the past, there have been several conflicts over ideology and power. Women are destined to occupy the lower rungs of the ladder because of their innate ability to preserve our traditional identity and cultural values. They will carry on with the task of protecting and fostering our national identity while also fighting for our own and modernizing everything.

> Partha Chatterjee contends that political nationalism and nationalism are not the same thing because many anti-colonial nationalists establish their own sovereignty within colonial society prior to starting their political struggle against imperial power. (Chatterjee, *The Nation and Its Fragments* 158-173)

These nationalists separated the spiritual and material spheres of their culture. While males were taking care of their material selves by functioning in the outside world, women were forced to represent spirituality through culture, caste, and traditional ethos. Chatterjee demonstrates how these middle-class elites prepared for the political conquest after first imagining the country to be playing in a spiritual dimension. Chatterjee speaks in Bengali while providing a wealth of examples taken from Indian sources. He presents a contradiction between the private and the public, the material and the spiritual, and ultimately discovers postcolonial modernity, which connects earlier resistance to modernity.

In the end, he discovers postcolonial modernity, which connects earlier battles against modernity, and offers a paradox of private against public—material versus spiritual. In his introduction title, "Whose Imagined Community?" Chatterjee challenges Anderson's imagined communities in the opening section of the book. In Bengal, for example, the book illustrates how nationalist movements have shaped subcontinental history and how "anti-colonial nationalism creates its own domain of sovereignty within colonial society well before its political battle with imperial power." (Chatterjee, *The Nation and Its Fragments* 6) He explains his reasoning for it. Because of the requirements of comprehending the nation exclusively through public, political action, the "prehistory" of nationalism is overlooked.

When it came to colonial nationalism, two structures were established: the material and the spiritual, which were reinforced by anti-colonial resistance to western civilization. India's population was, therefore, adjusting to the contemporary world, which was the effect of colonialism, manifesting in the "material" realm while also expressing their customs and civilizations, which were embodied by their women and family in the inner spiritual realm made up of traditional religions and caste hierarchy. Between "national" and "western," binaries were established; hence offering an idea centred on uniqueness and distinction rather than a notion of mankind as a whole.

The "national" community's identity is, therefore, in opposition to other groups in this regard. Negotiations over dualism is another topic covered in his work. In addition, he discusses the reform of women's education and the memoirs written by educated women about how they adapted to their new roles at home and in society. Therefore, the job of female emancipation is linked to and placed on women as a new social obligation in order to achieve independent nationhood. The foundation of the new nation will be cultural distinctions encompassing both traditional and modern modes of subjugation.

Thus, nationalism asserted its sovereignty over the internal spiritual domains of language, religion, and caste, arguing for a fundamental distinction from the colonizer while simultaneously eliminating any indication of distinction in the external material domains of the state, such as law, administration, and so forth. Therefore, the communal idea of universality that has permeated the postcolonial state with the claims of "autonomous subjectivity" and the insistence on difference are at odds.

To conclude, the selected seminal readings in this chapter are based on similar aspects as they examine and critique the effects of colonialism in a number of social domains, such as nationalism, education, feminism, and literature, in the context of postcolonial discourse. Together, they advance knowledge of how postcolonial modern realities are nevertheless shaped by the dynamics of colonial authority. In colonial and postcolonial countries, while strategies of domination based on gender, race, class, and language intersect and reinforce one another, these writings illustrate the intersectionality of power structures. As an illustration of the interaction between colonialism and patriarchy, Mohanty's critique of Western feminist studies highlights how colonial discourses reinforce gendered stereotypes and denigrate women from the Global South. They provided insight into the hegemonic and cultural imperialist strategies used by colonial governments to keep conquered populations under control.

The imposition of Western education and language was employed as a tactic of cultural assimilation and colonial domination, bolstering the hegemonic position of the colonizers while marginalizing indigenous knowledge systems. Macaulay's "Minute on Indian Education" is an example of this. The selected reading also looks at ways that people have contested and rebelled against colonial authority institutions. For example, Altbach's critique of literary colonialism reveals the ways in which postcolonial intellectuals and writers contest Western literary domination and attempt to regain agency through cultural production. Similar to this, Viswanathan's examination of British Indian English literary education shows how native elites negotiated and opposed colonial educational initiatives to assert their cultural identities. They discuss the intricacies of nationalist movements and how national identities are constructed in postcolonial cultures. By exposing the shortcomings of Western forms of nationalism in non-Western contexts, Chatterjee's examination of nationalism in "Nation and Its Fragments" sheds light on the conflicts between colonial and indigenous conceptions of nationhood. These writings demonstrate how national identities are formed and how postcolonial people fight for their right to self-determination.

These seminal essays are related to each other within the postcolonial framework because of their shared endeavour to analyze the long-lasting impacts of colonialism on different facets of society and to shed light on the intricacies of identity, resistance, and power in postcolonial settings. Their contributions enhance our comprehension of the consequences of colonialism and the difficulties associated with decolonization. They provide insightful information to academics and activists working on the continuous endeavour to restore agency and sovereignty in the Global South.

Chapter 6

Postcolonial Caribbean Literature: Works by Derek Walcott and Jamaica Kincaid

6.1 Postcolonial Literature: An Introduction

Postcolonial literature refers to literary works written by authors from places that were formerly colonized by European powers or, more broadly, from areas that experienced colonization and its aftermath. This literary genre arose in response to the historical legacy of colonialism and the challenges of postcolonial countries. Identity, culture, power relations, resistance, and the impact of colonization on individuals and communities are common issues in postcolonial literature.

Postcolonial literature is distinguished by the following characteristics:

1. **Diverse viewpoints**: Postcolonial literature represents a wide range of voices and experiences, emphasizing the viewpoints of people who have previously been neglected or silenced.

2. **Cultural Hybridity**: Many postcolonial works highlight cultural hybridity, highlighting the merging and alteration of many cultural aspects in the context of colonial encounters.

3. **Colonial and Postcolonial Contexts**: These works frequently address the region's colonial history and its consequences in the present. They also investigate the decolonization process and its problems.

4. **Identity and Belonging**: Postcolonial literature usually addresses issues of identity and belonging, looking at how people sustain their cultural and national identities in the aftermath of colonization.

5. **Resistance and Agency**: Authors in this genre frequently examine themes of resistance and agency, emphasizing how people and communities express themselves against repressive colonial powers.

6. **Language and Representation**: Postcolonial writers may struggle with language and representation concerns, questioning Eurocentric ideas and attempting to reclaim and re-write their narratives.

7. **Global Perspective**: While postcolonial literature frequently addresses local and regional issues, it also has a worldwide component. It contributes to a greater understanding of interdependence and global influence.

Chinua Achebe, Salman Rushdie, Ngugi Wa Thiong'o, Derek Walcott and many others are notable postcolonial authors. Their works, which include novels, poetry, essays, and plays, play an important role in shaping discourses about colonialism, identity, and social justice. In essence, postcolonial literature serves as a forum for delving into the complexity of postcolonial society, celebrating multiple voices, and contributing to a better understanding of colonial legacies. As described by Katharine Burkitt in her phenomenal book *Literary Form as Postcolonial Critique* (2012): "The texts are all aware of the problematic nature of this moment in terms of the cultural and transnational shifts of identity and self-conscious of their own participation" (Burkitt 170). In her postcolonial narrative poems and verse-novels, Katharine Burkitt analyzes the relationship between literary form and textual politics. Burkitt contends that these works violate and undermine the traditions of specific forms and genres, most notably those associated with the prose books, poetry, and epic. Burkitt argues that this subversion of form is an important aspect of the postcoloniality of the text because they all concern themselves with issues of social, racial, and national identities in a world where these categories are inherently complicated. *The Long Space: Transnationalism and Postcolonial Form* (2010) by Peter Hitchcock is one of the most recent and challenging books into this reconstituted postcolonial field, in which nationalism is questioned and the very concept of nation is rendered constitutionally ambiguous, a "flag of evenness that must be studied for its unique process and not simply as the failed-state syndrome ideologically serving state dependency or neo-colonialism." (Hitchcock 6) Hitchcock theorizes the "open seriality of decolonization" as well as the postcolonial "novel in series," which spans numerous volumes and "interrogates the seriality of nation" (Hitchcock 25-26). The extended space's wide seriality is articulated in a "language of form" that exploits allegory, symbolic acts, and the aleatory destinies of desire (Hitchcock 62) and defies any fixed form or formula. Hitchcock's theory of the long space challenges the concept of comparative literature as well as the stable national identities that allow for the critical task of comparison.

As previously discussed, 'postcolonial studies' refers to an interdisciplinary set of viewpoints, theories, and approaches. The studies illustrate the deconstruction of colonial discourses and cognitive patterns that continue to have an impact even today. Many novels, short stories, and poems have been written with postcolonialism as an underlying study. Writings about decolonization, or the political and cultural freedom of cultures under colonial domination, are included. Through the incorporation of metaphors from indigenous culture with modern and current poetry, postcolonial poetry significantly expanded the canon of English literature. The resulting hybridization of the English muse with the muses of post-colonial nations in Africa, India, and the Caribbean and other third-world countries has produced rich and vivid poetry. Understanding the entire western enterprise of colonial domination, hegemony, and exploitation—which is ultimately responsible for the condemnation, damnation, and marginalization of the world's vast population—is essential to understanding postcolonial theory and literature. Jenni Ramone begins her book *Postcolonial Theories* (2011) with a short statement of what Postcolonial studies seeks to do; she states that "Postcolonial literature and theory react to colonial encounters, and the primary function of both is to critique the assumptions and representations on which colonialism is based." (1)

The world was brought together by colonialism, but it also contributed to the continuation of a biased and discriminatory system where ideas of superiority and inferiority—based on factors such as race, culture, ethnicity, language, colour, etc.—became the governing principles. A literary theory known as postcolonialism came into being following the end of colonialism. According to Bill Ashcroft et al., "The idea of 'post-colonial literary theory' emerges from the inability of European theory to deal adequately with the complexities and varied cultural provenance of post-colonial writing. European theories themselves emerge from particular cultural traditions which are hidden by false notions of 'the universal'." (*The Empire Writes Back* 11)

It represents the opposition to and deconstruction of imperialist rhetoric. It was an attempt to expose and externalize the logic and justification of colonialism and imperialism, and it arose as a reaction and resistance to the concepts and ideals of colonialism. A component of Western imperialism, colonialism was an international project of dominance and control. The philosophy known as imperialism defends the right of one country to govern over another on the basis of conquest, both militarily and politically. "The extension and expansion of trade and commerce under the protection of political, legal, and military control" (Childs et al., 227) is how author Peter Childs and author Patrick Williams define imperialism.

Since the seventeenth century, imperialism led to the colonization of several South American nations as well as those in Africa, the Caribbean, and Asia. The experience of colonialism emerged as the most influential and defining factor in these nations, influencing all aspects of their life, including language, culture, politics, law, customs, social conventions, and moral standards. For both the colonizer and the colonized, colonialism was a pervasive phenomenon. Both the colonizers and the colonized experienced changes in their socio-political and economic circumstances.

"Settlement of territory, exploitation or development of resources, and the attempt to govern the indigenous inhabitants of the occupied lands" (Boehmer, *Colonial and Postcolonial Literature* 2) is how Elleke Boehmer defines it. Three points are included in this definition. Territory colonization comes first, followed by resource development or exploitation and, finally, an effort to subjugate the native population. A more thorough analysis of this concept reveals that colonialism aims to dominate the colonized people's whole existence, including their political system, economics, and land. Therefore, colonialism was an all-encompassing, fully involved attempt by colonial powers to govern the colonized.

Following the official end of colonialism in the 20th century, this hegemony of discourse persisted because colonial narratives continued to instil value systems in the minds and cultures of the colonized people, and the binary opposition of superior/inferior, black/white, and colonial/colonized still dominated the psyches of both former colonizers and colonized people. In the words of Kirsti Bohata, in her prominent book *Postcolonialism Revisited: Writing Wales in English* (2004), as she says: "The categories of colonizer and colonized are, of course, far more complex than the simple binary suggested by these two labels might suggest." (Bohata 5) In the context of current debates concerning colonial and post-colonial cultures, Kirsti Bohata investigates how far postcolonial theory paradigms might be productively embraced and adapted to give an informative investigation of Welsh writing in English, while also exploring the issues that such writing may present to the postcolonial theory.

The writers and intellectuals of the former colonies attempted to refute the colonialist discourse and present the honest and objective realities of the colonized people, but these efforts remained the occasional contestations, and until postcolonial theory became recognized as a legitimate theory and reading practice, no theoretical framework could develop. Postcolonial authors have made serious attempts in modern times to 'write back' against colonial writers of history who have portrayed oppressed people as 'savages' and 'barbaric' to the civilized colonizer. As a result, it is critical for postcolonial writers to dispel the myths generated by colonial writers. There are various examples of Victorian book re-workings. *A Tempest* (1969) is a sequel to *The Tempest* (1611), *Things Fall Apart* (1958) is a prequel to *Heart of Darkness* (1902), *Foe* (1986) is a prequel to *Robinson Crusoe* (1719), and *Wide Sargasso Sea* (1966) is a prequel to *Jane Eyre* (1847). As described by Sarah Brouillette in her book *Postcolonial Writers in the Global Literary Marketplace* (2007): "Writers are compelled to resist, justify, or celebrate precisely this aspect of the postcolonial field's arrangement, in accordance with their own circumstances" (Brouillette 4). She further continues her discussion to summarize, several characteristics distinguish the most successful postcolonial literature in the contemporary market: It is English-language literature; it is relatively 'sophisticated' or 'complex' and frequently anti-realist; it is politically liberal and suspicious of nationalism; and it employs a language of exile, hybridity, and 'mongrel' subjectivity. (Brouillette 61)

6.2 Postcolonial Caribbean Literature

Postcolonial Caribbean literature is a rich and diverse body of work that reflects the Caribbean region's complicated historical, cultural, and social experiences in the aftermath of colonialism. In the postcolonial era, this literature emerged as a potent tool for conveying the struggles, identities, and aspirations of Caribbean people. Caribbean literature is firmly steeped in the historical background of colonization, slavery, and European colonial legacies. The narratives frequently deal with the horrific experiences of the transatlantic slave trade and the maltreatment of indigenous people. Brathwaite is a well-known Caribbean writer and cultural theorist who focuses on Caribbean identity, history, and culture. In *The Development of Creole Society in Jamaica, 1770-1820*, he provides a seminal examination of the socio-cultural factors that produced Jamaica's postcolonial society during the colonial periods. While this work is largely concerned with historical analysis rather than literary theory, Brathwaite's insights into Caribbean history and culture have had a considerable impact on the study of postcolonial Caribbean literature (Brathwaite 1-30).

Language, religion, music, and other facets of Caribbean life reflect this confluence of cultural influences. Language is frequently used in multilingual ways in Caribbean literature. To capture the richness of linguistic expressions in the Caribbean Literature, writers integrate local dialects, creole languages, and linguistic experimentation. Caribbean literature addresses issues of identity, belonging, and diaspora. Migration, displacement, and the search for a postcolonial identity are all common issues in Caribbean Literature. Many works of Caribbean literature examine the fights for independence and the challenges of nation-building that followed. The authors deal with the complications of postcolonial nationalism, such as governmental corruption and social injustice. Resistance and emancipation are prominent themes in Caribbean literature. Writers frequently glorify the Caribbean people's resilience in the face of persecution, portraying protagonists who oppose colonial control and fight for liberation.

The oral tradition is important in Caribbean literature. Many authors use storytelling techniques rooted in Caribbean folklore, myths, and oral histories to illustrate the region's cultural richness. Caribbean literature can be used to address societal injustices and inequality. The authors criticize power structures, economic inequities, and the long-lasting impact of colonial-era social hierarchies in Caribbean countries. Gender dynamics and feminism are frequently explored in Caribbean literature. Women writers, in particular, have played an important role in defying patriarchal conventions and giving voice to Caribbean women's experiences. In more recent works, Caribbean literature addresses globalization and its impact on the region. Here are some postcolonial Caribbean voices explored:

6.3 "A Far Cry from Africa"- Derek Walcott

The Nobel laureate and prolific Caribbean poet and playwright Derek Walcott has left an enduring impact on the literary world. Walcott's works, like as "Omeros" and "The Sea is History," which are set on the small island of Saint Lucia, flawlessly interweave Caribbean history, mythology, and the brutal legacy of colonialism. His poetry frequently deals with the conflict between cultural legacy and the influences of European colonization, providing a nuanced view of the Caribbean experience. Furthermore, Walcott's acute sense of language and imagery, which is profoundly anchored in the Caribbean terrain, lifts his lines to worldwide resonance. His poetic legacy transcends borders, offering a striking tribute to the long-lasting impact of postcolonial studies on the human mind. Examining Derek Walcott's writings reveals a significant literary voice that transcends geographical boundaries and enriches our understanding of the complex dynamics of identity and cultural memory. "A Far Cry from Africa" by Derek Walcott is a moving examination of identity and the lingering impact of colonialism. The poem discusses racial tensions and colonial occupation in Africa. The poem expresses the predicament of the indigenous people.

The poet received the Nobel Prize for his contribution to literature. He was born on the island of St Lucia in the British West Indies. As he grew older, he became aware of his hybrid grandparents, who were both white and black. His many poems are based on the idea of roots and division. In 1962, the poem "A Far Cry from Africa" was released. The poem delves into the history of Kenya in the 1950s, when the Mau Mau revolt, led by the Kikuyu tribe, fought for eight years against the colonists who were regarded as illegal trespassers by the locals. Colonialism shattered the cultural history of this place through brutality, cultural hegemony, and racial biases.

The poem, which is rooted in the historical background of Kenya's Mau Mau Uprising, navigates the difficulties of the poet's own identity as a person of mixed descent while diving into broader issues of postcolonial trauma. The poem provides a critical examination of colonial legacy, ambivalence about violence, cultural hybridity, the significance of language, and the personal and collective elements of pain. The poem begins with a reflection on the poet's identity, which is divided between African roots and European influences. The colonial heritage, with its historical wounds, becomes a key motif as the poet grapples with the ambivalence inherent in the collision of civilizations. Walcott's own mixed lineage becomes a microcosm of the larger postcolonial struggle, and his internal conflict serves as a metaphor for the friction between personal identity and external forces.

Violence emerges as a perceptible undercurrent, particularly in the setting of the Mau Mau Uprising. The poet does not take a clear moral stand on the violence, but rather conveys it with ambiguity, respecting the intricacies of the historical time. This sophisticated treatment challenges readers to consider the ethical quandaries of resistance and the blurring lines between oppressors and victimized. The poem's description of violence acts as a metaphor for the historical suffering of the colonized people.

The poet's mixed heritage represents a recurring theme of cultural hybridity. The poem portrays a sense of displacement, stressing the wound coiled in the grass as a metaphor for the poet's psyche's long-term consequence of colonialism. The picture depicts the continual struggle to reconcile the various parts of cultural identity, capturing the separation from African origin.

Walcott's use of language is critical in portraying the poem's emotional weight. The vivid imagery, sophisticated language, and free verse help to portray complicated emotions in a fluid manner. The language of the poem becomes a vehicle for exploring the poet's experience of beauty and harshness, echoing his reality.

The poet is deeply moved and asks himself a difficult question: "How can I face such slaughter and be cool?" (Walcott lines 32-33)

He adores the English language, but his ancestors were Africans who were persecuted by the English, whose native tongue he requires to survive as a poet. The poem's title appears to be peculiar as it appears that he wishes to convey the truth that he lives on the remote island of St Lucia, far from Africa, and that his cry must go a long distance to reach Africa. Or perhaps the ideal image of Africa is let down by the current reality of colonialism. He says:

"A wind is ruffling the tawny pelt of Africa.
Kikuyu, quick as flies,
Batton upon the bloodstreams of the veldt.
Corpses are scattered through a paradise." (Walcott lines 1-4)

The poem's setting on the African plain is depicted in the first line, and the country is contrasted with a lion. Kikuyu is the local clan in Kenya, yet the unadulterated representation of the African plain travels quickly, and Kikuyu is contrasted with the flies buzzing around and fortifying on blood as big as streams. The carcasses have covered Africa's heaven. Human material is represented by images of parasites and worms. The casualties are occurring through one or more means. The poet then paints a picture of the Kikuyu uprising against the English in the 1950s. They are unable to justify their actions. They were seen as savages, as useless as Jews were by the Nazis.

They were likewise seen as despicable. After making this vision, he returns to the wild land of Africa, where many varieties of brutes ruled before African and European development. The whites attempted to regulate and restrain the people who were represented as inhumane, untamed, or barbarians and savages for following the beat of the drum. The poet criticizes the comparison of the Mau Mau uprising to the Spanish Civil War (1936-39). These lines are difficult to understand. The forefathers of France and England wanted to avoid another war, so they signed an indifference agreement signed by twenty-seven countries and endorsed by the military leaders of Germany and Italy.

The Republicans, on the other hand, had no such backing. Despite their gallant efforts, they were defeated. The animalized Africans battled against the supermen in the Mau Uprising. The poet is caught between the current and the past. He's at a loss for words when it comes to the Mau uprising. He is a product of both African and English ancestors. He is not happy with what transpired in the past, but as readers, we can presume that Walcott will not give up either Africa or England.

Africa was a paradise before colonization. The poet reproduced the past and history by juxtaposing heaven littered with carcasses- the demise, death, corpses, and devastation. Worms may represent rot's lament over the destruction of the useless (blacks). Hitler also murdered millions of Jews because of their ethnicity. The poet sees a parallel with the unforgiving encounter of the West Indians with Spain. The fight was comparable to a gorilla vs. Superman. The gorilla represents the locals, while the superman represents the white men. He is divided between his feelings for two cultures:

> "The drunken officer of British rule, HOW CHOOSE
> Between this Africa and the English tongue I love?
> Betray them both, or give back what they give?" (Walcott lines 29-31)

The lyric depicts remorselessness and viciousness in the pursuit of a personality. The poet laments Kenya's past in the 1950s. A nationalist rebellion led to the deaths of 13000 individuals, predominantly Kenyans, as well as a large number of animals. He condemns man's inhumanity in enacting justice through bloodshed, as well as how deaths have been reduced to numbers and statistics. This obscures the reality of the deceased and their pain, regardless of whether they were whites or savages. He comes from a British Caribbean colony, a long way from Africa, but he hears a scream or anguish that has become universal and timeless, reverberating around the globe. The poet gives his poem vibrant force by vivid imagery and juxtapositions. The historical context of the Mau Mau Uprising provides a backdrop for the poem's political commentary. Walcott invites readers to reflect on the consequences of colonialism and the struggles for independence in various parts of the world. The poem becomes a testament to the enduring impact of historical injustices, urging a collective reckoning with the complexities of postcolonial existence.

Thus "A Far Cry from Africa" is a masterwork that deftly weaves together themes of identity and brutality of colonial legacy. Derek Walcott's poetic skill and sophisticated study of historical suffering contribute to the poem's ongoing prominence in postcolonial literature. Through its colourful imagery and complicated ideas, the poem urges readers to examine the nuances of personal and collective complexities of postcolonial existence.

6.3.1 Cries of Resistance: Themes in "A Far Cry from Africa"

"A Far Cry from Africa" by Derek Walcott is a beautiful canvas that weaves together many images, providing readers with a profound analysis of identity, brutality, and the continuing impact of colonialism. One of the poem's key themes is the examination of identity, specifically the poet's internal conflict caused by his mixed origin. The poet struggles with the conflict between his African ancestors and the colonial influences that shaped him. The complexities of postcolonial identity are revealed as Walcott reflects on his own dual background, symbolizing the larger problems experienced by individuals navigating the clash of cultures in a postcolonial world.

The poem delves into the history of Kenya in the 1950s, when the Mau Mau revolt, led by the Kikuyu tribe, fought for eight years against colonists who were regarded as illegal trespassers by the locals. Colonialism shattered the place's cultural history through brutality, cultural hegemony, and racial biases. Violence appears as a visceral and ambiguous motif, set in the historical setting of Kenya's Mau Mau Uprising. Walcott depicts the savagery of the fight, reflecting the turmoil and bloodshed that marked the independence struggle. However, the poet refrains from taking a firm moral stance on the violence. Instead, he employs ambiguity, recognizing the difficulties and ethical quandaries inherent in the fight against colonial oppression.

Another key issue in the poem is cultural hybridity and displacement. The poet's mixed origin serves as a metaphor for the experience of postcolonial nations coping with colonial legacy. The importance of language in communicating the emotional weight of the poem cannot be overstated. Walcott's use of vivid imagery and rich diction aids in the portrayal of complicated emotions. The language of the poem reflects the poet's diverse experience, portraying both the beauty and violence inherent in the clash of civilizations, as well as the difficulties of postcolonial identity. The poem's political critique is set against the historical backdrop of the Mau Mau Uprising. Walcott asks readers to consider the implications of colonialism as well as the larger struggle for liberation. The poem calls for a collective confrontation with the complexity of postcolonial existence as a monument to the lasting legacy of historical injustices. Following are the relevant themes addressed in the poem:

Split Identity: The poem's main theme is the poet's split identity. He couldn't choose between Africa and England. He has mixed sentiments toward Kenyan terrorists and counter-terrorists, as well as the white colonial administration. Both appear to be cruel to the man who slaughtered the common people. To him, both are savages. As a poet, he cannot support either of them because their blood runs through his veins. He adores the English language, but his ancestors were Africans who were persecuted by the English, whose native tongue he requires to survive as a poet.

Colonialism: Colonialism has shattered the place's cultural history through brutality, cultural hegemony, and racial biases. Africa was a paradise before colonization. The poet reproduced the past and history by juxtaposing heaven littered with carcasses- the demise, death, corpses, and devastation. Worms may represent rot's lament over the destruction of the useless (blacks). Hitler also murdered millions of Jews because of their ethnicity. The poet draws a parallel with the West Indians' bitter relationship with Spain. The fight was comparable to a gorilla vs. Superman. The gorilla represents the locals, while the superman represents the white men.

Devastation and Slaughter: The poet paints a picture of the Kikuyu uprising against the English in the 1950s. They are unable to justify their actions. They were seen as savages, as useless as Jews were by the Nazis. They were likewise seen as despicable. After making this vision, he returns to the wild land of Africa, where many varieties of brutes ruled before African and European development. The whites attempted to regulate and restrain the people who were represented as inhumane, untamed, or barbarians and savages for following the beat of the drum. The poet is saddened by Kenya's past in the 1950s. A nationalist rebellion led to the deaths of 13000 individuals, predominantly Kenyans, as well as a large number of animals. He condemns man's inhumanity in enacting justice through massacre and how deaths have been reduced to numbers and statistics. This obscures the reality of the dead and their pain, whether whites or savages. He comes from a British Caribbean colony, a long way from Africa, but he hears a scream or anguish that has become universal and timeless, reverberating around the globe.

Finally, "A Far Cry from Africa" provides a rich study of the issues that are profoundly embedded in postcolonial discourse. Derek Walcott's poetic ability enables readers to understand the complexities of identity, the ambiguity of violence, and the persistent legacies of colonialism. The poem becomes a meaningful portrayal of the vast postcolonial experience through its rich imagery and nuanced issues, not only a reflection of the poet's emotional concerns.

6.3.2. Title as Catalyst: Significance in "A Far Cry from Africa"

Derek Walcott appears to be attempting to convey the truth that he lives on the remote island of St Lucia, far from Africa, and that his lament must go a long distance to reach Africa. Or perhaps the ideal image of Africa is let down by the current reality of colonialism. The poem's title also includes an idiom, "far cry," (Walcott, "A Far Cry from Africa"), which signifies "impossible thing." However, there are numerous interpretations of this term. He is writing about an African issue from afar. He is writing from an island far away from Africa--both literally and metaphorically--it is vast and distant. It also appears that the poet hears the poem as a far cry coming from thousands of miles away. In the poem, the poet also employs animal images. He also depicts death and bloodshed, as well as mankind transformed into beasts and savages. Beasts fare better than humans and "upright man" (Walcott line 16). Violence is committed on the basis of skin colour.

Violence in Kikuyu, violence in "paradise," both result in devastation in the African continent. Because of his mixed blood, the poet feels divided and split at the end of the poem. He cannot find a way out. He can't choose one between Africa and England. He has mixed sentiments toward Kenyan terrorists and counter-terrorists, as well as the white colonial administration. Both appear to be cruel to the man who slaughtered the common people. To him, both are savages. As a poet, he cannot support either of them because their blood runs through his veins. He adores English language, but his ancestors were Africans who were persecuted by the English, whose native tongue he requires to survive as a poet.

6.3.3 Narrative Resonance: Probing the Writing Techniques of "A Far Cry from Africa"

"A Far Cry from Africa" by Derek Walcott has a distinct and powerful writing style distinguished by vivid imagery, deep symbolism, and rhythmic language. Walcott's command of poetic forms contributes to the poem's emotional intensity and thematic depth. Walcott's writing style is noteworthy for his adept use of vivid imagery. Throughout the poem, he uses words to construct compelling pictures, producing sensory experiences that allow readers to engage with the issues viscerally. The opening words, for example, give dramatic imagery of "the sun sought your body" and "the white safaris" that immediately immerse the reader in the landscapes and conflicts of colonial Africa. The use of concrete and specific imagery heightens the poem's emotional resonance.

Derek Walcott's poem "A Far Cry from Africa" discusses racial tensions and colonial occupation in Africa. The poem expresses the black poet's predicament. The poet received the Nobel Prize for his contribution to literature. He was born on the island of St Lucia in the British West Indies. As he grew older, he became aware of his hybrid grandparents, who were both white and black. The poem delves into the history of Kenya in the 1950s, when the Mau Mau revolt, led by the Kikuyu tribe, fought for eight years against colonists who were regarded as illegal trespassers by the locals.

The poem contains no regular rhyme system. The poem contains both full rhyme and slant rhymes. Iambic pentameter is the main meter used in the poem. The poem's title also includes an idiom, "far cay," which means "impossible thing." However, there are numerous interpretations of this term. His other poems are also based on the idea of roots and division. In the poem, Walcott employs religious imagery. He employs the contrasts of heaven and corpses. In the poem, he also connects life and death. "Kikuyu quick" employs cacophony by the poet. Alliteration is used in "Batten upon the bloodstreams" and "colonel of carrion cries." "How can I....How can I?" (32-33) also employs anaphora. The poem uses a scattered rhyme scheme of ABABBC and forced rhymes such as "again. ...Spain" (23-24) and so on.

Symbolism is important in Walcott's writing style because it adds layers of meaning to the narrative. The form and rhythm of the poem contribute to its overall artistic appeal. Walcott uses enjambment to allow thoughts and ideas to flow from one line to the next. This results in a dynamic and fluid movement that reflects the intricacies of the issues covered.

Walcott's writing style is distinguished by a deft use of language that depicts the poet's inner conflicts. The diction is both lyrical and forceful, conveying the poet's emotional struggle with identity as well as the tragedy of the colonial past. The word choices, such as "safari," "Mau Mau," and "Kikuyu," convey cultural and historical uniqueness, placing the poem in a specific location yet resonating with universal postcolonial concerns. Walcott's literary style is further emphasized by the poem's strong engagement with historical events and political discourse. He mixes personal contemplation with bigger social problems, resulting in a narrative that transcends the individual to explore the challenges of postcolonial existence.

This merging of the personal and the political is a compelling feature of Walcott's style, emphasizing the interdependence of personal experience with broader historical forces. In conclusion, Derek Walcott's literary style in "A Far Cry from Africa" is distinguished by vivid imagery, complex symbolism, rhythmic language, and sophisticated diction. These aspects come together to form a poem that not only tackles the poet's own difficulties with identity and violence, but also speaks to broader postcolonial concerns. Walcott's talent enables readers to negotiate the complexity of history and identity via a poetic prism, resulting in "A Far Cry from Africa" being a powerful and enduring work in the domain of postcolonial literature. In *Nobody's Nation: Reading Derek Walcott*, Paul Breslin (2001) provides a thorough examination of Derek Walcott's poetry, with a focus on themes of nationhood, identity, and postcolonial consciousness. Breslin's research focuses on how Walcott's work navigates the complexity of Caribbean history and culture, as well as broader issues of colonialism and globalization (Breslin 10-30). Breslin's research highlights the significance of Walcott's poetry in the context of postcolonial literature and thought.

6.4 "A Small Place"- Jamaica Kincaid

Jamaica Kincaid, a Caribbean-American writer, renowned for her evocative prose and moving explorations of postcolonial and feminist issues, has left an enduring mark on contemporary literature. Her works, such as "Annie John" and "A Small Place," negotiate the complicated terrain of identity, colonial legacies, and the deep relationships between individuals and their cultural traditions. Kincaid's work, distinguished by a distinct narrative style and astute insights, frequently dives into her characters' psychological and emotional landscapes, offering readers a comprehensive knowledge of the influence of colonization on personal and societal identities. Kincaid's elegant and, at times, piercing prose sheds light on the intersections of power, gender, and postcoloniality, leaving an enduring literary legacy that questions and broadens our ideas of the Caribbean and the human experience.

The postcolonial masterpiece "A Small Place" by Jamaica Kincaid is a compelling and personal analysis of the impact of colonialism and neo-colonialism on Antigua, the author's birthplace. Kincaid provides a critical indictment of the long-term impacts faced by Caribbean Island under colonial domination through a distinct narrative voice that blends rage, irony, and reflection. The unique structure of the work distinguishes it, as Kincaid confronts the reader directly and presents a critical perspective on the tourism business, corruption, and the history of colonial exploitation. The narrative voice conveys the author's rage and frustration, allowing her to express the complicated emotions associated with cultural identity, loss and the imposition of foreign ethos. Kincaid also addresses the psychological and cultural ramifications of colonization in "A Small Place," stressing how the Antiguan people deal with a warped sense of self and a broken relationship with their history. The book highlights the continuous neo-colonial dynamics that exist even after an official colonial rule has ended, looking at how economic dependencies and power disparities continue to define postcolonial reality.

Furthermore, Kincaid's use of language is important in portraying the postcolonial concerns. Her work is both evocative and incisive, with a personal and intimate tone that immerses the reader in the everyday experiences of the author and her people. Kincaid confronts the reader with harsh truths about the repercussions of colonialism and urges them to evaluate their role in perpetuating oppressive institutions through this intimate storytelling approach.

In conclusion, "A Small Place" is a moving postcolonial work that explores the complexity of the colonial past, its long-term consequences, and the ongoing struggles for identity and agency in the face of neo-colonial forces. Kincaid's distinct narrative style and unabashed assessment of her native region add to the work's significance in the context of postcolonial literature. Kincaid's narrative also calls into question traditional Western assumptions of history and cultural superiority. She exposes the reader to the terrible realities of exploitation, poverty, and corruption that continue to exist in postcolonial cultures. By doing so, she challenges the conventional narrative, which frequently romanticizes the colonial past, and calls into question the morality of the mechanisms that maintain such inequities. Hence. "A Small Place" is an appealing and impactful postcolonial work that employs a direct narrative voice, a critical examination of the tourism sector, and a unique use of language to show the lingering repercussions of colonialism on Antigua. Kincaid's work exemplifies the ongoing conflicts of identity, agency, and justice in postcolonial contexts.

6.4.1 Narrative Layers: Plot Dynamics in "A Small Place"

"A Small Place" is broken into four untitled pieces. In the first portion, we see Kincaid's narrative of natural beauty. The narrator is a tourist in Antigua who has fictitious opinions and experiences about this small island that is insulated from the harsher realities of life of the people who live there. An "insider" would be aware of the facts presented by the narrator. The narrator understands the reason for the operation of the expensive Japanese automobiles on the island, as well as the huge houses on the island; how they were obtained through illicit and corrupt operations. Even ten years after an earthquake, the library requires repairs.

The narrator's tour continues in the hotel, and this portion concludes with a discussion of her moral ugliness as a tourist. The second section transports us to colonial Antigua, where people were obedient to English culture. The narrator also recalls the casual bigotry prevalent during the period. The colonial occupation of Great Britain damaged indigenous culture and history. The white, affluent buildings at Mill Reef Club were built by wealthy foreigners. We can recall the history of Barclay's Bank. She recalls Princess Margaret's visit to the island when she was a child. Antiguans were oblivious to the racism. They were naive about colonial hegemony and its consequences.

Colonialism has instilled in Antiguans an inferiority complex. Thus, the second portion discusses the gradual poison of colonialism, as Antiguans readily accepted colonial rule and began expressing themselves in the colonial language with a high regard for English culture. The island has a colonial history, and capitalism and corruption are prevalent in the present. The final section of the book is comparably longer and focuses on the island's present. When the narrator compares the current to the past, the latter is more unsettling and gloomy.

She is saddened by the state of the library because she spent a lot of time there as a child and is now obliged to live in temporary accommodations above a dry goods store while repairs are being made. Kincaid has mixed thoughts about the ancient library. She recalls how the head librarian, who is now working to get funding to create a new library, suspected her of stealing books. The mill reef club has finances, but they can only assist the library if the new library is structured. This condition is not filled with genuine feelings of support, but rather with nostalgia for the colonial government. Antigua's minister is unable to administer culture. This is one of Antigua's most egregious ironies. Education has suffered more after independence. The writer also examines and observes the terrible speech habits of Antigua's younger generations. Her mother is also politically involved in her mission, working with the current minister, who has allowed the library to deteriorate.

Antiguans become oblivious to their government's corruption. They appear to be unconcerned with many wrongdoings committed as a result of power abuse, such as misappropriation of finances, drug smuggling, political violence, kickbacks, and so on. They are almost unknown to the typical Antiguan. Only hands have been switched for power from colonists to capitalists. Since its independence, Antigua has suffered greatly. Corruption has become an inseparable aspect of the island's political life. The bulk of the populace holds honest and ideal government officials in contempt, rather than respecting and honouring them. The general public regards them as idiots. This type of depressing and distressing condition may lead to dictatorship in the near future, resulting in numerous political upheavals. The fourth and last section of the book provides an overview of the island's fabricated beauty. The beauty appears "unreal," (Kincaid 76) as if it were a stage set or an artwork. The poverty of the Antiguans contributes to the beauty of the island. The beauty of the surroundings is a mixed gift for the people that live there. Slaves were brought to Antigua in the past, but their descendants have now become an integral part of the current and contemporary Antigua, who are simply human beings who share the common problems that all humans face.

6.4.2 Themes- "A Small Place"

Jamaica Kincaid's "A Small Place" dives into a plethora of subjects that compose a heartbreaking postcolonial narrative. Kincaid addresses the reader directly in an intimate and conversational tone, uncovering the various layers of influences of colonialism on Antigua. The implications of tourism, the disintegration of cultural identity, the lasting legacy of colonialism, and the function of language in forming narratives are among the subjects examined in the book. One of the key themes of "A Small Place" is a critique of the tourism industry and its exploitative character. Kincaid deconstructs the glorified image of the Caribbean paradise that is frequently maintained by the tourism industry. She exposes the monetization of indigenous culture for the enjoyment of foreign visitors, emphasizing the economic discrepancies and power imbalances that remain as a legacy of colonialism. Kincaid examines the ongoing neo-colonial dynamics through the prism of tourism, underlining how Antigua remains economically dependent on foreign interests. The disintegration of cultural identity is closely related to the theme of tourism. Kincaid investigates how the influence of European norms, education, and beauty expectations has led to the Antiguans' flawed self-perception. The author emphasizes the psychological consequences of colonialism, illustrating how the colonized absorb denigration of their history and heritage. This theme reflects the graver postcolonial battle for cultural identity recovery and preservation in the face of adversity. The lasting impacts of colonialism become a recurring issue throughout the narrative. Kincaid explains how colonial economic mechanisms continue to exist, sustaining a cycle of dependency and exploitation. She challenges the glorified myths that commonly accompany the colonial past by confronting the reader with the stark reality of poverty, corruption, and systematic injustices. This theme criticizes the neo-colonial factors that continue to affect postcolonial reality.

Language and its role in forming narratives is another important issue in "A Small Place." Kincaid participates in linguistic resistance by addressing the reader directly. She questions traditional Western beliefs on history and cultural superiority, upending the mainstream narrative, which frequently obscures the terrible reality of colonialism. The issue of language emphasizes the power relations inherent in storytelling as well as the significance of questioning and altering narratives in a postcolonial environment.

Moira Ferguson's book *Jamaica Kincaid: Where the Land Meets the Body* published in 1994, gives an in-depth analysis of Jamaica Kincaid's use of language and its link to themes of identity, colonialism, and gender in Kincaid's works. Ferguson investigates how Kincaid's writing style, which frequently employs aspects of Caribbean English and vernacular, reflects the complexity of Caribbean culture and history. Ferguson's work provides vital insights into the linguistic innovations and narrative tactics used by Kincaid to express Caribbean women's experiences and the influence of colonialism on their lives (Ferguson 1-30).

Thus "A Small Place" creates a web of ideas that offer a complex and insightful study of the postcolonial predicament. Kincaid challenges readers to critically explore the repercussions of tourism, the erosion of cultural identity, the lingering effects of colonialism, and the function of language in crafting narrative through her distinct style of storytelling. The art is a strong witness to the continuous battles for agency, justice, and cultural survival in the aftermath of colonialism.

The following are the major thematic concerns of the work:

Negative Image of Tourism

Kincaid represents a symbol of the moral depravity of tourism. It displays a physically terrible picture, the callous use of the poor for personal benefit and enjoyment of the capitalist government depicting their moral degradation. ("A Small Place" 17-20) According to her, one government officer operates a brothel, which is a form of direct exploitation of others, but she appears to be more interested in depicting spiritual enslavement. ("A Small Place" 33) When a tourist visits an area, he wants to get out of his dull routine and be drawn in by new places and new things, but it actually causes problems for the people who live there. For example, due to the clear and sunny sky and lack of rainfall, pure water in Antigua is a scarce and valuable commodity, but just the beauty draws tourists because drought is not their burden to cope with. Tourists find the modest cottages and shabby attire of the locals beautiful. Even exposed latrines seem appealingly "close to nature" (Kincaid 7) to them. These are the negative consequences for both residents and visitors. They are unable to assess the harsh reality of the environment in which they have been placed.

Colonization and Its Aftermath

Kincaid is astounded at the state of education and libraries since independence. ("A Small Place" 38-40) She, too, was a product of colonial Antigua, but her education was superior to that of contemporary existing children in the region. They are unable to express themselves clearly due to the influence of American pop culture. Because Antiguans were enslaved and later colonized by England, she grew up speaking English. She received a good education and read all of the classics written in English. Due to a lack of proper education, the indigenous people accepted their subservience to Britain. She regrets her colonial origins and the fact that they were simple objects of colonization. However, she adds that, due to Antigua's narrow bounds, she may be able to extend her worldview as a result of English imperialism. Thus, previous victims of imperialism joyfully welcomed imperialism ("A Small Place" 44-50). Kincaid does not feel at ease in either world. Whatever she reads is tinged with resentment for this dominant culture and their oppressive authority. She says: "Where the shelves of books used to be, where the wooden tables and chairs used to be, where the sound of quietness used to be, where the smell of the sea used to be, where everything used to be, was now occupied by costumes: costumes for angels from the realm." (Kincaid 46)

Because of her race and heritage, she will never be completely English. Antiguans were merely cogs in the vast colonial machinery. People from large spaces shape events, control history, and even control language. Local Antiguans were completely unaware of their legal rights. They accepted the ones who enslaved them.

Capitalism and Corruption

After independence, the oppression of colonization continues in newer forms of corruption. Government officials run brothels while purporting to use people's money for the betterment of Antigua. The populace has become indifferent to government programs and motivations. Whatever Antiguans witnessed during colonial rule, how their resources were mismanaged by colonizers is being replicated by capitalists in independent Antigua. "A People to Mold, a Nation to Build" (Kincaid 48) is their motto.

As a result, Antiguan history provides them with lessons to learn. Ministers claim to be working for the betterment of independent Antigua while enriching themselves.

6.4.3 Kincaid's Prose: Writing Style of "A Small Place"

"A Small Place" by Jamaica Kincaid is distinguished by a distinct and powerful literary style that blends elements of rage, irony, and an intimate conversational tone. The author's choice of language and narrative approaches substantially contributes to the work's impact and effectiveness. Kincaid's writing style is distinguished by her direct address to the reader. She establishes an immediate and personal connection with the audience by speaking directly to them, engaging them into a dialogue that feels both intimate and combative. This narrative decision has two functions: it involves the reader in the themes and concerns being covered, pushing them to confront their own involvement in the colonial heritage, and it reveals Kincaid's highly personal and emotional investment in the subject.

The writing is characterized by a pervading sense of rage and bitterness. Kincaid's dissatisfaction with the aftermath of colonialism is obvious throughout the work. This emotional tone emphasizes the importance of the ideas being discussed, giving the story a sense of urgency and sincerity. The author's rage is not simply an emotional outburst, but a calculated rhetorical approach designed to drive readers to interact with the author's exposé of injustices and inequalities. Kincaid's use of vivid imagery and detailed language heightens her writing's emotional impact. The text is descriptive, depicting Antigua and its inhabitants vividly.

"A Small Place" is a postcolonial critique of the island of Antigua's tourism impact. It is a work of realistic fiction written in the second person. The second-person narration is employed in a confrontational manner, presenting the readers as antagonists, which is highly tough, yet things become evident to the readers as they immerse themselves in the story. They become aware of the issues involved. The novel is a scathing assessment of Antigua's postcolonial society. The novel is a significant contribution to the postcolonial canon of Caribbean literature. Kincaid takes readers on a detailed and personalized tour of Antigua. She says: "You may be the sort of tourist who would wonder why a Prime Minister would want an airport named after him- why not a school, why not a hospital, why not some great public monument?" (Kincaid 3).

She offers a bleak view of the West Indian tourism business. Kincaid truthfully discusses her own love-hate connection with British colonial rule, which began in the 16th century in the West Indies and ended in the 1970s. She addresses both visitors to the island and readers as "you," depersonalizing them by addressing them directly. She employs the pronoun "you" to boldly challenge the colonial authority. In comparison to her prior works produced in the 1980s, her associations with the readers make her work bolder. Kincaid portrays tourism as a new colony, which is nothing more than the legacy of colonialism. Many postcolonial issues are included in the novel, such as adopting the colonial tongue and providing an alternate past, as well as how history has been rewritten by postcolonial writers.

Antigua's suffering, even after independence, exposes us to a greater panorama of neo-colonization via using communication tools such as tourism. The writer's educational situation and ambivalent attitude toward colonial speech show the dualism of oppression. Using colonial terminology, the writer attempts to undermine racial and colonial power systems by writing back to the centre. Kincaid describes in full the difficult journey from colonization to independence. In an endeavour to restore their civilization, the independent Antiguans fell into the trap of exploitation, yet another negative kind of colonization. The writer employs an assertive technique in her bright and forthright manner to depict Antigua's history, which most readers are unaware of.

The newly liberated Antiguans fell victim to the corrupt administration. One of these escapades is the tourism sector. The work is regarded as the most important in the postcolonial canon for exposing slavery, colonization, and tyranny after independence. Tourism contributes to an unequal distribution of income in Antigua. Mill Reef Club doesn't like Antiguans (black people) at all, the poetic voice declares. She says: "I knew of this woman, for she is notorious for liking Antiguans only if they are servants" (Kincaid 47). Kincaid also used parenthesis to indicate the narrator's inner thoughts. She appears to have mastered the "language of the criminal" that she despises. Her writing style is absolutely unique, and it looks to be quite intimate and casual at times. In her narration, she also employs a scathing sense of humour and complete fearlessness.

"A Small Place" has an unusual structure, like a stream of consciousness. Kincaid blends memories, critiques, and reflections together in a nonlinear method. This fractured framework reflects the complexities of postcolonial experience and underscores the personal, and subjective quality of the narrative. The lack of a linear timeline emphasizes the ongoing impact of colonialism, stressing that its consequences are not limited to a certain time period but continue to shape the present.

Kincaid's use of repetition is also remarkable as a stylistic element. Throughout the narrative, certain words and motifs are repeated, providing a rhythmic aspect that emphasizes and resonates with major topics. This repetition is a rhetorical device used to emphasize key points and to emphasize the cyclical nature of the issues being discussed. In summation, the writing style of Jamaica Kincaid in "A Small Place" is distinguished by direct address, emotional intensity, vivid imagery, unorthodox organization, and deliberate repetition. These aspects combine to form an engrossing and thought-provoking novel that forces readers to confront the complexities of postcolonial realities as well as their own culpability in the ongoing legacy of colonialism.

6.4.4 Persona Craft: Art of Characterization in "A Small Place"

Characterization takes on a unique and atypical form in "A Small Place" by Jamaica Kincaid, fitting with the work's particular narrative framework. The narrative's capacity to convey a vivid image of the people of Antigua is not diminished by the absence of typical characters with particular names. Kincaid, on the other hand, employs a collection of literary approaches that collectively contribute to a complex analysis of the community's collective identity, historical pain, and ongoing problems. The narrative voice, as embodied by the anonymous narrator, is central to the art of characterization. This first-person perspective acts as a conduit for the people of Antigua's collective experiences, memories, and emotions. The narrator builds an intimate and combative connection with the reader through direct contact, including the audience in the narrative and stressing the shared nature of the characters' troubles.

The absence of individually identifiable characters is a deliberate strategy that underscores Antigua's collective identity. Kincaid's portrayal, rather than focusing on specific individuals, revolves around the bigger themes and experiences that define society. The lack of individual names emphasizes the characters' connectivity, underlining that their hardships and resilience are part of a shared experience. The direct address to the reader is an effective narrative device that allows the narrator's emotions, disappointments, and recollections to become vital to the characterization process. This intimacy connects readers in a more direct and visceral way, allowing them to have a better grasp of the characters' experiences and perspectives. Characterization is thus created not through typical conversation or character arcs but through the immediate emotional impact of the narrator's thoughts. The Antiguan people's cultural identity appears as a fundamental feature of categorization. The deterioration of this identity as a result of colonialism and neo-colonial dynamics becomes a prominent issue. Readers gain insight into the characters' complex relationship with their own past and the difficulty of sustaining cultural identity in the face of external forces through the narrator's investigation of cultural battles and the imposition of Western values. Despite the absence of identifiable characters with unique personalities, the tourist acts as a symbolic figure reflecting neo-colonial exploitation. The visitor is portrayed as critical and mocking, stressing their role in sustaining economic inequities and cultural commodification. This symbolic figure serves as a lens through which the larger dynamics of power and exploitation can be observed.

Hence, the art of characterization in "A Small Place" demonstrates Jamaica Kincaid's ability of storytelling. Kincaid creates a vivid and poignant portrait of the people of Antigua through the first-person narrative, direct communication to the reader, and thematic examination of cultural identity and historical tragedy.

To conclude, this chapter gives us an insight into postcolonial Caribbean literature. This chapter specifically explores the post-colonial writing that emerged from the Caribbean. It places Caribbean literature in the larger framework of postcolonial literature, highlighting the distinct historical, cultural, and linguistic dynamics influenced by independence movements and colonial legacies. The poem "A Far Cry from Africa" by Derek Walcott provides a starting point for examining colonialism, history, and identity issues in Caribbean literature. The poem's engagement with the intricacies of postcolonial identity is examined in detail in the critical analysis, with special attention to the conflict between African and European influences in the Caribbean setting. "A Small Place" by Jamaica Kincaid is a biting indictment of colonialism and its effects in Antigua. This text's narrative layers, thematic investigations, writing style, and characterization are all examined in detail in this chapter, which emphasizes Kincaid's potent depiction of postcolonial Caribbean realities and the legacy of colonial exploitation. Two well-known writers, Derek Walcott and Jamaica Kincaid, offer a thorough analysis of postcolonial Caribbean literature. They shed light on the manner in which writers from the Caribbean struggle with the effects of colonialism, slavery, and cultural disarray while simultaneously claiming their own agency and sense of cultural identity. Readers acquire a fuller comprehension of the colonial experience in the Caribbean and its long-lasting effects on identity, culture, and society through these writings. Along with highlighting the Caribbean writers' tenacity and inventiveness in challenging colonial myths, they also confirm the region's vast cultural diversity. Overall, by elevating the voices and perspectives of Caribbean writers and illuminating the nuances of postcolonial identity, resistance, and cultural reclamation in the Caribbean setting, this chapter adds to the continuing discussion within postcolonial discourse.

Chapter 7
Postcolonial African Literature: Works by Chinua Achebe, Wole Soyinka, David Diop and Namwali Serpell

Postcolonial voices of African descent include a broad and diverse range of writers who address colonial legacies, the complexity of cultural identity, and the social and political difficulties which they reflect in their literature. Postcolonial African literature is a vast study field representing the issues of identity, struggle, and liberation. Chinua Achebe, N'gugi wa Thiong'o, and other African writers have constructed complicated narratives that examine the complexity of cultural hybridity, the fight for identity, and the collective resistance against colonial tyranny in the aftermath of colonial control. Their literary works delve into the complexities of liberation movements and the difficulties of nation-building, providing a painful perspective on the postcolonial African experience. Language, as a weapon for mental decolonization, plays an important part in this literary tradition, reclaiming indigenous languages and opposing colonial linguistic legacies. Hence, Postcolonial African Literature creates a comprehensive canvas that depicts the diverse, tenacious, and ongoing journey of African nations toward self-discovery and a liberated future. Here are some notable works from Africa:

7.1 *Things Fall Apart* as a Postcolonial Novel

Chinua Achebe's *Things Fall Apart* is widely considered as a foundational work in postcolonial literature. The novel, published in 1958, examines the influence of British colonization on Igbo society in Nigeria during the late nineteenth century. Here are some characteristics of the novel that show its significance in the context of postcolonial literature:

1. **Encounter with the Colonial Power:** *Things Fall Apart* depicts the arrival of European colonial forces, primarily the British, and the disintegration of traditional Igbo society that ensues. The novel depicts the

collision of civilizations as well as the deterioration of indigenous values and rituals.

2. **Cultural Collision:** Achebe depicts the confrontation between traditional Igbo values and the values imposed by colonists. The novel emphasizes the damaging effects of European colonization on indigenous civilizations, such as the destruction of social structures, religious beliefs, and familial bonds.

3. **Narrative Perspective:** The novel's narrative perspective is distinctive. Achebe narrates the story from the point of view of the colonized, not the colonizers. This movement calls into question the Eurocentric narratives that dominated literature at the time, and it offers voice to people whose voices were frequently neglected or suppressed.

4. **Resistance and Identity-** *Things Fall Apart* delves into issues of resistance and the fight to maintain cultural identity in the face of colonial influences. Okonkwo, the protagonist, becomes a symbol of resistance, but his terrible fate also illustrates the challenge of navigating change and resisting colonial forces.

5. **Language and Representation:** Achebe wrote the novel in English, the colonist's language. However, by doing so, he recovered the narrative and used the colonizer's vocabulary to portray the colonized's experiences and perspectives. This calls into question the idea that only colonizers had the authority to tell stories.

6. **Postcolonial Critique-** *Things Fall Apart* can be interpreted as a critique of colonial depictions of Africa and its people. Achebe challenges stereotyped and often degrading representations of Africa by mainstream writers. He portrays Igbo culture in a sophisticated and honest manner.

7. **Legacies and Influence:** The work has had a long-lasting influence on postcolonial writing, inspiring numerous writers to investigate the complexity of colonialism and its consequences. Achebe's work has become a reference point for conversations about decolonization, cultural identity, and the long-term consequences of imperialism.

In conclusion, *Things Fall Apart* is an important work in postcolonial literature because it provides a forceful critique of colonialism and its influence on African societies. Achebe's depiction of the complexity and implications of the colonial encounter has largely contributed to postcolonial ideas on identity, power, and representation.

7.1.1 The Rise and Fall: Plot Dynamics in *Things Fall Apart*

The narrative recreates 1920s Nigeria at the dawn of colonialism through the advent of Christian missionaries in Nigerian community. Okonkwo, the protagonist of the novel, is a warrior in the Igbo clan's village Umuofia. Okonkwo has won numerous titles in the past due to his gallantry and bravery. His father's cowardice, Unoka, tormented him. He did not want to be like his father, who was mistreated and died without paying his obligations. He acted in a reckless and impetuous manner. In a deal with a neighbouring tribe, he was given a fifteen-year-old boy named Ikmefuna.

Okonkwo was a well-known warrior and farmer. His real son's name was Nwoye, and he was discovered to be feminine and effeminate. Both young boys formed a deep bond with one another. Okonkwo began to perceive an ideal son in Ikmefuna, and the boy began to call him father, but Okonkwo restrained himself from lavishing affection on him. He disobeyed the commandment and beat his second wife, Ekwefi, during the week of peace. He surprised his community with his rash and impulsive behaviour, but he eventually had to make some compromises. Ikemefuna lived with the family for three years and became inseparable from them. But there was an announcement from the Oracle, and Ogbuefi told Okonkwo privately that Ikemefuna should be murdered, but because the youngster was calling him father, he should not participate in his sacrifice. Okonkwo lied to the little child about returning to his home village. Nwoye sobbed when he was separated from Ikemefuna. They went for several hours while Ikemefuna contemplated meeting his mother, but he was ambushed by clansmen wielding machetes. In a rage, the foster child, Ikmefuna, ran to Okonkwo for assistance, but he decapitated him because he did not want to appear weak in front of his clansmen.

Thus, despite the Oracle of the Cave's warning, Okonkwo actively participated in Ikemeguna's sacrifice. He was unable to eat or sleep after this incident, and he became depressed. He went to his friend Obierika to feel lighter, and he began to feel slightly revitalized. His daughter, Ezinma, became unwell but recovered after harvesting herbs for her treatment. Ogbuefi's death was proclaimed using the musical instrument ekwe. Okonkwo was disappointed since he had ignored Ogbuefi's last warnings. There was a great and magnificent funeral with men banging drums and firing guns, but Okonkwo's exploded gun accidentally killed Ogbuefi's sixteen-year-old son. Killing a clansman is a crime against Mother Earth, so Okonkwo was forced to relocate his family to Mbanta, his mother's birthplace. Following his departure, his obi and animals were burned and killed to atone for the transgression committed in the hamlet. It was all done by folks from the Ogbuefi quarter. Uchendu, Okonkwo's uncle, welcomed him heartily. He assisted him in the construction of his new huts and also loaned him yam seeds to establish a farm. Okonkwo was depressed at his tragedy, but he relaxed into his new role. Okonkwo was in exile, and during his second year, Obierika arrived with a bag of cowries to give to Okonkwo, which he organized after selling Okonkwo's yams. He also informed them that the white man had demolished their neighbouring hamlet, Abame. Six missionaries came to Mbanta shortly after this tragedy. Mr Kiaga, one of them, worked as an interpreter. Mr Brown, the missionaries' leader, persuaded the people to convert to Christianity by claiming that their gods were untrue since they worshipped more than one God. The peasants couldn't see how the Holy Trinity could be regarded as a single God. Mr Brown advised his followers not to be harsh with the locals and to try to persuade them to become Christians without coercion. The converts were relieved to have escaped Mr Brown's policy. When a convert named Enoch dared to unmask an egwugwu at the annual ceremony to honour the soil deity, he was charged with murdering an ancestral spirit. The following day, Enoch's compound was set on fire, as was James Smith's church. This news enraged the district commissioner, who requested a meeting with Umuofian elders. He treated the leaders with contempt. They were handcuffed and thrown in jail, where they were subjected to physical violence and insults. Following their release, they had a meeting with other clansmen, during which five court messengers approached and told them to stop. Okonkwo, believing that his clansmen would assist him in the insurrection, killed their leader with his machete. As he watched the other messengers flee, he understood that his people were unwilling to go to battle. When the District Commissioner came to Okonkwo's compound, he saw him hanging. Obierika declared that suicide was a great sin in their clan and that they could not touch his body in accordance with their culture. The commissioner was writing a book on Africa and thought Okonkwo's uprising was worthy of a line or two in his book. He had already settled on and picked the title of his work, "The Pacification of the Primitive Tribes of the Lower Niger." (Achebe, *Things Fall Apart* 188)

7.1.2 Culture in Flux: Thematic Explorations in *Things Fall Apart*

Chinua Achebe's *Things Fall Apart* deftly weaves together thematic issues that reveal the devastating influence of British colonialism on Igbo society in the late nineteenth century. The story depicts the disintegration of indigenous rituals and societal institutions as a result of the clash between traditional Igbo culture with the forces of change brought about by the colonial encounter. Individual challenges, particularly those faced by the tragic hero Okonkwo, unfold against the backdrop of societal expectations and changing gender roles within this framework. As traditional beliefs clash with the arrival of Christianity, Achebe deftly explores the intricate interplay between religion and spirituality. The story also delves into the complexities of justice, language, and communication, highlighting the power dynamics inherent in the colonial imposition of English. *Things Fall Apart* stands as a profound investigation of the deep layers of culture, power, and society development in the face of colonialism, as generational conflicts erupt and fate intertwines with human choices.

Representation of Igbo Culture

The work depicts Igbo culture and its complexities. Their pumpkin festival, marriage rites, various deities, food production, and religious views are diametrically opposed to European culture and belief. The Igbo culture celebrates with a yam feast. They have a custom of offering Kola nuts to their guests. They have a well-organized society, which is reflected in the Oracle of the Cave's announcements. Their tradition is oral, with folk culture in its most rudimentary form. They keep the peace in their clan. Their social system is extremely powerful, with shared leadership for the community. These are the intricate and dynamic characteristics of Igbo culture that Chinua Achebe recreates in this novel.

Cultural Conflict: East vs. West

On the one hand, the story depicts the complexities of Igbo culture, which are disrupted by the rapid arrival of Europeans via Christian missionaries. Western culture has the concept of the Holy Trinity, which contrasts sharply with Africans' concept of numerous deities. Africans believe in myths and folk tales, which Europeans critique. The python is regarded revered in African tradition, yet diabolical in European society. Africans are referred to as "heathens" by James Smith (Achebe, *Things Fall Apart* 135). Through this novel, Achebe wishes to express to the mainstream writers how indigenous people have been misrepresented by Europeans in their writings.

Tragedy and Destiny

With the death of its leader, the novel depicts the catastrophic defect of the Igbo clan. Throughout the novel, he acted in a reckless and impetuous manner. He kills Ogbuefi's sixteen-year-old son due to his unintended and hasty actions and behaviour, even after the Oracle of the Cave admonishes him, and it appears that he is doomed to self-destruction. He is primarily to blame for his fall. Such a warrior and hero hangs himself abruptly, and his body is not even touched by his clansmen. The colonial arrival hastens his demise. He was extremely resistant to accepting and adapting to new changes. His rigidity and inflexibility, along with his impulsiveness, bring him disaster, and he is eventually abandoned by his clansmen.

Okonkwo can be compared to his friend Obierika, who is a highly rational and reasonable figure. He opposes the use of might and force to drive settlers from their territory. He is a thoughtful individual. He accepts changes because of his adaptability. He said of the foreigners, "Who knows what will happen tomorrow?" (Achebe, *Things Fall Apart* 142) He is quite foresighted about the changes that have occurred in Umuofia. The entire structure of Igbo culture collapses due to the lack of a core figure as a leader. The British culture, on the other hand, was ambitious, and their aims were fuelled by the false "white man's burden" notion, which was bringing them to self-enrichment and trespassing the liberty and freedom of the Igbo clan.

The concept of fate and destiny is explored on both an individual and societal level. This idea is regularly brought up for the readers by Chi, the particular and personal deity. Okonkwo feels certain of his fate. He goes on to say: "when a man says yes, his chi says yes also." (Achebe, *Things Fall Apart* 27) He is confident that his chi will never fail him. He also understood that a man cannot ascend above his chi. Looking at the societal level of fate and destiny, we can observe that Igbos lack a unified self-image and leadership, which has been used against them. The lack of centralized power and image caused the things to fall apart.

Tradition vs. Change in Tradition

Okonkwo opposes the new political and religious orders. He is also concerned about losing his social standing. His sense of self-worth is based on ancient patterns and structures, but if his village embraces Christianity, his people and culture would perish, and new Christian converts will enjoy a lofty and elevated social status. Nwoye, his own son, was converted to Christianity. As a result, the community is torn between a new and an ancient culture.

Many villages were ecstatic about having one God and one church, as well as new chances and ways for harvesting, constructing, and cooking. Traditional procedures that were formerly necessary for survival are now obsolete. The abolition of Igbo culture and language results in the abolition of old and traditional techniques.

Masculinity

The novel also addresses a significant issue of masculinity. Okonkwo was preoccupied with the concept of masculinity. In an attempt to avoid being like his feminine father, Unoka, he became an overly masculine figure. There came a pronouncement from the Oracle, which Ogbuefi told Okonkwo privately, that Ikemefuna should be murdered, but since the young boy was calling him father, he should not participate in his sacrifice. Okonkwo lied to the little child about returning to his home village. Despite the Oracle of the Cave's warning, Okonkwo actively participated in Ikemeguna's sacrifice. He was unable to eat or sleep after this incident, and he became depressed. His persistent efforts to transcend his father's history aided him in becoming a masculine figure. His masculinity was prone to rage, violence, and rashness. He was unable to exhibit his fatherly love and affection for his children since he was unable to verbalize his emotions.

Language- A Sign of Cultural Difference

We hear many interwoven African folk-tales in the novel, which contradicts Joseph Conrad's depiction of Africans in *Heart of Darkness*, in which Africans were not given a voice (Conrad 32). Africa is not a silent and incomprehensible continent; rather, the Igbo language is too complex to be translated directly into English. The same is true of Igbo culture. It was quite complicated for the Europeans. Umuofians mocked Mr Brown's translator, Mr Kiaga, because his language was a little different from theirs. Achebe wrote the work in English because his intended audience and readers were the English, whom he wished to educate about African culture and history, which had been misrepresented by atrocious European writers. Africa has several diverse languages that the Europeans could not understand. African folktales, proverbs, and songs translated from Igbo are included. Achebe attempted to preserve African rhythm, symphony, and cadence in his writing.

7.1.3 Storytelling Craft: Achebe's Writing Style in *Things Fall Apart*

Chinua Achebe's literary style in *Things Fall Apart* is distinguished by a brilliant blend of vivid imagery, oral storytelling skills, and a subtle investigation of cultural issues. Achebe uses clear and remarkable prose, making the story accessible to a broad audience while conveying profound issues. His language is rich in metaphor and symbolism, allowing readers to interact with the text on a variety of levels. Achebe's use of Igbo proverbs and idioms enhances the narrative's authenticity and cultural complexity, providing a sense of immersion in the traditional African milieu. Achebe's meticulous use of language not only conveys a gripping story but also challenges dominant colonial narratives by providing a counterbalance to Eurocentric ideas. As a result, the author has developed a distinct and powerful literary style that captures the essence of Igbo culture while tackling universal issues such as identity, change, and the effects of historical forces.

Achebe employs numerous tactics and incorporates them to such a degree in his narrative that the readers start sympathizing with the African culture. He shows a vast representation of Igbo society as self-contained and harmonious. They value their way of life and their cultural heritage. The writer does not translate numerous African words, such as obi, chi, ekwi, egwuwu, and so on, as translating them into English loses their cultural value, and he also wishes to convey and keep an African flavour and sensibility in his narrative. The novel emerges as an African narrative written in English through the use of irony, comedy, imagery, and cultural symbols. With the coming of the whites, Achebe has well chronicled the truth with his narration, showing how their privacy and serenity are jeopardized. The work depicts Igbo culture and its complexities. They have a well-organized society, which is reflected in the Oracle of the Cave's announcements. Their tradition is oral, with folk culture in its most rudimentary form. There are intricate and dynamic characteristics of Igbo culture that Chinua Achebe recreates in this novel. This idea is regularly brought up for the readers by Chi, the particular and personal deity. Okonkwo feels certain of his fate. He goes on to say: "when a man says yes, his chi says yes also." (Achebe, *Things Fall Apart* 27)

He is confident that his chi will never fail him. He also understood that a man cannot rise beyond his chi. Looking at the societal level of fate and destiny, we can observe that Igbos lack a unified self-image and leadership, which has been used against them. The lack of centralized power and image caused the things to fall apart.

Okonkwo expected help from his clansmen, but he didn't get it. That's why he committed suicide at the end of the novel. On the one hand, the story depicts the complexities of Igbo culture, which are disrupted by the rapid arrival of Europeans via Christian missionaries. Western culture has the concept of the Holy Trinity, which contrasts sharply with Africans' concept of numerous deities. Africans believe in myths and folk tales, which Europeans critique. The python is regarded revered in African tradition, yet diabolical in European society. Africans are seen as "heathens" by James Smith. "And he told them about this new God, the Creator of all the world and all the men and women. He told them that they worshipped false gods, gods of wood and stone." (Achebe, *Things Fall Apart* 145)

Through this story, Achebe wishes to express to the centre how they have been misrepresented by Europeans. Their culture is not backward or slavish; rather, it has been portrayed by racist Europeans who saw Africans as nothing more than primitive niggers. The narrative is linked with various proverbs and maxims that share a photographic perspective: "If I hold her hand she says, 'don't touch!' If I hold her foot, she says, 'don't touch!' But when I hold her waist beads she pretends not to know." (Achebe, *Things Fall Apart* 118) This song depicts the young woman's hesitancy and then sudden willingness to love. It depicts the Nigerian code of conduct and ideals visually.

The novel is written in the third person omniscient point of view, which allows the reader to get inside the thoughts and ideas of any character, with a concentration on the main characters, Okonkwo, Ikemefuna, Nwoye, Ekwefi, and others. We gain a profound understanding of the lives, values, and customs of the Igbo people via the story. Africa is not a silent and incomprehensible continent; rather, the Igbo language is too complex to be translated directly into English.

The novel provides a three-dimensional characterization rather than simply repeating stereotypes. The wide use of dialect adds authenticity to the narrative by allowing a thorough penetration into all levels of African characters with their whims and fancies. The decadence of the locusts symbolizes the advent of the locusts. Just as the Igbo did not perceive this as a threat, they did not recognize the difficulties posed by the advent of the Christian missionaries. The novel takes place during the close of the nineteenth and beginning of the twentieth centuries. With the entrance of Christians in the village, the story progressively takes on an ominous tone. The novel is structured into three sections, one for each stage of Okonkwo's journey. Part One is about his life as a warrior trying to redeem his name from his father's past and then accidentally killing the headmen's son. Part two illustrates colonization and its commencement, which the naïve people do not understand. Part three deals with Okonkwo's return and his understanding that his culture has been defeated by an alien and new foreign culture. He recognized that his village had succumbed to the colonists, and consequently, he committed suicide. Thus, the readers witness the story of Okonkwo's downfall from glory to obscurity, and the fall of Okonkwo represents the decline of African culture and tradition.

7.2 Narrative Threads in *Anthills of Savannah*

Anthills of Savannah by Chinua Achebe emerges as a remarkable literary investigation of postcolonial Africa, deftly integrating political allegory, cultural introspection, and social critique. The novel is a profound meditation on the intricacies of power and politics in a fictional African setting, mirroring the larger challenges confronted by newly independent African countries. Achebe deftly examines the abuse of authority, moral quandaries confronting political leaders, and the resulting impact on the lives of regular citizens. Through characters such as Beatrice, the story challenges gender conventions and celebrates women's perseverance in a changing society. The novel's historical setting in post-colonial Nigeria gives credibility to the story, making it both a timeless piece of literature and a timely commentary on the ongoing struggles for justice, identity, and cultural preservation in post-colonial cultures. *Anthills of Savannah* exemplifies Achebe's creative prowess and dedication to depicting the complicated weave of African life and politics.

Anthills of Savannah is a novel about a chaotic political uprising in the fictitious setting of Kangan. Sam, Chris Oriko, and Ikem Osodi are the novel's main characters. The three were childhood friends who rose to power and are now carrying out their duties. Sam is the Republic of Kangan's de facto leader, the President. Chris becomes the head of the Information Ministry, while Ikem becomes the editor-in-chief of the widely circulated and government-controlled daily, National Gazette. The story begins with the regime's president and his cabinet convening in Kangan, a western African country. The prior dictator was deposed, and current government has been in place for two years. Three characters, Sam, Chris, and Ikem, wield power. Ikem is an outspoken poet who is also an intellectual who wants to see political improvements. Chris serves as a go-between for Sam and Ikem. Sam wants more power without respect for his people.

According to Ikem and Chris, Sam is gradually becoming a dictator. He becomes blinded by the power he wields and uses to dominate over the people. Elewa, Ikem's pregnant girlfriend, was semiliterate and used to work in a shop. Beatrice, Chris' fiancée, was a well-educated woman who worked as an administrator for one of the state departments. She had known Ikem since she was a child, and she had also worked for Sam. Her ties include almost all of the important players. She observes government activity and also watches Chris and Ikem's reactions; she understands every circumstance due to her sensitive disposition. She also wants Ikem and Chris to connect the dots.

In the second part of the novel, Sam orders Chris to fire Ikem from his position as an editor, but Chris does not appreciate Sam's command and refuses to follow his orders. Chris knows more about Ikem and whether he was participating in the Abazon delegates' protest. Nonetheless, Ikem was fired from his position, and he later spoke to a student group at a university. He was highly passionate and vocal about the regime. He made no attempt to conceal his disdain for the government. He was making a joke about minting coins with Sam's head on them, which turned out to be propaganda alleging that Ikem wanted to behead Sam. Ikem was removed from his home and killed by state police in the middle of the night.

In the third phase, Chris realized that Sam had become quite dangerous. He planned to use his relationships with international institutions to spread the word about Ikem's murder. Chris was able to flee the city with the assistance of Abdul, a cab driver, and Emmanuel, a student leader who admired Chris much. He was able to flee Bassa and make his way to Abazon. The authorities issued an arrest warrant for him and warned anyone concealing information about him. Chris felt a sense of oneness in his heart during his bus ride with the natives, but the bus was ambushed by a frenzied mob celebrating the news that Sam had been killed and his rule had been overtaken by another. When Chris and the other passengers wanted to get the news and confirm it, they spotted Adamma, a student, being taken away by a soldier to be raped. But, in his attempt to save her, Chris was slain by the soldier.

Part four depicts Emmanuel, Adamma, and Abdul's return to Bassa to inform Beatrice and others about what has occurred there. Her heart was heavy, but she continued to celebrate the naming ceremony for her baby girl, who was born after Ikem's murder. She named her child Amaechina, a boy's name that meant "May the path never close." Thus, the narrative concludes on the novelist's magical imagination.

The style combines flashbacks and alternating perspectives to provide a thorough understanding of the characters' backgrounds and motives. Achebe's use of indigenous proverbs, folklore, and linguistic variety enriches the narration, adding layers of cultural authenticity to the plot. *Anthills of Savannah* concludes with a tragic yet redeeming conclusion. The protagonists deal with the consequences of their actions, and the novel finishes with observations on the cyclical nature of power and the people's enduring resilience. Achebe's plot is essentially a canvas of political intrigue, personal issues, and societal reflections artfully stitched together to create a narrative that connects with the complexity of post-colonial African politics as well as the universal themes of power and humanity.

7.2.1 Thematic Explorations in *Anthills of Savannah*

Chinua Achebe's *Anthills of Savannah* resonates with significant themes that reflect the intriguing issues of post-colonial African civilization. The work digs into the difficulties of government and the moral quandaries faced by political leaders, and one prominent theme is the investigation of power relations. Resistance is also a significant theme, as exemplified by individuals like as Ikem, Osodi and Beatrice Okoh, who oppose authoritarian regimes via dissent and human agency. As people battle with the tension between retaining traditional values and adapting to the demands of modernity, the story highlights the ongoing struggle for cultural identity. Gender dynamics are portrayed through Beatrice's character, illustrating women's changing roles in a changing society. Achebe also weaves a story on the cyclical nature of power and the resilience of the people. The deep interaction of these themes takes *Anthills of Savannah* above and beyond a political allegory, transforming it into a devastating reflection on the intricacies of postcolonial African existence. While Ato Quayson's work "Relocating Postcolonialism", published in 2002, is not solely about *Anthills of Savannah*, he does explore Achebe's novel from the perspective of postcolonial literature and theory. In *Anthills of Savannah*, Quayson explores subjects such as power, politics, and the legacy of colonialism, providing insights into Achebe's critique of postcolonial

African governance and societal dynamics (Quayson 89). Quayson's analysis helps us comprehend the novel's significance in the context of postcolonial discourse.

The novel's themes are:

Political Upheaval and Abuse of Authority

The novel depicts a catastrophic political upheaval in the fictitious setting of Kangan. Sam wishes to increase his authority at the expense of his people. According to Ikem and Chris, Sam is quickly becoming a dictator. He becomes blinded by the power he has and uses it to dominate over the people.

Lower-class Corruption and Oppression

The Kangan government is corrupt, as evidenced by its treatment of Abazon's destitute people and land. Ikem is assassinated because he spoke out against corruption and impoverished people's persecution. Because of his desire for power, Sam began to question those close to him. Ikem was slain as a result of his alert voice, and Sam felt frightened by him. On his way to Abazon, Chris noticed that people were living in oppressive conditions. He also recognized the gravity of the situation and the government's failure to address it. When he saw the anthills on the side of the road, he recognized the calamity that his friend Ikem had seen and acknowledged before him.

Relationship Betrayal

The work depicts the issue of betrayal in human relationships. Three characters, Sam, Chris, and Ikem, wield power. Ikem is an outspoken poet who is also an intellectual who wants to see political improvements. Chris serves as a go-between for Sam and Ikem. Sam becomes blinded by the power he has and starts to overthrow the people. According to Chris, he was a "baby monster" who became plagued with paranoia, rage, and insecurity when his political ambitions failed.

Relevance of Storytelling

The character of Ikem in the novel emphasizes the significance of storytelling. He spoke out against corruption as the editor of The National Gazette. He also goes into great detail about the job of the storyteller while speaking to a group of students. He also emphasizes the job of a writer in his speech, saying, "Writers don't give prescriptions. They give headaches!" (Achebe, *Anthills of the Savannah* 138)

Women's Power and Role in Society

The novel emphasizes the female characters as well. The novel has a number of strong female characters. Beatrice Okohis, Chris' fiancée, is a multidimensional character explored by Achebe in this novel. She is the main character in the story and is heavily involved in the plot's action. She plays a crucial role in the novel's events while working with Sam and being an old acquaintance of Chris. She was an unwelcome child for her parents because she was the fifth daughter when they were anticipating a boy child. So, she was given the name Nwanyibuife, which means "A Woman Is Also Something" (Achebe, *Anthills of the Savannah* 90). She worked as an administrator in a state office. Her character was defined by her sophistication, intelligence, and independence. She was the woman who preferred to be alone and unnoticed. She is personified as the goddess Idemili, who was sent to man to oversee morality. Her character is likewise elevated in this mythical tradition. Though she does not believe in stories, she grows in dedication, understanding, knowledge, and compassion for her people and the region of her birth. She attends the naming ceremony for Ikem and Elewa's daughter and names her Amaechina, a boy's name that means "May the Path Never Close." (Achebe, *Anthills of the Savannah* 132)

7.2.2 Narrative Cadence: Achebe's Writing Style in *Anthills of Savannah*

The literary style of Chinua Achebe in *Anthills of the Savannah* is embedded with language complexity, cultural nuance, and narrative subtlety that reflects the complexities of postcolonial African literature. Achebe skilfully blends English with local proverbs and idioms, producing a linguistic landscape that reflects Kangan's cultural variety. The narrative lends credibility to the story by immersing the reader in linguistic intricacies and reflecting the intricate network of traditional and modern influences. Achebe's prose is distinguished by its clarity and directness, expressing profound ideas with ease. His narrative framework is multi-perspective, allowing different characters to express their experiences and points of view. This not only provides a comprehensive grasp of the complex social and political context, but also demonstrates Achebe's ability to create different voices for each character. The novel's use of flashbacks enhances the narrative by providing insights into the backgrounds and motives of the characters. The literary style of Achebe in *Anthills of the*

Savannah becomes a cultural and linguistic inquiry, enabling readers to interact with the difficulties of identity, power, and societal transformation.

The novel is written in the first person. Various characters deliberate at various points throughout the chapters. For example, in the first chapter, the story is narrated by Chris, who is speaking in the first person, but when the story portrays Ikem, he begins speaking in the first person, but we also notice a blend of narration as a third person point of view with the first person narration. Readers feel close to the characters portrayed because of the close narration. With the publication of the novel, Achebe also broke his silence, which had lasted twenty years since the publication of *A Man of the People* published in 1966. In the meantime, he wrote short stories, essays, and juvenile literature. Many opponents thought that he was following in the footsteps of an acclaimed fellow countryman, Wole Soyinka, who was honoured with the Nobel Prize in Literature in 1986.

Achebe uses the English language to write back to the centre in order to improve and correct the inaccurate image of Africa in Joseph Conrad's novella *Heart of Darkness*. In one of his essays, he characterizes his position as an educator by saying: "I would be quite satisfied if my novels...did no more than teach my readers that their past- with all its imperfections- was not one long night of savagery from which the first Europeans acting on God's behalf delivered them." (Achebe, "The Novelist as Teacher" 45)

Anthills of the Savannah is set in Kangan, a postcolonial African setting. The old traditional dignity and mythological oral culture are imprinted in the province of Abazon, from which a delegation and its leader have come to Bassa, the capital city, to appeal for help owing to the drought-ridden region. The central idea in the title is taken from his speech, which will be delivered later to the group of students by Ikem. The truth cannot be defined by a single culture, nor can it belong to a single political party, race, or society. Rather, as the tribal elder puts it, "What is true comes in different robes." (Achebe, *Anthills of the Savannah* 74)

Following the publication of *A Man of the People* in 1966, a group of Nigerian army officers transformed the writer's vision into reality by seizing control of the state from civilian leaders. The current novel *Anthills of the Savannah* is likewise a fictional reflection of a terrible incident in the political drama. The military dictatorship has already reached a critical juncture. Corruption and tyranny are already widespread. The prior dictator was deposed, and current government has been in place for two years.

The events in the course of action of the novel take place through speech, memories, reminiscences, and inner monologue, which add to the narrative's beauty. The work is complex due to the paradoxes and ambiguities inherent in ordinary life, which are shared by three narrators. We see a variety of perspectives in the novel as we see Achebe's alter ego in the story within the individual orthodoxy and lack of disagreement coupled with political philosophy and art. Sam's control over Kangan fails because he attempts to ban paradoxes. He was trained as a military officer, which made him impervious to compromise and converted him into an absolute despot. He also believed that his two closest friends' loyalty had turned to betrayal. Fearful of the insurgencies, he left the chamber and sought private counsel from Okong. Sam was increasingly sceptical, so he summoned his Attorney General to validate the story, who was an even greater master of sycophancy than Okong. Long after colonialism has ended, we can see that the psychic vestiges continue to influence the Attorney General's attitude. By mocking such attitudes, Achebe hopes to contribute to their extinction.

Beatrice, who is continually hostile to orthodoxy, is alive at the end of the novel. She is the woman who prefers o be alone and unnoticed. She is personified as the goddess Idemili, who was sent to man to oversee morality. Her character is likewise elevated in this mythical tradition. She was raised to reject her family's sexism. Achebe also incorporates the myth of creation into the novel's prosaic occurrences by employing archetypal outlines in her character. According to this old belief in African myth, the Almighty limits the rampages of power in his creation by sending his daughter Idemili to Earth "to bear witness to the moral nature of authority by wrapping around Power's rude waist a loincloth of peace and modesty." (Achebe, *Anthills of the Savannah* 61) Thus, Idemili restrains all earthly forces morally by managing the evils of her personality--pride, avarice, acquisitiveness, and aggression.

Though Beatrice develops apart from the world of the tales and legends of her ancestors, she has inherited the role of Idemili as a result of collective wisdom. Beatrice performs the civilizing role for which her country has trained her. She embodies Achebe's best hope for people's survival in the face of violence and avarice, both of which have become typical in modern African states.

The writer establishes a link between the past and the present by establishing a kinship between Ikem and Elewa. Their union gives birth to a child, who leads to a relationship and bond in the future. As a result, their daughter becomes a living representation of their love. Elewa's mother and uncle arrive for the naming ceremony following Ikem's murder and are horrified when the child is named Amaechina, which means "May the path never close." The name is meant for a boy, so they interpreted it as a violation of custom, and the uncle laughed at it, but Beatrice claimed parenthood of the child for everyone in the room. Only gradually did he embrace the name and interpret it as a metaphor for a pious kid, implying "may this child be the daughter of all of us." (Achebe, *Anthills of the Savannah* 136) As a result, the uncle mixes a harsh exterior with an instinctive ability to adapt to change.

Achebe also used pidgin English and African proverbs and parables to show and illuminate the rich history of African culture. He appears to be more interested in portraying society as a whole than in characterizing individuals. Since the work employs several narrators, readers can form their own opinions rather than relying on a narrator or a single character. Kangan is a fictitious setting in the novel that is similar to Achebe's home Nigeria, although many commentators see it as a counterpart of Idi Amin's Uganda. The author depicts a modern postcolonial nation fighting to establish peace and security. There is a sharp blend of tradition and modernity, with parts of tradition reflecting consistency among the people. The novel shows two segments: government and business, which are immensely affluent, and the other is the community in which the people of Kangan live in harmony. The means for discovering the location of the government is the press, and this is how the regime is administered. The novel's essence is the expert blending of African customs, folklore, myths, and proverbs with current political views and Christian theology. Due to the complete disarray and disorder of the present, the belief in the former system has been empowered. The convention of storytelling is also maintained in this novel by the writer, who has a deep sense of the past and oral heritage.

7.3 "Telephone Conversation"- Wole Soyinka

The Nigerian playwright, poet, and essayist Wole Soyinka is regarded as a towering figure in African literature and global intellectual discourse. Soyinka's writings, including "Death and the King's Horseman" and "A Dance of the Forests," which won the Nobel Prize in Literature in 1986, demonstrate a profound engagement with the intricacies of postcolonial identity, political opposition, and the collision between tradition and modernity. Soyinka's literary achievements transcend beyond the region, displaying a genuine dedication to social justice as a zealous champion for human rights and political activity. His writing contains a unique synthesis of Yoruba cultural components and Western literary traditions, making Soyinka a global literary light and a compelling voice for the continuing search for justice.

Biodun Jeyifo's book *Wole Soyinka: Politics, Poetics, and Postcolonialism*, published in 2004, delves deeply into Wole Soyinka's literary career, political involvement, and cultural contributions. Jeyifo's analysis goes into Soyinka's poetry, plays, essays, and political writings, examining the connections between politics, poetics, and postcolonialism in his work (Jeyifo 65). Jeyifo's study provides vital insights into Soyinka's involvement with subjects such as power, oppression, identity, and cultural resistance in postcolonial Nigeria and across the African continent.

Wole Soyinka's poem "Telephone Conversation" is a brief but powerful exploration of racism, prejudice, and the power dynamics. The poem, set in the apartheid era of South Africa, portrays the terrible and degrading experience of a black man trying to rent an apartment. Soyinka's use of the telephone as a communication medium becomes a potent metaphor, emphasizing the distance and anonymity that technology can both create and bridge. The poet uses crisp and vivid language to expose the landlady's racial intolerance and hatred when she learns about the speaker's racial identity.

Wole Soyinka's poem "Telephone Conversation" is a literary satire on racial prejudice, which persists even in today's world and society. A white lady and an African American man are speaking on the phone. The man is looking for a house at the start of the poem, and the landlady does not live under the same roof. The residence is in an unbiased and unprejudiced neighbourhood. He reveals to the lady about his identity and ethnicity because he has had racial experiences in the past. He does not want to waste his time travelling there if she refuses on the basis of race. The man assumed he had misheard the lady, so he asked her to repeat her question, which she did with varying emphasis. He could smell the deception in her words. He felt like a machine, like the telephone in front of him. The words made him feel humiliated, and he saw crimson all around him.

He was embarrassed by the awkward silence that ensued and sarcastically inquired whether she was assisting him by providing options to pick from. She sought to embarrass him by repeating her query as if she were comparing him to a chocolate--dark or light. She responded objectively, and he clarified that he was a West African Sepia, which kept her quiet for a time. She became intrigued and inquired as to what it was, to which he said that it was comparable to brunette and she emphasized that it was dark. He had had enough of her insensitivity, so he disregarded all formalities and openly mocked her, noting and clarifying that he was not fully dark in his body. The soles of his feet and the palms of his hands were white, but due to friction from sitting on his bottom, they had turned black. Many impactful literary devices are used in the poem. The first two pictures are at the start of the poem, when the male is envisioning the woman: "lipstick coated, gold rolled cigarette holder piped." (Soyinka lines 8-9) She also appeared to be of a higher socio-economic status to him. When asked how dark he was, he felt ashamed and humiliated, recalling the sight of a massive bus squelching the black tar. This graphic illustrates the domineering attitude of the whites toward black minorities. The poem also employs irony when the man is forced to "self-confession" (Soyinka line 4) while revealing his skin colour to the lady. The colour is something over which one has no control. Being black or dark-skinned is not a sin. He expresses regret about his skin colour. The irony in the poem portrays humorous and grotesque racism. The lady continues to describe her high breeding and top class. The readers may detect her insensitivity and partiality toward skin colour. She's superficial and deceitful. She demonstrated her callous nature by asking him crude questions. Only her speech was polished. Her intellect was a ruse she was hiding behind the mask of mannerism.

The man is also well-mannered, debunking the stereotype that black people are savages and barbarians. The man retained better manners and vocabulary than the woman, using words like "spectroscopic" (Soyinka line 23) and "rancid," (Soyinka line 12), whereas she had no idea about West African Sepia and was judging a man's intellect and character solely on his skin colour. The poem is a caustic commentary on society's racial behaviour. It is written in an extremely passive tone. The writer appears to be writing from personal experience. The poem, which depicts the emotions of humility, fury, hatred, shame, embarrassment, and disgust, examines the sense of apathy and inhumanity of persons who can turn down a man because of the colour of his skin. Hating a race because of its colour or ethnicity will not help a society flourish. In today's world, racism is a dying worry. Discrimination against minorities has not been eliminated. People continue to harbour irrational fears and prejudices that they cannot understand. The poem has a general viewpoint, but it is timeless and applies to all forms of discrimination that exist in the world. Though the poem begins on a tranquil note, expressing the narrator's satisfaction:

"The price seemed reasonable, location indifferent." (Soyinka line 1)

The speaker decides to make a self-confession to reveal his identity as per his prior experience. He says: "Madam," I warned, "I hate a wasted journey- I am African." (Soyinka lines 4-5)

The language used in the poem is embedded with timeless message. Toward the end of the poem, he employs the metaphor of the telephone to mock racial bigotry with a sense of humour.

7.3.1 Racial Discourse: Central Themes in "Telephone Conversation"

Wole Soyinka's "Telephone Conversation" delves into various significant issues, with racial discrimination taking centre stage. The poem powerfully shows racial discrimination as the speaker strives to find accommodation. Through the passionate debate between the speaker and the landlady, Soyinka deftly unravels the issue of racism. The poet illustrates the ridiculousness of racial bigotry, illustrating how the landlord's perception changes just by mentioning the speaker's black identity. The poem becomes a microcosm of the larger socio-political landscape, delivering a profound remark on apartheid. Apart from racism, the poem also addresses power relations. The telephone, ostensibly a tool for communication, becomes a weapon that emphasizes the disparities between the speaker and the landlady, demonstrating how technology can be a double-edged sword in perpetuating injustice. In essence, "Telephone Conversation" is a dramatic investigation of racial discrimination, societal injustices, and the difficulties of genuine connection in the face of deeply ingrained preconceptions.

Following thematic issues are the major concerns in the poem:

Racism and Xenophobia

The poem's main issue is racism and xenophobia, which Wole Soyinka is raising awareness about. One's ideology should be open-minded and progressive. The difficulties of "light" and "dark" should not prevent a person from going about their daily lives. A white woman and an African American man are having a discussion over the phone. The man is looking for a house at the start of the poem, and the landlady does not share the same roof. The residence is in a neutral and unprejudiced neighbourhood. He reveals to the lady about his identity and ethnicity because he has had previous racial experiences. He does not want to waste his time travelling there if she rejects because of his skin colour. But she asked him how much black he was. He felt like a machine, comparable to the telephone in front of him. He was embarrassed by the remark and saw crimson all around him. He was embarrassed by the awkward silence that followed and sarcastically inquired whether she was assisting him by providing options to pick from. She sought to embarrass him by repeating her query as if comparing him to a chocolate--dark or light. She responded objectively, and he stated that he was a West African Sepia, which made her quiet for a time. Toward the end of the poem, he employs the metaphor of the telephone to mock racial bigotry with a sense of humour.

The Battle of White and Black

The poem shows a conflict between white and black people. The lady continues to describe her high breeding and top class. The readers may perceive her insensitivity and bigotry toward skin colour. She's superficial and deceitful. She demonstrated her callous nature by asking him crude questions. Only her speech was polished. She was merely pretending to observe proper etiquette and manners as if she had no care for colour. The white-skinned race objectifies and commodifies black bodies. This subject is raised in the poem as a result of the poet's own experience.

To sum up, Wole Soyinka's "Telephone Conversation" masterfully encapsulates issues of racial prejudice, structural injustice, and communication hurdles in the face of established biases. The poet navigates the harsh realities of racism, clearly depicting the speaker's humiliating experience while seeking accommodation. The poem is a forceful critique of apartheid-era racial tensions, shedding light on the absurdity and injustice of discrimination based on skin colour. Soyinka digs into broader themes of power dynamics and the impact of technology on interpersonal communication in addition to race. The telephone, a symbol of connection, becomes a harsh reminder of the isolation and alienation that racial discrimination perpetuates. Hence, "Telephone Conversation" echoes a resonance to introspection in its brevity, asking readers to consider the continuing repercussions of discrimination as well as the necessity for genuine empathy and understanding in daily encounters.

7.4 "Africa"- David Diop

The Senegalese-French poet David Diop rose to literary fame with his innovative and emotional portrayal of the African experience during World War I. "The Vultures," his celebrated work, conveys the horrors of combat, the dehumanizing impact of colonization, and the tremendous sense of loss experienced by African troops (Diop lines 217-218). Diop's poetry is a moving combination of historical awareness and a plea for African identity and emancipation. Diop's lyrics, as one of the important personalities in Negritude literature, reflect a powerful affirmation of African history as well as a criticism of the violence perpetrated by colonial forces. His significant contributions have left an indelible impression on the language of African identity, challenging dominant narratives and praising the spirit of perseverance of African in the face of adversity. Chinua Achebe's essay "The Novelist as Teacher", published in 1965, discusses the themes of resistance, identity, and cultural pride in African Literature (44). While Achebe's comments are not primarily about Diop, it does provide useful insights into the literary and cultural significance of African poetry. Abiola Irele's paper "Negritude: Literature and Ideology in Africa and the Caribbean", published in 1965, looks at the Negritude movement (Irele 499), which included David Diop, and its impact on African and Caribbean literature. While not exclusively focused on Diop's poem, Irele's analysis of Negritude sheds light on the cultural and ideological settings that shaped the creation and reception of "Africa" and other works linked with the movement. Irele's analysis sheds light on the importance of Diop's poetry in the larger context of African literary and intellectual history.

In the midst of colonial persecution, David Diop's poem "Africa" stands as a heart-breaking and evocative monument to the African continent's continuing fortitude, endurance, and cultural pride. This critical examination delves into the fundamental themes, literary strategies, and emotional resonance that make "Africa" such a powerful song of resistance. At its heart, "Africa" explores themes of identity and resistance to colonial tyranny. Diop portrays Africa as a symbol of a common heritage, a reservoir of history, and a rallying point for resistance, rather than just a geographical entity. The poem arises from a historical environment distinguished by the struggle for African decolonization, and its verses become a battlefield on which the poet fights not only against oppressors but also for the reclamation of Africa.

David Diop is a West African poet renowned for his work in the Negritude movement. He hopes that via his poems, Africa would be liberated from colonialism. His poetry was published in the Presence Africaine when he was only fifteen years old. His poems demonstrate his intense resentment of Europeans for the exploitation of his land and population. Essentially, Africans suffered as a result of colour prejudice, and these distinctions may still be seen today. The poet fantasizes about a liberated African land that his grandmother used to celebrate and sing about in her songs.

The poem "Africa" depicts the poet's goal and hope for a free and independent country, but Africa has only had a "bitter taste of liberty." (Diop line 23) The poet praises his countrymen for not crumbling under the weight of disgrace. Even after colonialists have left Africa, their imprints can still be felt. In the hands of the British, Africa has been deprived of its glory and dignity. They have been humiliated and mistreated, but they are not broken. Even after obtaining freedom, Africans continue to face barbaric treatment because of their skin colour, which only a native can understand. The poet portrays postcolonial turmoil and the brutality of the British for their own selfish objectives. When it comes to African labour, blood, slavery, everything was used by the British for their own benefit and selfishness.

According to the poet, the black is no longer twisted. They no longer need to submit to the British rule. They can now pursue their own ambitions. But they still feel the pressure and psychological turmoil. They are attempting to break out from the conventional image of themselves that has been represented, or rather misrepresented, by whites for a long time. They are striving to break free from the conventional image of themselves that has long been portrayed, or rather misrepresented, by whites. When they look back in time, they can see that they were humiliated. They remain "trembling with red scars, and their spirit is weak." (Diop line 14) They must now discover their 'self' and break free from the physical shackles imposed by the British. They must seek their 'self' and forget the colonial past that has stripped them of their originality and reality. The poet paints a picture of suffering Africans during the colonial era and the pressure to work for their independence in the postcolonial stage. The poem is a contribution to the Negritude movement in which the poet speaks about the glory and strength of Africans in their struggle for liberation.

The poem is a postcolonial composition that speaks about the effects of colonialism on African Indigenous, which will take many years to recover from. The colonial history was chaotic, which shaped the self-image of Africans. Thus, it is critical to celebrate Africans' new identity--their new independence. Africans must rise above the humiliation of the past and focus on their identity and the liberation that they can bring about in the future. The poem is a conversation between a youthful poet and an older intellect. The poem's theme is patriotism, which depicts "the bitter taste of liberty" (Diop line 23) for Africa.

The poem recalls the poet's grandfather's magnificent savannah songs praising warriors, as Africa was a proud warrior nation. The poet, on the other hand, has never met the country, but he is proud of the African blood that runs through his veins. Their black blood drenched the crops. They used to do farm work. They cultivated this land by sweat and servitude. Their hard work and contribution enhanced the grounds. Under colonial domination, Africa was bent beneath the weight of humiliation, and its back trembled with crimson wounds. For fear of penalty, they were forced to labour during the day.

The poet has a young voice that is curious about his country's history, and his question was answered by a solemn and mature voice. This voice is metaphorical and exceedingly optimistic, implying a supreme sacrifice on the side of the youth referred to as "impetuous child." (Diop line 26) The solemn voice advises the questioner to have revolutionary patience in order to obtain liberty. The solemn voice is enigmatic and perplexing, effectively silencing the sophisticated interlocutor.

David Diop, a black African born in France in 1927, wrote the poem as a dramatic monologue. Since his father was from Senegal and his mother was from Cameroon, he was familiar with the cultures and traditions of both France and West Africa. He was highly concerned with the issue of freedom from colonial control. Pre-colonial Africa, colonial Africa, and postcolonial Africa are the three sections of the poem. The poem makes extensive use of martial imagery, depicting Africa as a battleground and her inhabitants as soldiers. Diop's depiction of Africans as warriors is a call to arms, an assertion of power, and a declaration of the tenacious spirit that refuses to surrender to the degrading effects of colonization. The choice of words conveys a strong sense of urgency, determination, and the importance of taking collective action in the face of adversity. The idea of blood, a powerful symbol that resonates throughout the verses, is central to the poem's thematic investigation. The blood becomes a metaphor for sacrifice, endurance, and the enormous expenses associated with the pursuit of liberty.

The sun, another reoccurring element in "Africa," represents optimism, endurance, and the possibility of a brighter future. In the context of historical struggles, the sun becomes a figurative source of light that pierces through the darkness of colonization. This imagery adds dimensions to the poem, implying that, despite historical shadows, the possibility of regeneration, rejuvenation, and the creation of a new period persists.

Diop's use of rhythmic language reveals a strong affinity for the oral traditions that are common in many African societies. The tone and repetition of the poem contribute to its oral nature, making it appropriate for recitation and communal interaction. Throughout "Africa," there is a strong sense of national pride. Diop highlights the importance of Africans reclaiming their past, asserting their cultural identity, and rejecting Eurocentric viewpoints that seek to devalue the worth of African civilizations. The poetry is transformed into an anthem of cultural pride, honouring Africa's rich history and contributions to the globe. The poem's elegiac tone adds a dimension of emotional impact. It is a lament for the losses incurred as a result of colonial control, but it is also a call to action. The elegy transforms sadness into a booming declaration of resistance, becoming a forceful affirmation of African agency. This emotional resonance results from the confluence of pain, pride, and determination, resulting in a profoundly moving experience for the audience.

7.4.1 Thematic Analysis of "Africa"

With his profound and evocative works, Senegalese poet, David Diop has made an everlasting influence on African literature, and one of his most acclaimed poems, "Africa," serves as a dramatic study of important issues that resonate deeply with the continent's history and identity. A heartbreaking contemplation on the impact of colonialism on Africa is at the heart of Diop's poetry. In "Africa," he goes into the harsh realities of African nations under European dominance, depicting the difficulties of people striving for freedom and independence. The poem becomes a rallying cry against the continent's historical injustices, with vivid imagery and powerful language illuminating the breadth of the collective African experience. A wide panorama of compelling themes flows through David Diop's poem "Africa," expressing the poet's deep connection to the continent and a fervent response to the impact of colonialism. The celebration of African identity and perseverance is a significant subject. Diop depicts Africa not only as a geographical reality, but also as a symbolic depiction of a communal legacy that is robust in the face of colonial forces. The poem becomes a rallying cry for resistance, underlining the African people's resilience and determination in the face of historical misfortune. The appeal for cultural pride and reclamation is another prominent subject. Diop encourages Africans to declare and embrace their cultural identities, rejecting Eurocentric viewpoints that seek to belittle the importance of African cultures.

Following are the major thematic concerns of the poem:

Colonial Oppression

The poet portrays African turmoil and the brutality of the British for their own selfish objectives. When it comes to African labour, blood, and slavery, everything was used by the British for their own benefit and selfishness. He says:

> "The blood of your sweat
> The sweat of your work." (Diop lines 8-9)

Africans were forced to work in the burning heat of the day's sun due to fear of punishment by the colonists. Under colonial domination, Africa was bent beneath the weight of humiliation, and its back trembled with crimson wounds.

Exploitation and Humiliation

The poet praises his countrymen for not crumbling under the weight of disgrace. Even after colonists have left Africa, their imprints can still be felt. In the hands of the British, Africa has been deprived of its glory and dignity. They have been humiliated and mistreated, but they are not broken. Even after obtaining freedom, Africans continue to face barbaric treatment because of their skin colour, which only a native can understand. The poet portrays postcolonial African turmoil and the brutality of the British for their own selfish objectives.

> "The work of your slavery" (Diop line 10)

The cruel treatment has left scars to the Africans. He says:

> "This back that breaks under the weight of humiliation
> This back trembling with red scars
> And saying yes to the whip under the midday sun." (Diop lines 13-15)

Patriotism

The poem's theme is patriotism, which depicts "the bitter taste of liberty" for Africa. The poem recalls the poet's grandfather's magnificent savannah songs praising warriors, as Africa was a proud warrior nation. The poet has a young voice that is curious about his country's history, and his question was answered by a solemn and mature voice. This voice is metaphorical and exceedingly optimistic, implying a supreme sacrifice on the side of the youth referred to as "impetuous child" (Diop line 26). The solemn voice advises the questioner to have revolutionary patience in order to obtain liberty. The solemn voice is enigmatic and perplexing, effectively silencing the sophisticated interlocutor. He says:

"I have never known you
But your blood flows in my veins (Diop lines 5-6)
...
Splendidly alone amidst white and faded flowers
That is your Africa springing up anew." (Diop lines 19-20)

7.4.2 Unravelling the Writing Style in "Africa"

"Africa" by David Diop is a beautiful poem that demonstrates the poet's great craftsmanship. Diop constructs a lyrical canvas that examines issues of colonial oppression, cultural pride, unity, and historical consciousness through a peculiar literary style distinguished by vivid imagery, rhythmic language, emotional intensity, repetition, and symbolism. This poem digs into the nuances of Diop's craftsmanship, evaluating how each contributes to the poem's complexity and impact. The poem "Africa" by David Diop is a remarkable literary masterpiece that dives into the nuances of the African experience, blending themes of resistance and identity together. Diop tackles the consequences of colonial oppression and the resilience of the African people through colourful imagery, rhythmic language, and a celebration of cultural heritage.

As the lines progress from monosyllables, i.e., sweat, work, to trisyllables, i.e., slavery, and disyllables, i.e., children, the organization of the speech sounds emphasizes the message of the poem. The poem is a contribution to the Negritude movement in which the poet speaks about the glory and strength of Africans in their struggle for liberation. The poem is broken into three sections: pre-colonial Africa, colonial Africa, and postcolonial Africa. The following lines of the poem make extensive use of alliteration: "...this back that is bent/ This back that breaks under the weight of humiliation." (lines 12-13)

This line highlights the questioner's arrogance, which draws our attention to Africa's colonial subjugation. When Mother Africa's back is 'trembling with red scars,' the poet is saddened and disturbed. The poetry is a reproduction of his mother's personal pains, which is indicative of the African continent's fear. These phrases also foreshadow the exploitative effects of the 1958

Referendum, when Senegal became a neo-colonial country under the administration of France, led by first president Leopold Senghor.

Africa, like the Tree of Life, will expand and evolve. The poem concludes with a lovely tone and effect with a sound effect. The final phrases are contradictory, as liberty is associated with bitterness. The poem's tone and mood are shifting. It is happy at the beginning. It becomes melancholy in the middle. The poem is written in a nostalgic style, with an optimistic tone that ends on a cheerful and pleasing note. The poem employs anadiplosis, a technique in which the last phrase of one line becomes the beginning utterance of the next, as in the following lines:

> "The blood of your sweat
> The sweat of your work
> The work of your slavery" (Diop lines 8-10)

The poem also makes extensive use of symbols such as "scars," "whips," and "blood" to portray colonial tyranny. In the following line, the poem also offers a rhetorical question that does not require a response:

> "Is that you this back that is bent?" (Diop line 12)

With the images of taste, heat, the poem is exuberantly embedded. The poet says:

> "Bitter taste of liberty" (Diop line 23) and "The sweat of your work." (Diop line 9)

The poet used personification in his message to Africa as if Africa were a living human being. The phrase 'Africa' is repeated seven times throughout the poem, utilizing reiteration. "Africa, my Africa" (line 1) also employs anaphora. The poet has a young voice that is curious about his country's history, and his question was answered by a solemn and mature voice. This voice is metaphorical and exceedingly optimistic, implying a supreme sacrifice on the side of the youth referred to as "impetuous childs" (Diop line 26). The solemn voice advises the questioner to have revolutionary patience in order to obtain liberty. The solemn voice is enigmatic and perplexing, effectively silencing the sophisticated interlocutor.

Diop's use of vivid imagery is a pillar of his poetic art. The poem's phrases, such as "black blood," (line 7), evoke vivid mental imagery, letting readers to experience the physical and emotional struggles of Africans during the colonial era viscerally. The imagery acts as a visual anchor, anchoring the poem's themes in the harsh realities of the continent. Diop's literary style is distinguished by the purposeful use of repetition, most notably with the phrase "black." This repetition creates a rhythmic pattern that reflects Africa's heartbeat, underscoring the continent's collective identity. It becomes a rhetorical device, affirming the African spirit's tenacity and strength. Diop leaves a long and vivid impression on the reader through repetition. The rhythmic language in "Africa" demonstrates Diop's abilities as a poet. The rhythm reflects Africa's throbbing vitality, providing a sense of urgency and passion. The poem becomes a visceral experience as a result of its rhythmic nature, engaging readers on both emotional and cerebral levels. The cadence heightens the emotional effect of the verses, making them truly resonate. Kwame Dawes' paper "David Diop's Poetry: Language, Race, and Form", published in 1995, examines David Diop's poetry, focusing on language use, racial concerns, and poetic form (Dawes 53-72). He investigates how Diop's literary style reflects larger issues like African identity, resistance, and cultural legacy. Dawes' research sheds light on the aesthetic and stylistic features of Diop's poetry, as well as its significance in African literature and postcolonial studies.

Diop infuses the poem with tremendous emotional intensity, a driving force that emphasizes the poet's affinity to the subject matter. The explosive words convey Diop's passion, prompting readers to empathize with Africa's past atrocities. The poem's emotional intensity elevates it above a literary statement to a heart-breaking call to acknowledge and heal the wounds of the past. Diop's writing style embraces African culture and tradition while exploring problems. His pleasure in the variety of African cultures is palpable, striking a beautiful balance between addressing historical oppressions and highlighting the continent's continuing spirit. This dual viewpoint lends depth and richness to the poem, transforming it from a lament to a celebration of cultural resilience.

David Diop's skill emerges as a force in "Africa," transforming words into an immersive experience. Diop develops a literary masterwork that connects with themes of resistance and identity through vivid imagery, rhythmic language, emotional intensity, repetition, and symbolism. This poem serves as a call to connect with the complexity of African history and to honour the resilient spirit that defines the continent. Diop left an everlasting stamp on the landscape of poetry with "Africa," proving the enduring power of words to illuminate the human experience.

7.5 *The Old Drift*- Namwali Serpell

Namwali Serpell is a Zambian writer and professor who has received widespread recognition for her literary achievements. She is most known for her debut novel, *The Old Drift*, which was published in 2019. The novel spans generations and intertwines the tales of three Zambian families, examining issues such as colonialism, nationalism, migration, and technology (Serpell 23). *The Old Drift* gained considerable critical praise, garnering Serpell multiple awards and nominations, including the Los Angeles Times Art Seidenbaum Award for First Fiction and the Windham-Campbell Prize in Fiction. Namwali Serpell is not only a fiction writer, but also a recognized scholar and intellectual. She received her Ph.D. in English from Harvard University and is currently a Professor of English at Harvard, where she teaches courses on African literature and postcolonial theory.

Namwali Serpell's main contribution to postcolonial writing is her acclaimed debut novel, *The Old Drift*, which provides a comprehensive and diverse analysis of Zambia's colonial and post-war history. *The Old Drift* takes place over a century, beginning with the colonial era in Zambia (then Northern Rhodesia) and continuing into the near future. Serpell skillfully incorporates historical events and people into her narrative, giving readers a comprehensive grasp of Zambia's complex socio-political terrain. The novel covers the lives of three interwoven families across several generations, providing a comprehensive glimpse of Zambian society. Serpell addresses questions of identity, belonging, and cultural shift in the aftermath of colonialism. Her work explores a variety of postcolonial issues, including colonial legacy, the struggle for independence, and the obstacles of nation-building after colonization. She investigates power dynamics, racial hierarchies, and the long-term legacy of colonialism in Zambian society.

The Old Drift exemplifies Serpell's creative style of storytelling, which combines aspects of historical fiction, magical realism, and speculative fiction. The work employs a variety of narrative genres, including epistolary portions, oral histories, and future vignettes, showcasing Serpell's versatility as a writer. While *The Old Drift* is set in Zambia's specific historical context, it covers universal themes of love, sorrow, and human perseverance that will appeal to readers around the world. Her story asks readers to consider the interconnectivity of world histories, as well as the long-lasting effects of colonialism in many cultural contexts. *The Old Drift* contributes significantly to postcolonial writing by providing a thought-provoking and well-researched examination of Zambia's past, present, and future. Serpell's storytelling prowess and thematic depth enrich the literary world with an engaging and informative narrative.

7.5.1 Plot Analysis- *The Old Drift*

Namwali Serpell's *The Old Drift* is a sweeping, multigenerational novel that spans more than a century and chronicles the interwoven lives of three Zambian households. The novel begins with a prologue set in the early 20th century at Victoria Falls. Percy Clark, a British colonialist, finds a mosquito carrying the malaria infection. This interaction triggers a series of events that resonate throughout the narrative. The story follows three families: the descendants of Percy Clark, the Aga family (Indian immigrants), and the Matha family (indigenous Zambians). The fates of these families become entwined over generations. The novel explores Zambia's history from colonialism to independence, focusing on the impact on indigenous populations and the quest for self-determination. The characters deal with the complications of colonial subjugation, racial prejudice, and nationalism movements. The novel focuses on love and relationships as important themes. Serpell investigates interracial and multicultural relationships, illicit love affairs, and familial links that cross socio-economic and cultural lines. These relationships form the identities of the characters and guide their decisions. It also explores issues of science, technology, and progress. The story chronicles the evolution of technology across time, from the construction of the Kariba Dam to the rise of digital communication and genetic engineering. In the narrative, "Jacob had been the driving force behind the reconnaissance mission to this gentrified wasteland. Ever since he had learned about the Zambian Space Programme... Who knew technology was a family tradition- in his very blood!" (Serpell 477)

Serpell's narrative combines magical realism and speculative fiction, blurring the line between fact and myth. The work contains magical events, such as a woman whose hair grows uncontrollably and a man who speaks with mosquitoes, which adds a depth of enchantment to the plot. Her narrative examines issues of legacy, memory, and time. The characters struggle with the weight of history and their predecessors' legacies, addressing issues of identity, belonging, and the unavoidable nature of change.

The novel concludes with a futuristic vision of Zambia in the near future, in which the descendants of the three families deal with the consequences of their previous deeds and face the challenges of an unknown future. Serpell concludes with a moving comment on the enduring power of human connection and the tenacity of the human spirit. Thus, *The Old Drift* is a detailed and philosophically sophisticated work that provides a broad overview of Zambian history and society. Namwali Serpell's rich narrative structure and captivating characters create a sweeping epic that captivates readers and leaves an indelible impression.

7.5.2 *The Old Drift* as a Postcolonial Novel

This novel contains several postcolonial elements that reflect Zambia's complex past and ongoing conflicts with colonial legacy. The story begins with a British imperialist seeing a mosquito near Victoria Falls, signifying colonial forces' encroachment into African countries. Serpell's narrative delves into the long-term consequences of colonialism on Zambia's social, cultural, and political landscape, such as racial hierarchy, economic exploitation, and Indigenous community marginalization. The book explores the problems of identity development in a postcolonial milieu. Characters like Sibilla and Agnes negotiate numerous identities created by their colonial ancestry, ethnic origin, and personal experiences. Serpell illustrates the fluid and hybrid nature of identity, challenging essentialist concepts of race, country, and belonging.

The novel depicts several kinds of resistance against colonial oppression and racial prejudice. Characters like Matha Mwamba and Agnes struggle for independence and social justice by joining nationalist movements and questioning colonial authority. Serpell emphasizes the resilience and agency of underprivileged groups in the face of imperial violence and exploitation.

The Old Drift explores language as a tool for power and resistance. Serpell combines numerous languages and linguistic registers into the story, highlighting Zambia's linguistic variety and the difficulty of communication in a postcolonial country. Language becomes a space for negotiation and contestation, shaping relationships and identities. Serpell examines the effects of globalization and modernization on Zambian society, stressing contradictions between tradition and advancement. The construction of the Kariba Dam, the introduction of digital technology, and the expansion of Western consumer culture are all examples of globalization forces that transform local populations and disturb traditional lifestyles. The novel explores environmental justice via postcolonial lens, highlighting the ecological impacts of colonial exploitation and industrialization. Serpell examines the negative effects of projects such as the Kariba Dam on local ecosystems and communities, emphasizing the links between environmental degradation, socio-economic inequality, and colonial history. The writer features it in the following remarks: "The Colonel, who had plenty to say about the political interferences he had suffered while building Kariba Dam, might have objected to this, but he had fallen asleep in his chair, his empty stein nestled in his lap." (Serpell 308)

Serpell employs literary techniques that combine historical fiction, magical realism, and speculative fiction. This narrative innovation represents a postcolonial worldview that questions traditional storytelling conventions and breaks linear concepts of time and location. Through its engagement with these postcolonial aspects, *The Old Drift* provides a deep and diverse analysis of Zambia's colonial and post-war history. The writer says: "As for The Old Drift, Which once had the dignity of a place on the map- well, it has been swallowed by swamp." (Serpell 30) She invites readers to consider the intricacies of power, identity, and resistance in a globalised world.

To conclude, we find an in-depth examination of the complexities and nuances of African identity, culture, and history in the aftermath of colonialism when we read in this chapter through the prism of postcolonial literature. The chapter explores the major themes and narrative devices that define postcolonial African literature through an analysis of works by Chinua Achebe, Wole Soyinka, David Diop, and Namwali Serpell. The chapter examines the lasting effects of colonialism on African societies, emphasizing how literary masterpieces like *The Old Drift* and *Things Fall Apart* examine how colonial encroachment affects customary practices and societal systems. These books shed light on the challenges of cultural adaptation, resistance, and transition following colonial dominance through their convoluted plot dynamics and thematic issues.

The hybrid character of cultural identities in colonial and postcolonial contexts is frequently reflected in postcolonial literature. The chapter clarifies how African writers use linguistic and narrative tactics to portray the diversity and fluidity of African cultural experiences through an examination of Achebe's writing style in *Things Fall Apart* and Serpell's creative storytelling in *The Old Drift*. The idea of resistance against injustice and oppression is central to postcolonial literature. The works "Telephone Conversation" by Soyinka and "Africa" by Diop are potent examples of defiance and fortitude in the face of racial discrimination and colonial cruelty.

Reclaiming African agency and voice is central to Postcolonial African literature. The chapter emphasizes the significance of placing African perspectives and experiences front and centre in the conversation about colonialism and its consequences through the examination of narrative threads in *Anthills of the Savannah* and thematic investigations in "Africa." The tenacity, inventiveness, and fortitude of African people against colonial domination are validated by these writings. In the end, the chapter adds to the current discussion on postcolonial literature by emphasizing the richness and diversity of African literary traditions.

The chapter invites readers to critically engage with the legacies of colonialism and the opportunities for collective resistance, renewal, and transformation in the postcolonial African context by examining the works of Achebe, Soyinka, Diop, and Serpell. This helps to illuminate the complexities of postcolonial African identity, culture, and history. To sum up, this chapter provides a critical analysis of African postcolonial literature, shedding light on its themes, narrative techniques, and socio-political resonances within the larger context of postcolonial discourse. The chapter expands on our knowledge of the intricacies of African colonial experiences and their continuing influence on modern African society and cultures by analyzing important writings and authors.

Chapter 8

Postcolonial Voices from Indian Descent: Works by M K Gandhi, Jhumpa Lahiri, Mahashweta Devi and Kancha Ilaiah

Indian Postcolonial Literature is distinguished not just by cultural blending but also by a powerful spirit of dissent against the persisting remnants of imperialism. Through the perspective of Indian dissent, a distinct and strong narrative emerges in the literature that confronts, critiques, and redefines postcolonial identity. This study digs into the postcolonial elements inherent in Indian literature born of rebellion, examining how writers handle the complexities of resistance, identity, and autonomy. Indian Postcolonial Literature is a potent way of resisting colonial narratives that tried to homogenize and suppress indigenous perspectives. Writers use their creative skills to disrupt and question established power structures, providing a counter-narrative to colonial domination.

Dissenting voices in Indian literature are aggressively questioning the colonial past. The authors critically evaluate and deconstruct Eurocentric readings of India's past, offering alternative viewpoints that highlight the colonial agency. It extends beyond the colonial era to investigate neo-colonial strategies and practices. Writers address themes of economic exploitation, cultural imperialism, and political hegemony, putting light on the numerous kinds of colonialism that exist today. It also becomes a potent instrument for speaking the realities of oppressed people in Indian literature. While representing caste prejudice, tribal displacement, or gender inequality, writers magnify the voices of the historically oppressed, contributing to a larger social dimension of justice and equity. Language, a powerful weapon of colonial authority, becomes a source of contention in Indian literature. Nuances of Language are navigated by writers, who incorporate regional languages, dialects, and vernacular idioms. This language diversity threatens the hegemony of English and reclaims linguistic sovereignty. It also addresses the erasure and distortion of Indigenous identities as a result of colonization.

Authors investigate the intricacies of postcolonial identity, attempting to reconstruct and reinforce a sense of self that transcends the colonial gaze of confining narratives.

Some of the writers are actively involved in the revitalization and celebration of indigenous cultures and customs. Writers become cultural guardians through their creative expressions, protecting and promoting pieces of heritage that were threatened or suppressed throughout the colonial period. Postcolonial literature in India frequently intersects with political engagement, blurring the barriers between fiction and reality. Writers utilize their art to advocate for social and political change, connecting their stories to larger movements for justice, human rights, and democracy. It also transcends national borders, encouraging worldwide solidarity with other postcolonial conflicts. Writers find analogies between the Indian experience and those of other colonized nations, adding to a shared narrative of imperial resistance. Despite the difficulties highlighted, Indian postcolonial literature frequently weaves stories of hope and empowerment. Writers imagine alternate futures in which characters overcome adversity, oppose oppression, and contribute to the collective battle for a more just and equitable society.

As a result, a complex panorama of resistance, identity development, and cultural reclaiming is emerging. Literature becomes a potent vehicle for challenging the status quo, reclaiming agency, and forging a postcolonial identity that is aggressive, dynamic, and deeply entrenched in the spirit of resistance through the different narratives of opposing voices. Dissent in Indian literature is a monument to the continuing human spirit that resists, persists, and attempts to reconstruct itself beyond the shadows of colonial history.

8.1 *Hind Swaraj*- Mohandas K. Gandhi

Mohandas K. Gandhi's *Hind Swaraj* written in 1909, is a classic postcolonial work that articulates Gandhi's vision for India's freedom from British colonial control. While the term "postcolonial" is typically linked with the time following decolonization, *Hind Swaraj* might be seen as a proto-postcolonial text due to its severe critique of Western modernity and colonial ideology. Following discussions are important to have a postcolonial study of *Hind Swaraj*:

Rejection of Western Modernity

Gandhi is an outspoken opponent of the Western model of modernity, industrialization, and scientific advancement. He sees these features as not only harmful to Indian society but also as weapons of exploitation used by British colonial rulers. Gandhi's rejection calls into question the basic underpinnings of Western colonial domination.

Spiritual and Cultural Opposition

Gandhi's postcolonial vision is centred not only politically but also spiritually and culturally. He promotes a return to traditional Indian principles that emphasize self-sufficiency, simplicity, and a strong connection to the earth. This emphasis on cultural resistance is consistent with postcolonial philosophies that seek to recover indigenous identities while opposing cultural assimilation.

Mental Decolonization

Gandhi's condemnation of colonization extends beyond the political and economic arenas to include mental and cultural components. He advocates for the decolonization of the Indian mentality, asking his fellow Indians to reject the Western education system, which perpetuates colonial beliefs. This is consistent with postcolonial discourse, which emphasizes the significance of questioning Eurocentric narratives and reclaiming indigenous views.

Swaraj and Self-Determination

The term, "Hind Swaraj," means "Indian self-rule." Gandhi's definition of swaraj comprises not only of political freedom but also of all-encompassing vision of self-determination that includes economic, social, and cultural liberty. This is consistent with postcolonial aspirations for complete sovereignty and control over a nation's fate.

Nonviolent Conflict Resolution

Gandhi's nonviolent resistance concept, or "satyagraha", is an important part of *Hind Swaraj*. This approach departs from Western conceptions of armed resistance and corresponds with postcolonial efforts that prioritize resistance without copying the colonizer's violent means. Many postcolonial movements have been influenced by Gandhi's commitment to nonviolence as a means of resistance.

Examining Western Civilization

Gandhi's critique extends beyond politics to call into question the fundamental structure of Western civilization. He calls into question the ethics, morality, and sustainability of Western ways of life. This investigation is consistent with postcolonial viewpoints that deconstruct Western superiority myths and call into question the perceived benefits of Western ideologies.

Global Importance

While *Hind Swaraj* is set against the backdrop of British colonialism in India, the predominant ideas are universal. Gandhi's critique of Western modernism and urge for a return to traditional values is shared by postcolonial movements around the world. The book serves as a model for other colonial countries to reconsider their connections with the West and seek alternate paths to development and self-determination.

In conclusion, *Hind Swaraj* can be seen as a forerunner of postcolonial thinking due to its strong condemnation of Western colonialism, demand for cultural resistance and self-determination, and vision of a comprehensive, peaceful road to independence. Gandhi's ideas in *Hind Swaraj* continue to shape postcolonial discourse and are relevant in conversations about decolonization, cultural identity, and alternative development paths.

8.1.1 Gandhi's Philosophical Manifesto: A Critical Examination of *Hind Swaraj*

Hind Swaraj is a collection of Gandhian concepts with a fresh intellectual bent. This book is made up of 20 small chapters written in the form of a dialogue between the reader and the editor of a newspaper. Gandhi is the editor here, and he uses dialogic form to examine a wide range of subjects, each with its own consequences and complexities. *Hind Swaraj* critiques current civilization as well as the nature and structure of Indian Swaraj, as well as the means and techniques for achieving it. India has evolved as a result of long British administration, and under the influence of British authority, India has forgotten its religion. India is becoming an 'irreligious' country. Gandhi reflects: "Religion is dear to me, and my first complaint is that India is becoming irreligious. Here I am not thinking of the Hindu or the Mahomedan or the Zoroastrian religion but of that religion which underlies all religions. We are turning away from God." (Gandhi, *Hind Swaraj* 38)

Gandhi is not referring to a certain faith. Rather, he emphasizes all religions. However, as in the case of railways, these improvements have increased the British grip on India. These technological developments are causing us to become increasingly impoverished. They are also to blame for the rise in famines and epidemics. While considering the rise of Indian nationalism through railways, it is important to remember that India existed long before the British arrived. Lawyers also took advantage of Hindu-Muslim schisms, allowing the British to maintain their position by sucking the blood of poor India. He says: "My firm opinion is that the lawyers have enslaved India; have accentuated Hindu-Mahomedan dissensions and have confirmed English authority." (Gandhi 49)

Doctors have also been mostly responsible for encouraging individuals to be self-indulgent and to take less care of their bodies. He compares modern civilization to an "Upas tree", a toxic plant that consumes everything in its path. According to him, "One writer has likened the whole modern system to the Upas tree. Its branches are represented by parasitical professions, including those of law and medicine, and over the trunk has been raised the axe of true religion. Immorality is the root of the tree." (Gandhi 52) The education introduced by the British in India is a 'false education' (77) because the basic goal of education should be to learn to control our senses and to imbibe ethical behaviour in life, but the emerging elitism, which appears to be a by-product of the Macaulay system of education, has enslaved India.

The means for achieving Swaraj is urgently needed and is the fundamental issue of Swaraj. We should design a basic formula for transferring power from British to Indian hands, but this cannot be true Swaraj because it would result in "English rule without Englishmen." (Gandhi 27) We cannot achieve true swaraj until we are free as individuals. He attempts to define 'swaraj'. It is inextricably linked with a sense of freedom. Swaraj means "rule by yourself," "self-government," (22) or "self-rule." Swaraj means self-rule, which we must all experience. To achieve 'swaraj,' Indians must first become self-governing individuals. Changing the government is not enough; we must also make millions of people feel free. And how would it be accomplished--via armaments and violence? He attempts to analyse the situation and concludes that if thousands of Indians become violently rebellious, they must be armed, and India's holy country will become an unholy place owing to violence and bloodshed. In this circumstance, India will be worse off than Europe. He opposes the use of violence and guns to achieve swaraj. Since there is a close relationship between methods and ends, he rejects the use of arms and violence to achieve Swaraj. Furthermore, he does not agree with the belief of the Moderates that Swaraj can be obtained through mere prayers and supplications. To advance toward Swaraj, India requires a calm yet resolute form of opposition. Passive resistance is a love-force, soul-force strategy based on 'relative truth' through 'personal sufferings' (Gandhi 69).

Passive resistance is a weapon of the strong, not a tool or weapon of the weak. Thus, via passive opposition, true home rule or 'swaraj' can be achieved. Passive resistance requires absolute chastity, boldness, and the pursuit of truth. He also promotes the concept of Indian nationalism in this work. India existed as a nation long before the British arrived. Gandhi makes the argument that Hind Swaraj is not concerned with one religion, but rather with the fact that different religious people live in India, which strengthens the idea of Hind Swaraj because numerous Mohemmedans were already living in India previous to the coming of the British. Different religions should interact with each other in order to preserve Indian nationhood. He makes a profound statement:

> If the Hindus believe that India should be peopled only by Hindus, they are living in dreamland. Hindus, Mohammedans, Parsees and Christians who have made India their country are fellow countrymen, and they will have to live in unity if only for their own interests. In no part of the world are one nationality and one religion synonymous terms, nor has it ever been in India. (Gandhi 45)

As a result, he opposes the British notion that India never existed as a nation. Rather, it has always been a melting pot of diverse religions and communities. Since ancient times, pilgrimage centres in four corners of India have sparked the idea of nationhood in the minds of Indians. Thus, Gandhi emphasizes nationalism, for which he lived and died. Moral behaviour grants someone control over his psyche. It can lead a man down the path of truth and righteousness, strengthening and fortifying him. The current modern culture is deviating from the genuine path of morality. It is getting too self-indulgent. He also discusses Brahmacharya, swadeshi, means and ends, and other issues in the book. He believes that the new satyagrahis should serve as role models rather than vanguards. He also declares at the end of the book that he will spend the rest of his life as a Satyagrahi, which he sees as moral and self-fulfilling.

It is worth noting that *Hind Swaraj* did not originally pique the interest of scholars, but this changed after the release of the English edition in 1910, and then again in 1935. Gandhi sent a copy of *Hind Swaraj* to Wybergh soon after its publication in 1910, however Wybergh opposed many things in *Hind Swaraj*, especially that Western civilization is nothing more than a Satanic dominion that ought to be destroyed. According to him, Gandhi's prescription for 'freedom' to the majority of the population would do more harm than good. He also mentioned Anne Besant, who stated that Indians must expand their ambitions and activities in order to avoid stagnation and subjection. Western civilization was irrelevant to India for all of these reasons. He also claimed that passive resistance was nothing more than moving the conflict from the physical to the mental realm. As a result, it was neither spiritual nor non-coercive. He expressed significant opposition to Gandhi's use of soul force to achieve political and physical goals. Gandhi answered to Wybergh's letter by clarifying several things and stating that his major goal was to abolish violence from both private and public life.

He further highlighted that obtaining home rule by violence differs from obtaining it through passive opposition since the means determine the end, not the other way round. Only external force can bring about reforms, whereas passive opposition can bring about internal growth. It is possible to achieve it through the process of self-suffering and self-purification. As a result, while passive resistance is essentially founded on one's command over oneself, it has both moral and spiritual components. He also criticized Western society, which he saw as nothing but wickedness. He also disputed Wybergh's position on the need for people to be awakened by a "lash of competition."

He also advocated for Indians' quick liberation, even if this may not be achievable at the same moment. Gandhi also stated that he was attempting to bridge the gap between religion and politics, and that he would make all decisions on the concept of ethics and morals. *Hind Swaraj* is written in such a way and manner that it conveys a specific point of view. A quick reading of the book reveals it to be blatantly assertive and even absolutist in the extreme. It was written primarily to keep Indians from slipping into the trap of Western civilization. Only ethics and morality can serve as the basis for a new India in the post-independence age.

The book is a scathing critique of modern culture. He seeks an alternative to the modernist strategy. After 100 years, reading *Hind Swaraj* reveals that Gandhi could readily forecast the harmful effects of modern civilization much more clearly than his contemporaries. His ideas on man, society, and nature endured the test of time. History bears witness to this. Much scientific and technological progress brought a slew of obstacles on the road, which he detected at an early stage. Satyagraha was Gandhi's only option, and it became world famous for showing the correct method to right a wrong. The book is both timely and timeless.

Ideologies stated *Hind Swaraj* are always referenced in order to live a better and more meaningful life. It is at the heart of Gandhian thought since he offers a solution to the challenges that plague modern India. The book might be regarded as a plan of action or a manifesto. *Hind Swaraj* discusses the Gandhian idea of reconciling opposites inside and beyond traditions. This text is regarded as the cornerstone for comprehending the man and his mission. Gandhi has complete faith in Swaraj, which is nothing more than a moral victory; it is the love force and the soul force. He strives for ideological independence.

8.1.2 Swaraj as Spiritual Freedom: Themes in *Hind Swaraj*

Mohandas K. Gandhi's *Hind Swaraj* addresses a number of interwoven issues that make a comprehensive critique of Western colonialism and define Gandhi's vision for India's independence. The rejection of Western modernism and industrialization is a prominent subject. Gandhi sharply condemns the materialistic and technological progress associated with the West, seeing it as a tool of exploitation and a threat to Indian society's moral and spiritual richness. The concept of cultural resistance is linked to this, in which Gandhi urges for a return to traditional Indian values, emphasizing self-sufficiency, simplicity, and a healthy relationship with the soil.

Gandhi emphasizes nationalism, for which he lived and died. Moral behaviour grants someone control over his psyche *(Hind Swaraj* 94). It can lead a man down the path of truth and righteousness, strengthening and fortifying him *(Hind Swaraj* 68). The current modern culture is deviating from the genuine path of morality. They are getting too self-indulgent. He also discusses Brahamcharya, swadeshi, means and ends, and other issues in the book. He believes that the new satyagrahis should serve as role models rather than vanguards. He also declares at the end of the book that he will spend the rest of his life as a Satyagrahi, which he sees as moral and self-fulfilling.

He also promotes the concept of Indian nationalism in this work. India existed as a nation long before the British arrived. Gandhi makes the argument that Hind Swaraj is not concerned with one religion (*Hind Swaraj* 16), but rather with the fact that different religious people live in India, which strengthens the idea of Hind Swaraj because numerous Mohemmedans were living in India previous to the coming of the British (Hind Swaraj 38). Different religions should not fight with each other in order to preserve Indian nationhood.

The mind's decolonization emerges as a key issue, reflecting Gandhi's opinion that political freedom alone is insufficient without concurrent liberation from Western-educated mentalities. He promotes an education system based on Indian principles, opposing Eurocentric narratives that perpetuate colonial ideology. The overriding notion of self-determination, represented in the term "swaraj," includes not just political autonomy but also economic, social, and cultural autonomy.

Nonviolent resistance, or 'satyagraha', is a central discussion throughout the book. Gandhi's idea of peaceful resistance becomes a potent instrument for confronting colonial tyranny, aligning with the broader postcolonial emphasis on achieving independence through nonviolent means. Another key issue is Gandhi's questioning of Western civilization as a whole, in which he examines the ethics, morality, and sustainability of Western ways of life, challenging the assumed superiority of Western ideals. The emphasis on different paths to growth and freedom in *Hind Swaraj* emphasizes its worldwide relevance, providing a model for other oppressed nations. Gandhi's vision transcends India's freedom struggle, resonating with postcolonial movements around the world. Finally, the ideas in *Hind Swaraj* collectively contribute to a holistic and visionary critique of colonialism, providing insights that continue to impact postcolonial discourses on decolonization, cultural identity, and the search for genuine self-determination. In the article, "Gandhi, the Philosopher," published in 2003, Akeel Bilgrami provides a philosophical examination of Gandhi's ideas, concentrating on important topics from *Hind Swaraj*, such as nonviolence, self-sufficiency, and a critique of modern civilization. Bilgrami examines Gandhi's ideas through the lens of postcolonial theory, taking into account their relevance to current discussions about globalization, cultural identity, and political agency (Bilgrami 4159-4162). Bilgrami's analysis sheds light on how *Hind Swaraj* continues to impact discourse in postcolonial studies and provides insights into Gandhi's legacy in the postcolonial world.

The book's three recurring themes are colonial imperialism, industrial capitalism, and rationalist materialism.

Colonial Imperialism

Gandhi feels that the English did not seize India, but rather that we gave it to them. Their presence in India is thriving not because of their strength, but because we are keeping them. First and foremost, we can combat colonialism through our conscience. Through our recovery of self, we must make our personal foes feel exorcised and exiled. If we do not reclaim our authority, we will always be enslaved by some force, foreign or domestic. Internal colonialism cannot replace external colonialism. A white sahib, a brown sahib, they are all interchangeable. Imperialism in any state can be defeated by raising one's consciousness. We should not use Englishtan to compensate for the loss of Hindustan. British colonialism began in the name of enlightenment, as a Christianizing mission, and as a civilizing mission. Gandhi is attempting to undermine the legitimacy of the colonial enterprise at its foundation by rejecting modern civilization. The colonizers recognized that raw force could not be used to govern over India, therefore they maintained their power by civilizing missions.

Ranajit Guha's book *Dominance without Hegemony: History and Power in Colonial India*, published in 1998, provides a critical analysis of colonial power relations in India, challenging standard interpretations of colonialism and nationalism. While Guha's attention extends beyond "Hind Swaraj," he explores Gandhi's ideals and their significance for comprehending colonial authority and resistance in India (Guha 138-140). Guha's analysis sheds light on the complex interplay between colonial power, nationalist ideology, and the aspiration for self-rule stated in Gandhi's landmark text. Guha's research relates to the current discussion in postcolonial studies about colonial legacies and decolonization possibilities.

Hind Swaraj critiques current civilization as well as the nature and structure of Indian Swaraj, as well as the means and techniques for achieving it. India has evolved as a result of long British administration, and under the influence of British authority, India has forgotten its religion. India is becoming an 'irreligious' country. Gandhi is not referring to a certain faith. Rather, he emphasizes all religions. We are becoming atheists by rejecting God. Many modern developments have occurred, such as the railway and the creation of new elites such as doctors and lawyers.

However, as in the case of railways, these improvements have increased the British grip on India. These technological developments are causing us to become increasingly impoverished. They are also to blame for the rise in famines and epidemics. When considering the rise of Indian nationalism through railways, it is important to remember that India existed long before the British arrived. Lawyers also took advantage of Hindu-Muslim tensions, allowing the British to strengthen their position by sucking the blood of poor India. Doctors have also been mostly responsible for encouraging individuals to be self-indulgent and to take less care of their bodies. He compares modern civilization to an 'Upas' tree, a toxic plant that consumes everything in its path.

Industrial Capitalism

The driving force behind colonial imperialism is capitalism. Gandhi opposes capitalism because it degrades labor, devalues humans, and values machines in order to profit the upper class and deepens the gap between rich and poor. Modern civilization is a carbon copy of the machinery system that has eliminated handicrafts and small industries in India. As it leads to unemployment, it becomes a symbol of sin. Technology alienates and dehumanizes society. The impoverished are excluded from the benefits of industrialization, capitalism, and other professional services. *Hind Swaraj* is written in such a way that it conveys a specific point of view. A quick reading of the book reveals it to be blatantly assertive and even absolutist in the extreme. It was written primarily to keep Indians from slipping into the trap of western civilization. Only ethics and morality can serve as the basis for a new India in the post-independence age. The book is a scathing critique of modern culture. Gandhi seeks an alternate to modernity strategy.

Rationalist Materialism

According to Gandhi, technology is a manifestation of science that has evolved into an unwavering rationalism in modern society. This appears to be a threat to humanism. When rationality is misdirected, it transforms into madness. There is no limit to the number of reasons why one should be cautious. Gandhi believes that faith is more important than reason. He defends his faith with logic, but he never lets logic destroy his faith. Technological progress is nothing more than reasonable materialism. It is a defective materialism that denies the inner voice, spirituality, the transcendent, or religious perspective. Science and technology cannot penetrate the depths of truth. To him, reality extends beyond what the senses experience. The ultimate, transcendent reality provides significance and worth to the present, as does the Hindu aesthetic tradition. Rationalist materialism has left no room for human liberty. The author writes: "That which you consider to be the mother of Parliaments is like a sterile woman and a prostitute." (Gandhi, *Hind Swaraj* 29) He claims that the Indian parliament is ineffective because it achieves nothing. It is led by ministers who change. English administration features such as railways, attorneys, and doctors have only wreaked havoc on India. It cannot be called upon to bring about progress. In India, all machinery is decommissioned.

8.1.3 Gandhi's Prophetic Pen: Writing Style Analysis of *Hind Swaraj*

Hind Swaraj, authored by Mohandas K. Gandhi in 1909, has a distinct and important writing style that matches the text's profound concepts. The writing of Gandhi in *Hind Swaraj* is distinguished by clarity, simplicity, and a purposeful rejection of Western literary traditions. Gandhi authored *Hind Swaraj* on a steamship from London to South Africa. Originally written in Gujarati, it was not well received until it was translated into English. Gandhi, through the editor's voice in the book, wants home rule--Indian government, not British Indian.

Gandhi's writing style is notable for its simplicity and accessibility. Gandhi chooses a clear and conversational tone above sophisticated jargon and intricate phrase constructions. This choice is consistent with his ideal of making his ideas accessible to a wide range of people, including those without a formal education. The simplicity of his language amplifies the power of his message, allowing people from many backgrounds to understand it. To drive home crucial arguments, he employs rhetorical strategies such as repetition and forceful remarks, producing a convincing and emotional tone. This argumentative language was purposefully chosen to elicit thought and inspire critical inquiry.

Gandhi's writing reflects his convictions and principles. He writes with moral authority, which shows his dedication to truth, peace, and simplicity. His prose reflects the clarity of his vision for a self-sufficient and spiritually grounded India. This connection of his writing style and philosophical beliefs improves the credibility and persuasiveness of his arguments. Gandhi's writing style is also distinguished by the incorporation of personal anecdotes, examples, and connections to life experiences. He frequently uses his own observations and encounters to illustrate larger ideas, basing his views in real-world scenarios. This utilization of real-world examples helps to make his thoughts more relevant and practical to his readers' daily lives.

To summarize, Gandhi's writing style in *Hind Swaraj* is an intentional and successful technique of communicating his visionary ideas. The writing style is both accessible and persuasive due to its simplicity, directness, polemical tone, alignment with moral values, and utilization of personal tales. This stylistic approach heightens Gandhi's critique of Western modernity and his articulation of an Indian self-rule vision.

8.2 "Interpreter of Maladies"- Jhumpa Lahiri

Jhumpa Lahiri, a Pulitzer Prize-winning author of Indian origin, has distinguished herself through emotional and intricately woven narratives that examine the complexity of immigrant experiences and the dynamics of cultural identity. Lahiri's storytelling, known for works such as *Interpreter of Maladies* and *The Namesake*, deftly navigates the intersections of tradition and modernity, familial expectations, and the search for belonging. Lahiri's work is distinguished by its evocative simplicity, conveying with remarkable insight the delicate subtleties of human interactions. She contributes to the global literary scene as a diasporic writer, providing readers with a view into the emotional landscapes of individuals crossing the cultural barrier. Lahiri's work is notable not just for its portrayal of the Indian-American experience, but also for its universal themes of love, loss, and the search for one's identity.

Jhumpa Lahiri's *Interpreter of Maladies* is an intricate weaving of short stories, each giving a nuanced investigation of the complexity of human connection and the ways in which individuals face cross cultural and emotional barriers. The central plot is around the complexities of human relationships, with a particular emphasis on the experiences of Indian-American characters. Lahiri's stories take place in a variety of places, from the busy streets of Kolkata to tranquil suburban homes in the United States. Through works like "A Temporary Matter," "Sexy," and the title story, "Interpreter of Maladies," Lahiri dives into the numerous layers of intimacy, communication, and identity. The characters struggle with feelings of isolation, longing, and the consequences of cultural dislocation. "Interpreter of Maladies," the title story, delves into the relationship between an interpreter and a visitor on a journey to India, uncovering a narrative of unsaid yearning and squandered opportunities. Lahiri's storytelling is distinguished by its delicacy and emotional resonance, prompting readers to ponder the universal themes of love, sorrow, and the yearning for belonging that run throughout this remarkable collection.

Jhumpa Lahiri's "Interpreter of Maladies" chronicles the vacation of the Das family in India, which consists of Raj, Mina, and their three kids, Tina, Ronny, and Bobby. Mr. Kapasi is the tour guide they use. Mrs. Das discloses to Mr. Kapasi that Bobby was conceived through an affair and that she feels detached from her family during their visit to the Sun Temple (Lahiri 43). Mr. Kapasi recognises the deep loneliness and misconceptions that characterise their lives after experiencing a fleeting, erroneous connection with her. Bobby and several monkeys get into an incident at the end of the story, which represents the family's vulnerability and loneliness.

Mr Das told Mr Kapasi about his teaching job in New Jersey. Mr Kapasi also told him about his five-year tour guiding experience. Mr Kapsasi saw that the couple was arguing with each other while on this tour. They acted more like siblings to their children than parents. Mrs Das was upset with her husband for not arranging for an air-conditioned vehicle for the tour. She was eating her snacks without sharing them with anyone. Mr Das asked Mr Kapasi to halt the car after seeing the malnourished villagers.

They also noticed monkeys along the road, which was not unusual in that area. Mr Kapasi divulged to the Dases about his prior job as an interpreter at a doctor's office, which piqued Mrs Das's curiosity, and she described the position as romantic. Mr Kapasi was a superb scholar who knew numerous languages, but he had to limit himself to English because it provided him with financial rewards. In order to pay his son's medical bills after he died at the age of seven, he became an interpreter rather than a teacher. His marriage had been arranged, and he and his bride had very little in common. Mrs Das' statements about Mr Kapasi's work being "romantic" enticed him.

He began fantasizing about Mrs. Das. When they paused for lunch, Mrs Das insisted on having Mr Kapasi to join them. Mr Das shot their picture together when they were eating lunch, and Mrs Das collected Mr Kapasi's address to send a copy of the image to him. Mr Kapasi began wondering about their passionate letters and how she would confess her sad marriage to him through letters from this point forward. Mrs Das was appreciating the poses and legs of women while looking at the sensual photographs. Mr Kapasi was looking at the friezes depicting women in sensual postures. Before driving them back to the hotel, Mr Kapasi suggested them to go to a monastery. The area was crawling with monkeys. Mrs Das did not come out because her legs got hurt. She took the front seat and revealed the mystery of her younger son, Bobby, who was born eight years ago as a result of her affair. Because she felt lonely as a housewife, she slept with Mr Das's buddy who came to see them once. She never mentioned it to anyone. She believed that because Mr Kapasi was a disease interpreter, he might assist her.

Mr Kapsi's crush on her vanished as soon as he heard this. Mrs Das also confided to him that, despite the fact that she and her husband had known each other since childhood, she no longer loved him. She considered her children to be a burden and had a negative inclination toward them. She wished to find a solution to her agony and begged Mr Kapasi's assistance. He told her that what she was experiencing was more than just guilt. Mrs Das got out of the car and walked over to her family. While walking, she left a trail of puffed rice, which enticed monkeys, who attacked Bobby. In his anxiousness, Mr Das took an unintentional photograph, and Mrs Das begged for Mr Kapasi's assistance in rescuing Bobby from the monkeys. Mrs Das applied a bandage to Bobby's knee before reaching into her handbag for a hairbrush to straighten his hair, and the paper with Mr Kapasi's address fluttered in the air.

8.2.1 Cultural Crossroads: Themes in "Interpreter of Maladies"

Jhumpa Lahiri's "Interpreter of Maladies" dives into a rich variety of issues that run throughout the collection of short stories. One frequent issue is the investigation of cultural displacement and the resulting identity conflicts. Lahiri highlights the conflict between the characters' cultural background and their attempts to assimilate into new contexts, echoing the broader experiences of the Indian diaspora. Another painful issue is the complexities of communication and connection. The stories highlight the difficulties of communicating emotions, wants, and weaknesses, which are frequently hampered by linguistic and cultural boundaries. Love, in its numerous forms and expressions, is a recurring theme, reflecting the universal yet personal aspect of human interactions. Lahiri deftly investigates the impact of secrets and hidden facts, delving into the ramifications of unspoken feelings and the emotional toll of unspoken words. In addition, the story addresses the subject of isolation, both within marriages and in the broader context of immigrant experiences. Lahiri's treatment of these issues as a whole results in a compelling and powerful writing that challenges readers to consider the delicate threads that link and occasionally unravel the fabric of human connection. In "Interpreter of Maladies," Jhumpa Lahiri demonstrates a mastery of characterization, depicting her characters with a nuanced and empathic touch. Each protagonist is thoughtfully built with psychological depth and realism, whether stranded between cultural realms or negotiating the complexities of human relationships. Lahiri's characters, such as Mr. Kapasi in "Interpreter of Maladies" and Mrs. Das in "Sexy," encapsulate the intricacies of the immigrant experience, contending with cultural dissonance, personal needs, and unspoken longings. Lahiri's attention to detail goes beyond physical characteristics, going into the individuals' thoughts, feelings, and unspoken longings. The subtle nuances of their interactions, driven by cultural expectations and individual quirks, bring the story to life. Lahiri uses a fine balance of showing and hinting to provide readers with insights into the characters' inner lives. Lahiri's artistic portrayal not only depicts the various dimensions of the Indian and Indian-American experience, but also creates universally recognizable characters, making "Interpreter of Maladies" a heart-breaking investigation of the human condition in all its complexities.

Following are the relevant thematic concerns of the story:

Communication Barrier

The present story's main issue is communication. Almost all of the characters struggle with communication issues, which might have negative effects. Mr Kapasi has lost his ability to communicate in multiple languages and is now limited to English. His marriage is devoid of affection. There is little communication between the couple. He is also concerned that he does not communicate as well as his children. We also see an absence of communication between Mr. and Mrs. Das. The pair does not have a language barrier; instead, Mrs Das hides behind her shades most of the time, and Mr Das keeps himself busy with the guidebook. There is also a communication barrier between parents and children. They rarely pay attention to their parents. They do not heed Mr Kapasi's directions regarding monkeys. This huge communication chasm has many negative consequences. Even Mr Das and Mr Kapasi do not achieve the level of friendship that they could establish but do not do so. With the fluttering of the paper on which Mr Kapasi's address was written, all future possibilities of reaching out to one another vanish. Thus, the story addresses a significant communication difficulty that exists among humans.

Identity and Cultural Displacement

"Interpreter of Maladies" explores cultural displacement and its tremendous impact on identity as a primary theme. Lahiri's characters negotiate cultural expectations and personal identity while straddling the borders between their Indian origin and the American milieu. Whether in suburban America or returning to Kolkata, the protagonists struggle with a sense of belonging and the difficulties of bridging distinct cultural backgrounds.

Romanticism: A Potential Threat

The work is centred on the issue of romanticized beliefs that fail to mend broken marriage relationships. Mr Kapasi developed love feelings for Mrs Das, believing that this lonely woman could alleviate the loneliness of his sad marriage. She would be an ideal partner for him. He'd had enough of fantasizing and romanticizing. He was more focused on Mrs Das, her purse and sunglasses, and her naked legs. He couldn't help but think of her Americanized version of herself, in which she was more concerned with her own desires than her children's. On the other hand, she wished to resolve her marital problems with her husband with the assistance of Mr Kapasi, who served as a father figure, mentor, and guide to her. As a result of over-romanticization and a lack of adequate communication, grave consequences occur. Mr Das is passionate about taking pictures. He was unconcerned with the poverty and malnutrition of the peasants on the roadside; instead, he was only interested in photographing. He was still in the illusory realm of travelogues and refused to confront the reality of this real world. He could rarely visit his father's country and city; India was merely a tourist destination for him, with no connection to the concept of his father's land or original town. He was taking a photograph throughout the vital event of entanglement with the monkeys as well, as it was only a romanticized picture because he couldn't see the reality. He could only visit India as a tourist. India has no meaningful connection to him in terms of culture or history.

Secrets and Hidden Truths

The topic of secrets and unspoken feelings adds drama to the story. Lahiri's characters struggle with unstated personal truths, leading to emotional isolation and detachment. The unsaid becomes as strong as the stated, demonstrating the deep influence of concealed secrets on the emotional landscapes of the individuals.

Isolation and Alienation

In the context of marriages and immigrant experiences, Lahiri tackles the subject of isolation. Even in the most intimate partnerships, characters frequently find themselves emotionally alienated. The cultural divide contributes to a sense of alienation, particularly in stories like "The Third and Final Continent," in which the protagonist navigates the difficulties of adapting to a new society while retaining his sense of self. (Lahiri 183-188)

8.2.2 Intricate Narrative: Lahiri's Writing Style in "Interpreter of Maladies"

Jhumpa Lahiri is a master of storytelling, evoking deep pathos in her works. She represents the broken marriage of two characters in "Interpreter of Maladies". She maintains connections between two civilizations due to a flawless synthesis of two cultures- Indian and American. She overlays her topics and helps her readers react to the scenario. Lahiri's imagery is a stark and compelling manner that connects her readers with pathos. The imagery of the cab, pregnant wife, fall foliage, monkey gathering, and so on takes the readers on an emotional journey. She avoids sentimentality in her writing, instead relying on pathos to elicit emotions from her readers through vivid imagery.

    Her story is multi-layered, reflecting issues such as loneliness, homesickness, cultural integration, cultural clash, disastrous marriages, and so on. Thematic issues of the story are perfectly balanced with the narrative technique. Her style and themes are consistent. The stark feature in her writing is the short, sharp starting phrases that immediately introduce readers to information that is critical to the narrative. Her short stories can be read in a single sitting because she creates a sense of coherence in her works. She focuses on a single incident in a character's life before delving into that character's relationships with others. She creates an atmosphere that evokes emotions in the readers. As a result, we cannot separate action from her stories; they are really important.

    The book *Interpreter of Maladies* follows a consistent framework. Mr Kapasi's marriage was loveless, and he felt lonely. Mrs Das's comments enticed him. Mr Kapasi romanticized Mrs Das, believing that she may alleviate the loneliness of his miserable marriage. She would be an ideal partner for him. He'd had enough of fantasizing and romanticizing. He was more focused on Mrs Das, her purse and sunglasses, and her naked legs. Later, he became uneasy after Mrs Das revealed her adultery. The portrayal of the characters is based on their migrant experience and the cultural clash between the two countries. Mr. Kapasi represents the great rift between India and America. He was amused by the fact that these guys "appeared Indian but dressed like foreigners." (Lahiri 49) According to him, they were all so immersed in American culture that they acted more like siblings to their children than parents.

The Das pair is portrayed as undisturbed by India's social realities. Taking images of beggars sitting on the roadside was only playing tourist. By taking such images, they hoped to add local features to their journey. Mrs Das was fully preoccupied with herself. She was uninterested in her tourist experience. She became immediately interested in Mr Kapsi after he shared his previous experience as a language interpreter for a doctor. She idealized the concept and developed an unexpected interest in Mr Kapasi as a mentor in her life to fix her marital problems. Mr Kapsi, on the other hand, felt his job as thankless, but Mr and Mrs Das saw him as carrying a lot of responsibility. Mr Kapsi's task was to assist this family on their tour, but he was also suffering from marital discord with his wife, which led him to the conclusion that human behaviour is the same throughout countries because Mr and Mrs Das are not suited to one other. The same is true for him and his wife. Thus, Mrs Das's attentiveness flatters him, offering hope to the apathy in his troubled marriage.

As a result, "Interpreter of Maladies" explores a wide range of concerns and ideas, from unrequited love to the agony of loss. Jhumpa Lahiri's stories are all essentially humanistic. They have broad appeal despite dealing with Indian sensibilities in general. She uses vibrant characterization in her writings, making her writing an example of the true and authentic voice of the Indian diaspora. She abruptly shifts from the complexity of her words to a simpler, and often colloquial style. She goes on to say that the monkey's long grey tails dangled like a series of ropes among the leaves. She reflects: "All along the path, dozens of monkeys were seated on stones, as well as on the branches of the trees. Their hind legs were stretched out in front and raised to shoulder level, their arms resting on their knees." (Lahiri 67)

Consequently, one can find that her writing is direct and uncomplicated, lacking an in-depth style. It occasionally leaves readers with nothing to imagine. The story is told in the third person, with a limited point of view. The narrator is objective, not omniscient, and exposes Mr Kapasi's perceptions but not those of other characters. The narration focuses on Mr Kapasi rather than Mrs Das. For example, when Mrs Das exits the taxi to go to the temple, the plot does not follow Mrs Das until she returns to Mr Kapasi's view. Similarly, when Mrs Das accompanies Tina to the restroom, the narrator remains in the taxi with Mr Kapasi, who waits inside the car alone while the boys and Mr Das exit. The story's focus is on Mr Kapsi, through whom we examine other individuals. Mrs Das, for example, is not addressed by her first name, Mina, as her husband and children are. We do not learn much about the Das family from this narrow perspective. In truth, we are unable to determine Ronny and Tina's exact ages. Mr Kapasi perceived Mrs Das's statements as flirty, and Mrs Das also confesses her secrets about her affair and marital strife, which startles and shocks Mr Kapasi. In her anguish, she imagined Mr Kapasi as a mentor. Because of her experience as an interpreter, he would offer her some cures. However, every relationship formed between Mrs Das and Mr Kapasi is conceived in the imagination rather than in actuality.

We learn about Mr and Mrs Das's irresponsible behaviour and qualities through Mr Kapasi's story. Indian parenting styles contrast sharply with those of immigrant Indians. Indian Americans, unlike Indian parents, are not preoccupied with the concept of child safety. Indian American parents appear to act like their children's older brother and sister. Jhumpa Lahiri's stories are global in that they deal with a wide range of political and social concerns concerning the country and its people. The characterization is done mostly on ethnic grounds, providing her readers a real voice as a modern writer. Each story provides emotional output in an attractive manner while honestly exposing the psyche of the characters. The author portrays her characters with symbolic nuances using plain and direct language, which results in a lack of poignancy. Her writings provide value to people's lives by showing engaging and dynamic personalities, although providing little enticement through language.

8.2.3 Symbolic Threads in "Interpreter of Maladies"

There are numerous symbols employed throughout the story. They allow writer to add an additional degree of significance to her story. Meanings in a text might be literal and self-evident, or they can be symbolic and have deeper and more profound connotations. "Interpreter of Maladies" has various symbols, including Mrs Das' sunglasses, the slip-on on which Mr

Kapsi's address was scribbled, and Mr Das' camera. The young woman "lifted her pinkish brown sunglasses and arranged them on top of her head like a tiara." (Lahiri 56) They appear to be protective weapons for her, allowing her to relax in her comfort zone. Sunglasses are also referred to as shades, which stresses her secret that Bobby was not Mr Das' son, in order to protect her family. Mrs Das' sunglasses represent her hiding from the world. Her glasses shield her from the tiredness of the world around her. They also show her stylish personality. Another important symbol in the narrative is the piece of paper with Mr Kapasi's address scrawled on it, which represents the method of communication between him and Mrs Das. The slip of address represents a romantic vision that Mr Kapasi had when presenting his address to Mrs Das. Finally, the slip flutters away, indicating the end of their communication, which does not worry Mr Kapasi in the end. Before the slip fluttering, Mr Kapasi was anticipating a suitable form of connection through letters in which Mrs Das would write to him about her marriage's failure, and he would respond elegantly. As both of them had failed marriages, this would strengthen their bond and eventually lead to a relationship. Another remarkable symbol in the novel is Mr Das's camera, which represents his incapacity to see the world without a lens. He wanted Mr Kapasi to stop the automobile so he could photograph the destitute peasants instead of assisting them. As a result, he had become oblivious to the sufferings of others. He was also watching over the gorgeous surroundings of the mountains while he was busy taking shots. He intended to capture his family's happiness in these photos while ignoring his wife's inner bliss. Thus, through his photographs, he attempted to depict a perfect family, which is rare in this world. His children seemed to be uninterested in him, and his wife was unconcerned about closeness with her spouse.

As a result, we can observe that symbols play a crucial role in the "Interpreter of Maladies," which provides a more accurate interpretation of the text. The novel examines the predicament of a person caught between two cultures: Indian and American. Mr Kapasi's narrative exemplifies psychological turmoil in real-life situations. The characters have been raised in one culture and have matured and established in another. The author's works also highlight the cultural distinctions between the United States and India. Irony and melancholy are entwined with the narrative's heart and soul in her writings. "Interpreter of Maladies" is more than just a collection of stories; rather, all gathered works unite to form a "Short Story cycle." (Brada-Williams 451). Themes and motifs are interconnected in order to have a cumulative effect on the reader.

8.2.4 Jhumpa Lahiri's Linguistic Complexity

Jhumpa Lahiri's works are remarkable because of their linguistic complexity. Lahiri, an outstanding novelist recognized for her moving explorations of the immigrant experience and cultural identity, approaches linguistic intricacy in a variety of ways. Lahiri frequently shows characters that live in bilingual or multilingual environments, mirroring the reality of many immigrants who must traverse various languages and cultures. Her characters may code-switch between languages, negotiate linguistic identities, or face the difficulties of translating and communicating across linguistic boundaries.

In *The Namesake*, Lahiri delves into the language issues that the protagonist, Gogol Ganguli, faces as he navigates his identity as a second-generation Indian immigrant in the United States. Gogol struggles with his name, which both signifies his cultural past and distinguishes him in American society. Lahiri uses words to represent the friction between Gogol's Bengali roots and his American upbringing, as he struggles with his sense of belonging and self-identity.

English is frequently the dominating language in Lahiri's books, reflecting the colonial and postcolonial backgrounds of her characters. The language dualism deepens Lahiri's investigation of cultural hybridity and the intricacies of identity creation. Lahiri's work frequently digs into the complexities of intercultural communication, emphasizing the misconceptions, miscommunications, and moments of connection that occur when people with different linguistic and cultural backgrounds interact. In her short story "Interpreter of Maladies," Lahiri depicts the problems of communication and miscommunication among characters from various linguistic and cultural backgrounds (Lahiri 58-62). The Das family, hailing from India, employs Mr. Kapasi, an Indian interpreter, to join them on a sightseeing tour of India. As the protagonists seek to overcome their linguistic and cultural differences, misunderstandings and unspoken desires emerge, emphasizing the difficulties of intercultural communication.

The writer carefully depicts the difficulties of bridging linguistic and cultural boundaries, as well as the possibility of empathy and understanding across languages. In Lahiri's stories, language is crucial to shaping the identities of the characters. Language can be a source of cultural connection for immigrants and their offspring, as well as a marker of distinction in the host society. In her short story collection *Unaccustomed Earth*, Lahiri investigates the lives of Bengali immigrants and their children in the United

States. In stories like "Hell-Heaven," Lahiri digs into the complications of bilingualism and cultural adaptation, as individuals switch between English and Bengali and negotiate their two identities (Lahiri 38). Pranab Chakraborty, the protagonist, experiences sentiments of displacement and longing for his native language and culture while still embracing features of American life. (Lahiri 30-32)

Lahiri investigates how language impacts views of oneself and others, impacting characters' feelings of belonging, alienation, and cultural negotiation. In her own writing, Lahiri has experimented with language and form, stretching the frontiers of linguistic expression. For example, she has experimented with writing in Italian, a language she learned later in life, as a way to push herself creatively and explore themes of displacement and cultural adaptation in a new linguistic setting. In her nonfiction book "In Other Words," Lahiri discusses her own language journey and her determination to study Italian as an adult (Lahiri 33). Lahiri's study of language learning and cultural immersion sheds light on the transformational power of language and how linguistic identity influences personal and artistic expression. Lahiri's experience with Italian writing explores themes of dislocation, belonging, and the search for linguistic and creative fulfilment.

Jhumpa Lahiri's linguistic intricacy reflects her extensive research into the difficulties of the immigrant experience, cultural identity, and the interplay between language and belonging. Her subtle portrayals of linguistic diversity, bilingualism, and intercultural communication add to the richness and authenticity of her writing, which resonates with readers who face similar linguistic and cultural challenges. Through the experiences of her characters and her own language musings, Lahiri shows the rich canvas of linguistic diversity, as well as the common human desire for connection and belonging across cultural and linguistic borders.

8.2.5 Jhumpa Lahiri and Diaspora

Jhumpa Lahiri's work is frequently discussed in terms of diaspora, as her writing delves extensively into the realities of diasporic communities, particularly Indian immigrants and their descendants. Lahiri's stories effectively reflect the cultural displacement and dislocation experienced by diasporic individuals and families. Her characters struggle with sentiments of longing for their birthplace, as well as the difficulties of adjusting to a new cultural and social milieu. Through her nuanced portraits, Lahiri delves into the complexity of diasporic identity and how people navigate numerous cultural affiliations. Lahiri's characters frequently inhabit regions of cultural hybridity, navigating the intersections between Indian and Western cultures. In *The Namesake*, Lahiri depicts the Ganguli family's experiences as Indian immigrants living in the United States. Gogol Ganguli, the protagonist, tries to find a sense of identity and belonging as he navigates his Indian background and American culture (Lahiri 35-40). Lahiri powerfully illustrates the Ganguli family's cultural displacement and generational conflicts, emphasizing the complexity of diaspora life and the search for meaning and connection in a strange land. Lahiri investigates how diasporic people navigate their dual identities, combining components of their Indian background with Western lives and ideals. Through her works, Lahiri questions essentialist assumptions of cultural purity while emphasizing the flexibility and complexity of diasporic identities. In the short story, "A Temporary Matter" from "Interpreter of Maladies," Lahiri examines the issue of diaspora through the eyes of Shoba and Shukumar, a young Indian-American couple (Lahiri 10-12). As they deal with the loss of their unborn child and the dissolution of their marriage, Lahiri investigates how cultural differences and communication difficulties increase their feelings of alienation and detachment. Lahiri's experiences vividly show the difficulties of establishing a sense of home and belonging in a diasporic environment.

Lahiri's work investigates the conflicts and relationships between successive generations of diasporic families. She depicts the problems that develop between immigrant parents, who may adhere to traditional rituals and ideals, and their American-born children, who must negotiate many cultural influences. Lahiri's works frequently explore how diasporic families navigate generational divides and build new senses of identity and belonging. In her title story, "Unaccustomed Earth," Lahiri investigates the intergenerational relationships of a Bengali-American family. Ruma, a second-generation immigrant, struggles to reconcile her Indian background with her American lifestyle, while her father, Ashoke, experiences yearning for his homeland (Lahiri 200-205) and a sense of displacement in the United States. Lahiri skillfully depicts the complexity of diasporic identity, as well as the tensions between assimilation and cultural preservation within the family.

Lahiri's characters struggle with feelings of belonging and alienation as they traverse the challenges of diasporic life. Whether they are caught between two cultures or are struggling to reconcile their Indian background with their American identity, Lahiri's protagonists frequently experience displacement and a need to connect. Lahiri's writing skillfully conveys the emotional intricacies of diasporic experiences, giving light to the fundamental human desire for belonging and acceptance. In "The Lowland," Lahiri portrays the narrative of two brothers, Subhash and Udayan, whose lives diverge after Udayan joins the Naxalite movement in India. Lahiri delves into issues of political instability, exile, and diaspora as Subhash migrates to the United States and Udayan remains in India (Lahiri 150-180). Lahiri's portrayal of the difficulties of diasporic existence and the lingering relationships of family and homeland is multifaceted, owing to their experiences and the consequences of their decisions. Lahiri's stories focus on the transnational links and networks that build diasporic communities. Lahiri's protagonists keep in touch with their motherland and extended family members living overseas, whether through letters, phone calls, or visits back to India.

Jhumpa Lahiri's work provides a complex and nuanced analysis of diaspora within the context of postcolonialism, providing light on the cultural displacement, hybridity, and belonging experiences that diasporic people encounter around the world. Lahiri's perceptive representations of characters negotiating the intricacies of diasporic life urge readers to consider issues of identity, hybridity, and home in an increasingly interconnected and globalized world.

8.3 "Dopdi"- Mahasweta Devi

With her profound and socially conscious works, Mahasweta Devi, the acclaimed Indian writer and social crusader, had an everlasting influence on literature. Mahasweta Devi's writing, which includes works like "Draupadi" and "Mother of 1084," is renowned for its devotion to addressing issues of caste discrimination, gender injustice, and the misery of underprivileged people. Her stories frequently feature strong and stoic female heroes who bravely fight against social injustices and inequities. Aside from her literary accomplishments, Mahasweta Devi's activism and support for tribal communities and oppressed people have made her a symbol of social consciousness in India. Mahasweta Devi shows the transformative power of literature as a weapon for social change and a method of expression via her literary and activist undertakings.

Mahashweta Devi is the author of numerous works, including novels, plays, and a collection of short stories. She depicts the struggle of the tribes living on the margins in India. Her depiction of tribal women and the atrocities inflicted on them paints a vivid image of their daily hardships and strife. Her short story 'Draupdi' or 'Dopdi' is about a Santhal tribal woman who suffers from social discrimination and abuse and fights back. Her unwavering determination to destroy centuries-old racial injustice and gender inequality distinguishes her as a radical feminist.

In this famous work, "Three Women's Texts and a Critique of Imperialism" published in 1985, Spivak examines the writings of Mahasweta Devi (Spivak 245-250) and two other Indian women writers through the lens of imperialism and patriarchy. She looks at how these writers question prevailing narratives (Spivak 245-248) and explain the realities of underprivileged communities, particularly Indigenous people and lower-caste women in India. Spivak's involvement with Mahasweta Devi's texts sheds light on the intersections of gender, class, and power in postwar South Asia, adding to larger discourse in feminist and postcolonial theory (Spivak 258-260). Gayatri Spivak has done the translation of the short story "Draupadi". Dopdi Mejhen is an ignorant and uneducated tribal woman who realizes her rights and joins the armed struggle against oppressors. She advocates for the freedom and rights of the tribal community. Mahashweta Devi is the most translated Indigenous writer working today. Her active involvement with tribal women in West Bengal and southeast Bihar allows her to provide a detailed account of their lives, including their difficulties and oppression through racial and gender hierarchies. She also works as a journalist and the editor of "People's Magazine." In the words of Gayatri Spivak, "Mahashweta Devi is as unusual within the Bengali literary tradition as Foucault or Derrida in the philosophical or political mainstream in France." (Spivak, *The Spivak Reader* 163) Spivak's essay "Scattered Speculations on the Question of Value" published in 1985, explores the themes of value, ethics, and representation in the context of globalization and postcoloniality (Spivak 155-160), using examples from Mahasweta Devi's writings. Spivak investigates how Devi's works question traditional concepts of value and provide alternative perspectives on social justice, human rights, and the environment. Spivak's analysis focuses on the ethical and political implications of Devi's literary interventions, as well as their relevance to current discussions in postcolonial studies.

When we compare the characters of Draupadi from the epic *The Mahabharata* (Book 1, Chapters 155-157) to Dopdi from Mahasweta Devi's short story (Devi 22-25), we can see that tribal women in India have significantly greater standing than women in mainstream Hindu society. They are mute and enslaved, yet Dopdi has equal rights to combat the oppression as her husband. She is not as denigrated as other women in society. She is battling side by side with her husband. Draupadi is portrayed in *The Mahabharata* as a victim of patriarchy and masculine hegemony.

However, Mahashweta Devi questions and probes this singularity. Draupdi's husband lost her as an object in the dice game. Dusshasan humiliated her, and divine Krishna saved her. Senanayak is rendered dumbfounded and practically scared in this story by the forceful and strong persona of Dopdi. Through the compelling characterisation of Dopdi, the story questions the patriarchal hegemony of Indian society. In the present story, a miracle does not occur with the arrival of the heavenly Krishna since Mahashweta Devi is not telling a fanciful story; rather, she is making us aware of the harsh and violent facts and realities of tribal society. With her composed and forceful demeanour, Dopdi appears to be a radical tribal woman.

Instead of defending her honour, Mahashweta Devi enables Dopdi to be raped several times since her nakedness becomes a weapon to offend the attackers' masculinity. "What is the use of clothes?" she asks. "You can strip me, but can you clothe me again...? There isn't any man here that I should be ashamed of." (Spivak, "Draupadi" 402)

In the book *Imaginary Maps: Three Stories by Mahasveta Devi* (1994), she says: "Among the tribals, insulting or raping a woman is the greatest crime. Rape is unknown to them. Women have a place of honor in the tribal society." (Devi & Spivak xviii). She goes on to raise the issue of selling tribal girls for cheap labour as a perennial issue, as mentioned in this book: "I made a story. I have named the village Seora. But there are such villages everywhere in Palamu. Now they cannot do this anymore wherever there is a movement against bonded labour. But the sale of girls for rape still goes on." (Devi & Spivak xx)

Ironically, raping a woman is considered as an epitome of manhood, masculinity, and women's dignity is closely adhered to her body, which the writer interrogates through Dopdi's repeated rapes. The story takes place during the Nexalite movement of 1967-1971, as well as the Bangladesh Liberation War (1971). Tribal rebellions occurred against affluent landlords, infuriating the government, prompting it to undertake Operation Bakuli, which tried to exterminate the tribal rebels. Dopdi, together with her husband Dhulna, murdered numerous tribal affluent landlords and seizes their wells, the sole source of water in the village. The government attempted to subjugate this tribal group through any terrible activity- kidnapping, murder, rape- and as a result, Dopdi was arrested by Officer Senanayak, who commanded army officers to rape her in order to extract information about the rebel group. Dopdi ripped off her clothing and marched naked towards Senanayak, who was startled by her resistance after being violated by the same officers who commanded her to cover up. "There isn't a man here that I should be ashamed of," she said, standing in front of him "with her hand on her hip" as "the object of (his) search." (Spivak, "Draupadi" 402)

The protagonist, in the story, is a strong-willed woman who fought the stigma associated with women's bodies and sexual assault. She is a voiced subaltern, as opposed to Draupdi of epic, who was not so voiced. Dopdi, the indigenous woman, is more conscious of her rights and knows how to struggle against persecution and torment perpetrated by the society. Dopdi defies the stereotyped notions attached to the female body. She rejects the myths of the moral, devout, decent, and chaste woman. She is not ready to accept patriarchal institutions of society. She is conscious of her subaltern identity standing in contrast to the powerful and hegemonic systems portrayed by the characters of the policeman and Senanayak. Her body takes on the appearance of resistance to male domination. She is violently attacked by numerous men, but she fights to save her people, her community. She refuses to be clothed in defiance of male desire and power.

Mahashweta Devi exemplifies how a woman's body may become a target of masculine tyranny. Both men and women were tortured throughout the Naxalite movement, but women were doubly stigmatized because of their sexual assault. Devi portrays tribal women as subalterns living on the outskirts of society who dare to challenge patriarchal norms in this story. Subalterns are rarely represented in mainstream literature. Devi does not allow her female heroes from the oppressed sections of society to be passive and docile before being conquered by a male-dominated society, as Draupadi did in *The Mahabharata*.

Dopdi soothes the army officers at the end of the story with her bare body, which has been humiliated and tormented by society. She prefers to use her body as a weapon. Despite being physically mistreated, she emotionally tortures the male counterparts in the narrative. She refuses to be harmed emotionally. We see in her a powerful and radical woman who defied conventional and sexual norms despite being marginalized and exploited. She converted her body's impotence into a formidable tool, resisting with furious displays of her damaged and inflicted body. Devi does not exaggerate or romanticize tribal women's conditions; rather, she paints a realistic and genuine picture of a tribal woman using simple words and complex emotions. Thus, in the story, the woman's body is not an objectified instrument, but rather a weapon used to resist male exploitation and abuse. Judith Butler's *Gender Trouble* (1990) looks at how bodily gestures and societal norms are used to establish and enact gender identities (Butler 122-135). She claims that the body is more than just a passive object, but also a location of political contestation and resistance. Butler's theory of performativity questions traditional notions of gender as stable and binary, arguing that gender is constantly enacted through repeated performances. Butler's theory emphasizes the body's potential as a place for feminist critique (Butler 147-150) and activity, pushing people to challenge traditional gender conventions and embrace the fluidity and multiplicity of identity. Spivak goes on to state that "the subaltern has no history and cannot speak, the subaltern as female is even more in deeply in shadow." (Spivak, "Can the Subaltern Speak?" 288)

8.3.1 Rhetoric of Resistance in 'Dopdi'

The short story 'Dopdi' was published in the collection *The Breast Stories*, which Mahasweta Devi authored for the underprivileged section of society. Her female characters are not silent and voiceless; rather, she offers them a voice in order to struggle against society's patriarchal and hegemonic institutions. Mahasweta Devi employs sarcasm, myth, history, legends, and folklore in her narrative and literary style. Through her recurring third-person narration, the author conveys a global and universal worldview. The oppression of women is not a specific concern, but rather a universal one. The author employs numerous dramatic methods of role transformation to demonstrate her narrative management.

She illustrates the master-slave relationship and how it has been repeated throughout human history regardless of nation, caste, class, and ethnicity. She uses unusual diction and colloquial idioms to bring veracity and authenticity to her narrative. She questions why women are objectified because of their subaltern origins. She attempts to build a canvas of India's pre- and post-independence eras, depicting history and culture that are unknown to mainstream society. Spivak's essay "The Politics of Translation" (1992) addresses the difficulties and implications of translating literary writings (Spivak 180-185), particularly those by Mahasweta Devi. While Spivak's critique of translation theory is not limited to Devi's writing style, it does address the problems of portraying Devi's narratives in various linguistic and cultural contexts. Spivak's research sheds light on how Devi's writing style conveys themes of marginalization, resistance, and social critique, emphasizing the political implications of her literary works (Spivak 191-195).

Women's conditions in tribal communities are often significantly better than in mainstream Hindu society. Premarital sex and re-marriages are accepted in most tribal societies. Devi attempts to re-evaluate the nation's past in light of these edges that were never considered in the mainstream. By re-mapping the edges, she is altering mainstream history. By championing the position of a subaltern speaker, she expresses her rage and wrath at their dispossessed as a result of Bourgeois' complacent consumerism. Readers might detect Mahashweta Devi's rebellious attitude in her writings. Dopdi's rebelliousness and resistance have left an imprint on the writer, which she shares with her character. She captures the abused condition of subalterns. Dopdi's refusal to conceal her body is a reflection of her defiant attitude against being subject to male hegemony and a gender-prejudiced culture that views women as mere objects of pleasure. The crime against her body exposes the corrupt psyche of the strong and self-absorbed men. Dopdi's excruciating pain and suffering are caused by the continuing injustice perpetrated by the upper-class people. The scene is described by the author as follows:

> The guard pushes the water forward. Draupadi stands up. She pours the water down on the ground...tears her piece of cloth with her teeth...Senanayak walks out surprised and seers Draupadi, naked walking towards him in the bright sunlight with her head high. Draupadi stands before him, naked. Thigh and pubic hair matted with dry blood. Two breasts, two wounds. She comes closer and pushes Senanayak with her two mangled breasts. (Spivak, *Draupadi* 402) As a result, she encourages them to look at the atrocities they have committed against her body. "What is the point of clothes?" she asks. "You can strip me naked, but how will you clothing me again? Are you a guy?...There isn't a man here of whom I should feel ashamed, and I won't let you put my cloth on me." (Spivak, "Draupadi" 402)

8.4 *Why I Am Not a Hindu*- Kancha Ilaiah

Kancha Ilaiah is a professor at Maulana Azad National Urdu University, Hyderabad and the director of the Centre for the Study of Social Exclusion and Inclusive Policy. He is also a member of the Dalitbahujan and civil rights movements. His most notable writings include *Buddha's Challenge to Brahminism, Buffalo Nationalism: A Critique of Spiritual Fascism, God as Political Philosopher: Buddha's Challenge to Brahminism, Untouchable God: A Novel.* One can feel his pain, wrath and violence in his works. He is scathing of Indian society's caste structure. He discovers numerous discrepancies between Dalitbahujans and Hindus in the contexts of their childhood, family life, social life, market relations, and power interactions. He attempts to integrate the thoughts and viewpoints of the Dalits to convey their vision of a more just society. In his book titled *The Idea of Freedom in Asia and Africa*, published in 2019, Sudipta Kaviraj engages with Ilaiah's work, particularly the concept of "dalitbahujan" (marginalized communities), highlighting the need to challenge dominant caste-based social structures. (118-119) Gopal Guru's article "Caste as a Problem: A Theoretical Exploration" (2001) delves into the concept of caste and its ramifications for Indian society, based on the writings of Kancha Ilaiah and others (Guru 178-182). Guru scrutinizes Ilaiah's claims about the social and economic dimensions of caste oppression, as well as his proposals for social transformation and equality. Guru's analysis provides insights into the theoretical underpinnings of Ilaiah's work, as well as its importance in comprehending the complexity of caste relations in contemporary India. Gopal Guru's engagement with Kancha Ilaiah's theories sheds light on the theoretical roots of Ilaiah's writings, as well as the ramifications for broader concerns of caste, identity, and social justice in Indian society. Similarly, K. Satyanarayana's article "Story of a Social Scientist: Kancha Ilaiah Shepherd" gives an account of Kancha Ilaiah's life and work, including his literary achievements (Satyanarayana 12-13). Kancha Ilaiah reminds us of the importance of ongoing discussion since his book is targeted at open minds, not closed ones. He also faced ridicule and verbal abuse from his adversaries. He also asks Banias, Brahmins, and neo-kshatriyas (upper-class sudras) to learn only what they need to educate others: the Dalitbahujans. But, for the sake of the country, they should now learn to listen to and read what we have to say. The author describes the origin of the book as a manifesto for oppressed Dalitbahujans. The book, along with Dr B.R. Ambedkar's *Annihilation of Caste*, was designated as a millennium book, and it was also translated into several Indian languages, becoming a weapon in the hands of Dalitbahujans.

Why I Am Not a Hindu is a scholarly book about religion that should be a required reading in all Indian institutions and universities. In contrast, in comparison to *Why I Am Not a Hindu*, Bertrand Russell's book *Why I Am Not a Christian* appears to be superficial, as Russell fails to provide sufficient and solid grounds for not being a Christian. When the editor first read *Why I Am Not a Hindu*, he noticed that Kancha was discussing his experiences as a kuruma, or shepherd caste. The expertise of diverse techniques of a shepherd to breed and care for sheep was unknown to Brahamins. Kancha's grief and suffering were shared by the editor, who was also from the weaver caste. As described in the book, it is a pity that Brahmins have taken away the gods of the Dalits. Dalits also celebrate their festivals and rites, such as pocchamma's festivals, which include sacrifice and revelry. They sacrifice buffalo, sprinkle their blood on them, boil and devour them. They also sing and dance the entire night.

When the editor first read *Why I Am Not a Hindu*, he was taken aback. They are not required to learn the classical music that the Brahmins popularized. Because of the devdasis system, their Bharatnatyam and classical music persisted. Why do they label Dalits as uncultured when they are unaware of their culture and rituals? Dalits' Gods are fed with meat instead of bananas and coconuts since Dalitbahujans eat meat. The Brahmins are barbarians and savages who forbid Dalits from sacrificing animals because they want to eradicate their culture; how they have forgotten that they were also meat eaters 2000 years ago. They only became vegetarians to conquer Buddhists. Buddhists were unable to understand the policy of freshly converted Brahmins and assumed that they were non-violent, therefore, Brahmins gradually assimilated with Buddhists. Brahmins are the hegemonic caste, and they will go to any length to maintain their monopoly, including changing their cuisine. Brahmins also persuaded Christian missionaries against animal sacrifice. Kancha never saw any Brahmin children in the countryside while he was a kid. He inquires as to where these Brahmin children were at the time. They spent the entire day at home eating and singing mantras. They had no interaction with nature. They had never touched mud and knew nothing about plants or animals. They still want to be known as intelligent.

Kancha also exposes the Brahmins' sex education practices. In their households, the Brahmins never discuss sex education as it does not exist. Unlike us Dalits, their children have no concept of sex. They are taught sex education in their homes as Dalits, but Brahmin youngsters are not taught about birds and bees. Even their own children are not touched by the Brahmins. Their mothers never touch or adore their children. Brahmins, according to Kancha, are nasty people. The world should be aware of the Brahmins' abuse of women and widows. He exposes their mistreatment of women and widows, demonstrating their inhumanity.

They burn the widows after their husbands die, yet they are not regarded as offenders for this heinous offence. He claims that the goddess Saraswati is illiterate. Why do Brahmins forbid their daughters from studying? He describes their Gods as violent because Ram murdered Dalits such as Shambuka and Ravana. Krisna was also an expert at deception. He was an expert in Chanakya's Arthshastra and Vatsyayana's Kamsutra. (Ilaiah 48) The Brahmin Gods constantly destroy the oppressed. When the Brahamins say, 'Aham Brahmasmi,' it means "I own everything." Why should Brahmins be given everything? Why are they regarded as the best of the castes? (Ilaiah 89) He says: "The Hindu Gods and Goddesses are made in the cultural image of Brahmins." (Ilaiah 59) The fruits of Sudras' or Dalits' toil and hard work cannot be given to Brahmins. Kancha went so far as to critique the scriptures and epics. He claims that in *the Mahabharata*, the superior caste Pandavas murdered their lower caste Kauravas. He reveals the Mahabharata's hypocrisy. According to him, *the Bhagvad Gita* should be outlawed since it influenced those who discovered the atomic weapon. They were all Jews. Bhatvadgita impacted Einstein and Oppenheimer. This book is extremely deadly, as millions of people were killed in Hiroshima and Nagasaki, Japan, as a result of its impact. The Japanese should seek restitution from the Brahmins and Jews who caused the destruction of the two cities. Manu developed the *Manusmriti*, and without any governmental power, the Brahmins rule over the Dalits. When Muslims and the British ruled India, the Brahmins ruled over the Dalits. They are the most devious and cunning people on the planet. They are powerful even without owning land because they chant mantras and have no relationship with nature. They control individuals by hypnotizing them with their mantras. Kancha reveals all of the wrongdoings of Brahmins. Now, the Dalits have banded together to oppose the Brahmins by exposing their deception. According to him, the Hindu religion is harmful and should be opposed. They can only have peace and justice after destroying Hinduism.

The oppression of Dalits inspires Ilaiah to write this book, which bears little resemblance to Hitler's *Mein Kampf*. The author expresses his rage and hostility toward Hinduism. He also criticizes the "Bania economy." (Ilaiah 44) He criticizes all Hindu deities for oppressing Dalits. Brahma is a light brown Aryan, Vishnu is blue, and this was the colour of the mixed race, Kshatriyas, while Shiva is black to deceive the indigenous pre-Aryan inhabitants of India. Thus, the entire history of Indians provides an overview of racism and casteism. *The Ramayana* is essentially about a racial conflict between the northern Aryans and the southern Dravidians. In an anti-semitic twist, Brahmins controlled all of India's political parties. The Brahmins appeared to be committing mass genocide against the Sudras. The difference between Hinduism and Buddhism, Islam, and Christianity can be described by the former having an "inborn spiritual fascist" nature, whereas the other three have a "basic characteristic" of spiritual democracy. (Ilaiah 105)

The book condemns casteism, which is a major issue in India. Discrimination against Shudras-Harijans and tribal people can be seen almost everywhere, according to the writer. Though legislation, social and religious reforms, and education have resulted in some progress, much more remains to be done. This evil manifests itself in the shape of mistaken elitist Dalit leaders, Anglophile Indian elites who continue to shoulder the white man's burden, and Western specialists who harbour great contempt for Hinduism and Hindus. Kancha Ilaiah's book is an example of this troubling trend. He has become a star for numerous Christian missionaries, Islamists, and Indian Marxists since the book's publication. The title of his book is similar to Ibn Warraq's *Why I am not a Muslim* and Bertrand Russell's *Why I am not a Christian*, however Ilaiah's book differs from these two works in that he communicates his hatred for the targeted community, Hindus, through misrepresentation of the facts.

The book informs unbaked notions and does not involve any field survey. He also omits several references and bibliographical details to back up his claims. It also shows his lack of academic enthusiasm and erudition as a result of an abundance of cheap rhetoric. The author has a misunderstanding of the faith and culture he is attempting to malign. The book suddenly becomes popular in American and European universities. Hundreds of books have been written about the hardships of Dalits and the weaker sectors of society, many of which have been written by individuals who are suffering, but in Ilaiah's story, he is not describing his class or caste's misery, but rather his personal hatred for Hinduism. According to his so-called personal story, he belonged to the backward kuruma caste and grew up in a backward Telangana village raising sheep. With his experience, he learned to discern between different types of sheep, such as Bolli gore, pulla gore, and nalla gorre. He also learned about the different maladies that used to afflict sheep, as well as their rustic diagnoses; herbal treatments. If the paltry drug failed, he would provide hot-iron medication. He also learned how to shear sheep's wool without injuring them. This caste-based profession provided him with information and expertise. In addition to this knowledge, he earned a doctorate in academic studies and was appointed Associate Professor of

Political Science at Osmania University. He developed his "DalitBahujan" beliefs and perspectives based on his accumulated knowledge and childhood experience. However, reading his writing, which is nothing more than a venomous outburst on Hinduism and Brahminism, critically examines his lack of factual verification and academic study in this regard. He never confirmed anything he heard or saw as a child. His underdeveloped abilities did not require him to verify, clarify, and correct the notions he obtained as a child through hearsay. His work is perceived to be biased and prejudiced. As per the critics, his views on Brahminism and Hinduism in general appear to be shady. His opinions appear to be the result of a discussion with one or two co-workers who share a similar contempt for everything associated with Hindu tradition and Brahminical birth. Whatever happened to him as a child, he did not try to grasp or study it clearly in his "enlightened" years.

8.4.1 Radical Prose: Writing Technique in *Why I Am Not a Hindu*

Why I Am Not a Hindu by Kancha Ilaiah emerges as a forceful critique of Hinduism, diving into social, economic, and political issues with an unwavering stance. The book's stylistic characteristics, in addition to its provocative subject, contribute greatly to its impact. The present section investigates the distinguishing elements of Ilaiah's writing style, ranging from his use of language to narrative structure, in order to shed light on how these choices increase the effectiveness of his critique. In her paper, "Revisiting the Telangana Rebellion: Gender, Caste, and the Social Question in Kancha Ilaiah's Work", published in 2018, Anupama Rao examines Kancha Ilaiah's writings (Rao 36-38) in light of the Telangana insurrection and their implications for comprehending gender, caste, and socioeconomic inequality in India. While Rao's attention is not primarily on Ilaiah's writing approach, her research of his texts sheds light on how he employs narrative strategies and rhetorical elements to address complicated social issues. Rao's analysis contributes to a better understanding of Ilaiah's works' literary elements as well as their broader sociopolitical implications. Anupama Rao's involvement with Kancha Ilaiah's writings offers yet another scholarly perspective on the literary features of his works, as well as its significance for the study of Indian politics and society.

Language Accessibility and Directness

Ilaiah's writing style is distinguished by its accessibility and directness. He avoids complicated vocabulary in favour of a direct and strong tone. This decision makes difficult sociopolitical ideas more accessible to a wider audience, which aligns with Ilaiah's objective of democratizing debate. The clarity with which he expresses himself strengthens the persuasive power of his arguments, inviting readers from various backgrounds to connect with the subject.

Personal Narrative and Anecdotal Evidence

Throughout the book, Ilaiah mixes personal narratives and anecdotal evidence to anchor his critique on lived experiences. This stylistic decision humanizes the intellectual analysis, making the book more approachable and emotionally resonant. Ilaiah enables readers to identify with the difficulties and perspectives of oppressed people by presenting human stories, and transforming abstract critiques into concrete critiques.

Rhetorical Tactics for Emphasis

The work is peppered with rhetorical tactics that serve to highlight important discussion issues. Repetition, parallelism, and strong wording form a rhythm that emphasizes Ilaiah's message's intensity. Ilaiah's use of these tactics not only confirms his points but also pushes readers to consider the gravity of the topics he discusses, leaving a lasting impression.

Interdisciplinary References

Ilaiah draws on a wide range of disciplines, including history and sociology, as well as economics and politics. His writing style reflects his interdisciplinary approach, elegantly combining insights from numerous subjects. This stylistic choice deepens the critique by emphasizing the interconnectivity of social issues and reinforcing Ilaiah's analysis's comprehensiveness.

Statements: Bold and Provocative

Ilaiah is not afraid to make statements that are bold and provocative, questioning conventional knowledge and disturbing established narratives. His writing style is strong, displaying an intellectual posture that is daring. The use of provocative language fosters a culture of intellectual inquiry by stimulating critical thinking and encouraging readers to rethink deeply rooted views. Hence, Kancha Ilaiah adopts a vibrant and meaningful writing style in *Why I Am Not a Hindu*, going beyond conventional exposition. His use of personal experiences, rhetorical tactics, interdisciplinary references, and forceful declarations all contribute to the indelible impact of his work.

Examining the writings of M.K. Gandhi, Kancha Ilaiah, Mahasweta Devi, and Jhumpa Lahiri in the postcolonial framework, this chapter provides a thorough examination of the Postcolonial Indian experience from a variety of viewpoints. The chapter critically examines how these writers' works represent the ongoing effects of colonialism in India. These literary works, which range from Gandhi's *Hind Swaraj*, a critique of Western modernity, to Ilaiah's *Why I Am Not a Hindu*, a radical deconstruction of Hinduism, explore the political, social, and cultural effects of colonial rule and illuminate the intricacies of postcolonial Indian culture. The chapter explores the intricacies of cultural identity, migration, and displacement within the Indian diaspora and marginalized populations through Lahiri's "Interpreter of Maladies" and Devi's "Dopdi." These pieces offer complex representations of the Indian experience both inside and outside of national boundaries by navigating the interconnections of culture, language, and identity. Devi's examination of oppression and resistance and Ilaiah's critique of the caste system challenge long-standing power systems in Indian society. Through elevating the voices of neglected people and questioning prevailing narratives, these writers add to the current discourse in postcolonial India about social justice, equality, and emancipation. The chapter also looks at the narrative strategies and stylistic devices employed by these writers to get their points across. Every author, from Gandhi's philosophical treatise to Lahiri's complex narratives and Devi's skilful rhetoric, uses a different literary strategy to draw readers in and encourage critical thought on issues related to colonialism, identity, and power.

To sum up, by emphasizing the postcolonial Indian experience and providing a range of viewpoints on colonial legacies, cultural identities, and social justice, the chapter contributes to the larger panorama of discussions on postcolonial literature. Gandhi, Ilaiah, Devi, and Lahiri challenge readers to confront the legacy of colonialism and envision alternative futures based on equality, dignity, and liberation while also deepening our awareness of the nuances and complexity of postcolonial India through their writings. It also highlights the significance of postcolonial literature in addressing the intricacies of cultural identities, power structures, and colonial legacies in the Indian context. Through their works, these authors add to a larger global discussion on decolonization, justice, and human rights while also shedding light on the challenges and subtleties of postcolonial India.

Conclusion

While concluding this book on postcolonial theory and literature, it is critical to cover the multiple recent voices coming from different contexts. Through the eight chapters of this book, a deep theoretical underpinning of postcolonial studies, with important concepts and terms that affect our understanding of postcolonial dynamics in Chapter 1, has been explored. This chapter aimed to shed light on the complexities of colonialism, its legacies, and its affinity with other social, cultural, and political phenomena while also acknowledging colonized people's agency and resilience in the face of oppression.

Chapter 2 began by setting postcolonial theory in its historical and intellectual framework, emphasizing its relevance to contemporary questions of power, identity, and representation. Major works such as Edward Said's "Representation and Resistance," Leela Gandhi's "Thinking Otherwise," and Chinua Achebe's "Colonialist Criticism," which established the framework for the investigation of postcolonial dynamics, have been discussed at length.

In Chapter 3, the intersections of history, culture, and geography have been explored, specifically how postcolonial writers "write back" to colonial narratives to recover their voices and histories. Deepesh Chakravarthy's "Postcoloniality and the Artifice of History" and Dennis Lee's "Writing in Colonial Space" demonstrate how literature may challenge prevailing narratives and establish alternative perspectives.

Chapter 4 delves into the other major aspects of postcolonial discourse, examining how bodies, ethnicities, subaltern voices, and languages intersect in colonial and postcolonial contexts. Through seminal texts such as Frantz Fanon's "The Fact of Blackness," Gayatri C. Spivak's "Can the Subaltern Speak?" and Ngugi Wa Thiong'o's "The Language of African Literature," Achille Mbembe's *Necropolitics* and Sabelo J. Ndlovu Gatsheni's *Epistemic Freedom in Africa: Deprovincialization and Decolonization*, we interrogated the ways in which colonialism inscribes itself onto bodies and languages, perpetuating oppression and resistance.

In Chapter 5, we looked at the interconnections of postcolonial feminism, third-world literacy, nationalism, and education, emphasizing the interwoven concerns and objectives that drive postcolonial cultures. We explored the issues of gender, race, and class in colonial and postcolonial contexts through works such as Chandra Talpade Mohanty's "Under Western Eyes" and Thomas Macaulay's "Minute on Indian Education."

Chapter 6 examined postcolonial Caribbean literature, providing insights into the region's complex historical, cultural, and social experiences. We investigated themes of identity, diaspora, and cultural memory using texts such as Derek Walcott's "A Far Cry from Africa" and Jamaica Kincaid's "A Small Place," shedding light on the intricacies of Caribbean identities and narratives.

In Chapter 7, we focused on postcolonial African literature, exploring the intricacies of cultural hybridity, identity formation, and resistance in the African environment. Chinua Achebe's *Things Fall Apart*, Wole Soyinka's "Telephone Conversation," and David Diop's "Africa", Namwali Serpell's *The Old Drift* all deal with themes of cultural conflict, colonial violence, and the assertion of identity and autonomy.

Chapter 8 focused on voices of Indian descent, delving into the intricacies of resistance, identity, and autonomy in the Indian setting. We experienced the intricacies of Indian identities and narratives, as well as the struggles for social justice and cultural regeneration, via texts such as M K Gandhi's *Hind Swaraj*, Kancha Ilaiah's *Why I Am Not a Hindu*, Mahashweta Devi's "Dopdi," and Jhumpa Lahiri's "Interpreter of Maladies."

Thus, we have encountered a diverse range of voices, perspectives, and narratives that question mainstream discourses and proclaim alternative worldviews. We have also explored how postcolonial theory and literature can be used as strong instruments for questioning power and oppression, recovering silenced voices and histories, and envisioning more just and equitable futures.

In conclusion, our exploration of postcolonial theory and literature has been both instructive and transformational. We have seen the long-lasting effects of colonialism and imperialism, as well as the perseverance and ingenuity of colonized people in the face of persecution. As we move forward, we must continue to engage critically with postcolonial theory and literature, recognizing their ability to question prevailing narratives, inspire social change, and create better understanding and solidarity across borders and cultures. We may work toward a more just and equitable future for future generations by engaging in continuous discourse, critical reflection, and collective action.

Conclusion

While postcolonial theory and literature have made enormous contributions to explaining the intricacies of colonial legacies and their impact on cultures around the world, it is critical to recognize some limitations and examine opportunities for future investigation and development. One limitation of postcolonial theory is that it favours certain locations and experiences over others. The field has typically concentrated on British and European colonialism, frequently overlooking other colonial histories and settings. Future study should aim to widen the geographical reach of postcolonial studies by including viewpoints from Latin America, and the Middle East, and indigenous groups worldwide. This more inclusive approach would provide a more complete knowledge of colonial dynamics and their long-term impacts on many nations. Furthermore, postcolonial theory has been chastised for its reliance on Western theoretical frameworks and its neglect of indigenous knowledge and epistemologies. Moving forward, scholars should focus on decolonizing the area by emphasizing indigenous viewpoints and connecting with non-Western theoretical frameworks. This includes developing communication and engagement with indigenous researchers and boosting their perspectives in postcolonial discourse.

Another weakness of postcolonial theory is that it tends to prioritize historical analysis over contemporary ones. While the field has made considerable contributions to understanding the historical roots of colonialism and imperialism, there is a need for more focus on contemporary expressions of colonial power relations, such as neocolonialism, globalization, and environmental degradation. Furthermore, postcolonial theory has been widely critiqued for its theoretical fragmentation and lack of coherence. The discipline contains a diverse spectrum of theoretical ideas and techniques, which can occasionally result in theoretical contradictions and conflicts. Future studies should strive to overcome these gaps and create interdisciplinary debate, using insights from sociology, anthropology, political science, and other subjects to improve our knowledge of colonial processes.

In terms of future impact, postcolonial theory and literature have the potential to continue impacting critical discussions about power, identity, and resistance in the twenty-first century. By highlighting marginalized perspectives, challenging dominant narratives, and pushing for social justice, postcolonial theorists and writers can help to advance global decolonization and liberation movements.

Works Cited

Achebe, Chinua. "An Image of Africa: Racism in Conrad's 'Heart of Darkness'." *The Massachusetts Review*, vol. 57, no. 1, Spring 2016, pp. 14-27.

Achebe, Chinua. "The African Writer and the English Language." *Morning Yet on Creation Day: Essays*, Heinemann, 1975, pp. 60-65.

Achebe, Chinua. "Colonialist Criticism." *Hopes and Impediments: Selected Essays*, by *Chinua Achebe*, Anchor Books, 1990, pp. 57-61.

Achebe, Chinua. "The Novelist as Teacher." *Hopes and Impediments: Selected Essays*, by *Chinua Achebe*, Anchor Books, 1990, pp. 40-46.

Achebe, Chinua. *A Man of People*. Heinemann, 1966.

Achebe, Chinua. *Anthills of the Savannah*. Picador, 1988.

Achebe, Chinua. *Things Fall Apart*. Heinemann, 1958.

Adichie, Chimamanda Ngozi. *Half of a Yellow Sun*. Alfred A. Knopf, 2006.

Adiga, Aravind. *The White Tiger*. Free Press, 2008.

Ahmed, Abdullahi Yusuf. *The Somali National Movement: A Study in Political Dynamics*. University of California Press, 1992.

Altbach, Philip G. "Literary Colonialism: Books in the Third World." *The Postcolonial Reader*, edited by Bill Ashcroft et al., Routledge, 1995, pp. 485-490.

Althusser, Louis. "Ideology and Ideological State Apparatuses." *Lenin and Philosophy and Other Essays*. Translated by Ben Brewster, Monthly Review Press, 2001, pp. 127-188.

Althusser, Louis. *On the Reproduction of Capitalism: Ideology and Ideological State Apparatuses*. Verso, 2014.

Ambedkar, B.R. *Thoughts on Linguistic States*. Siddharth Publications, 1929.

Ambedkar, B.R. "Writings & Speeches". Vols. 1-10. *Education Department, Government of Maharashtra*, 1987.

Ambedkar, B.R. *Annihilation of Caste: The Annotated Critical Edition*. Navayana Publishing, 2014.

Anderson, Benedict. *Imagined Communities: Reflections on the Origin and Spread of Nationalism*. Verso, 2006.

An-Na'im, Abdullahi Ahmed. *Islamic Law, International Law, and Human Rights*. Routledge, 1990.

Anzaldúa, Gloria. *Borderlands/La Frontera: The New Mestiza*. Aunt Lute Books, 1987.

Appadurai, Arjun. "Theory in Anthropology: Center and Periphery." *Comparative Studies in Society and History*, vol. 28, no. 2, Cambridge University Press, Apr. 1986, pp. 356-374.

Appadurai, Arjun. *Modernity at Large: Cultural Dimensions of Globalization.* University of Minnesota Press, 1996.

Appiah, Kwame Anthony. 'Cosmopolitan Patriots'. *Critical Inquiry,* vol. 23, no. 3, University of Chicago Press, Apr. 1997, pp. 617–639, https://doi.org10.1086/448846.

Ashcroft, Bill, Gareth Griffiths, and Helen Tiffin, editors. *The Postcolonial Reader.* Routledge, 1995.

Ashcroft, Bill, Gareth Griffiths, and Helen Tiffin. *Key Concepts in Post-Colonial Studies.* Routledge, 1998.

Ashcroft, Bill, Gareth Griffiths, and Helen Tiffin. *The Empire Writes Back: Theory and Practice in Post-Colonial Literatures.* Routledge, 1989.

Barker, Francis, et al., editors. *Colonial Discourse/Postcolonial Theory.* Manchester University Press, 1994.

Berman, Antoine, and Paul North. *Theories of World Literature.* Routledge, 2021.

Bethell, Leslie, editor. *The Cambridge History of Latin America, Volume 1: Colonial Latin America.* Cambridge University Press, 1984.

Bhabha, Homi K. "Cultural Diversity and Cultural Differences." *The Post-Colonial Studies Reader,* edited by Bill Ashcroft et al., Routledge, 1995, pp. 206-209.

Bhabha, Homi K. "The Commitment to Theory." *New Formations,* no. 5, 1988, pp. 5-23.

Bhabha, Homi K. *The Location of Culture.* Routledge, 1994.

Bilgrami, Akeel. "Gandhi, the Philosopher." *Economic and Political Weekly,* vol. 38, no. 39, 2003, pp. 4159-4165.

Boehmer, Elleke. *Colonial and Postcolonial Literature: Migrant Metaphors.* 2nd ed., Oxford University Press, 2005.

Boehmer, Elleke. *Stories of Women: Gender and Narrative in the Postcolonial Nation.* Manchester University Press, 2005.

Bohata, Kirsti. *Postcolonialism Revisited*: Writing Wales in English. University of Wales Press, 2009.

Brada-Williams, Noelle. "Reading Jhumpa Lahiri's 'Interpreter of Maladies' as a Short Story Cycle." *MELUS,* vol. 29, no. 3-4, 2004, pp. 451-464.

Brathwaite, Edward. *The Development of Creole Society in Jamaica, 1770-1820.* Oxford University Press, 1971.

Breckenridge, Carol A., and Peter van der Veer, editors. *Orientalism and the Postcolonial Predicament.* University of Pennsylvania Press, 1993.

Breslin, Paul. *Nobody's Nation: Reading Derek Walcott.* University of Chicago Press, 2001.

Brouillette, Sarah. "Postcolonial Writers in the Global Literary Marketplace." 30 June 2018.

Budd, Christopher Houghton. *Gramsci in the World.* Routledge, 1995.

Burkitt, Katharine. *Literary Form as Postcolonial Critique*. Ashgate Publishing Limited, 2012.

Butler, Judith. *Gender Trouble: Feminism and the Subversion of Identity*, Routledge, 1990.

Campbell, Kofi Omoniyi. *Literature and Culture in the Black Atlantic: From Pre- to Postcolonial*. Palgrave Macmillan, 2006.

Canny, Nicholas. *The Oxford History of the British Empire: Volume I: The Origins of Empire*. Oxford University Press, 1998.

Césaire, Aimé. *Discourse on Colonialism*. Translated by Joan Pinkham, Monthly Review Press, 2000.

Chakrabarty, Dipesh. "Postcoloniality and the Artifice of History: Who Speaks for 'Indian' Pasts?" *Representations*, no. 37, Special Issue: Imperial Fantasies and Postcolonial Histories, Winter 1992, pp. 1-26. University of California Press. *JSTOR*, http://www.jstor.org/stable/2928652.

Chandra, Chandra Talpade Mohanty. "Under Western Eyes: Feminist Scholarship and Colonial Discourses." *Boundary 2*, vol. 12, no. 3, 1984, pp. 333-358

Chatterjee, Partha. *Nationalist Thought and the Colonial World: A Derivative Discourse?* University of Minnesota Press, 1993.

Chatterjee, Partha. *The Nation and Its Fragments: Colonial and Postcolonial Histories*. Princeton University Press, 1993.

Childs, Peter, and Patrick Williams. *An Introduction to Post-Colonial Theory*. Routledge, 2016.

Conrad, Joseph. *Heart of Darkness*. Edited by Robert Kimbrough, W.W. Norton & Company, 2009.

Craps, Stef. *Postcolonial Witnessing: Trauma out of Bounds*. Palgrave MacMillan, 2013.

Dangle, Arjun, editor. *Poisoned Bread: Translations from Modern Marathi Dalit Literature*. Orient Blackswan, 1992.

Dawes, Kwame. "David Diop's Poetry: Language, Race, and Form." *Research in African Literatures*, vol. 26, no. 2, 1995, pp. 53-72.

Deloria, Vine, Jr. *Custer Died for Your Sins: An Indian Manifesto*. University of Oklahoma Press, 1988.

Deluze, Gilles. *Difference and Repetition*. Translated by Paul Patton. Columbia University Press, 1994.

Derrida, Jacques. *Of Grammatology*. Translated by Gayatri Chakravorty Spivak, Johns Hopkins University Press, 1976.

Desai, Gaurav. *Subject to Colonialism: African Self-Fashioning and the Colonial Library*. Duke University Press, 2001.

Descartes, René. *Meditations on First Philosophy*. Edited by John Cottingham, Cambridge University Press, 1996.

Devi, Mahasveta, and Gayatri Chakravorty Spivak. *Imaginary Maps: Three Stories by Mahasveta Devi*. Routledge, 1995.

Devi, Mahasweta. "Draupadi". *Breast Stories*, translated by Gayatri Chakravorty Spivak, Seagull Books, 1997, pp. 19-38.

Diop, David. "Africa." *All Poetry*, 1956.

Diop, David. "The Vultures." Translated by Simon Mondo, *The Penguin Book of Modern African Poetry*, edited by Gerald Moore and Ulli Beier, Penguin Books, 1998, pp. 217-218.

Eagleton, Terry, Fredric Jameson, and Edward Said. *Nationalism, Colonialism, and Literature*. University of Minnesota Press, 1990.

Eltis, David, et al., editors. *The Cambridge World History of Slavery, Volume 4: AD 1804–AD 2016*. Cambridge University Press, 2017.

Engels, Friedrich. *The Origin of the Family, Private Property, and the State*. International Publishers, 1972.

Fanon, Frantz. *Toward the African Revolution*. Translated by Haakon Chevalier, Grove Press, 1964.

Fanon, Frantz. *A Dying Colonialism*. Translated by Haakon Chevalier, Grove Press, 1965.

Fanon, Frantz. "The Fact of Blackness." *Black Skin, White Masks*, translated by Charles Lam Markmann, Pluto Press, 1986, pp. 109-112.

Fanon, Frantz. *The Wretched of the Earth*. Translated by Richard Philcox, Grove Press, 2004.

Ferguson, Moira. *Jamaica Kincaid: Where the Land Meets the Body*. University of Virginia Press, 1994.

Foucault, Michel. *The Archaeology of Knowledge*. Translated by A. M. Sheridan Smith, Pantheon Books, 1972.

Fraser, Nancy. *Justice Interruptus: Critical Reflections on the "Postsocialist" Condition*. Routledge, 1997.

Freire, Paulo. *Pedagogy of the Oppressed*. Translated by Myra Bergman Ramos, Continuum, 2000.

Galeano, Eduardo. *Open Veins of Latin America: Five Centuries of the Pillage of a Continent*. Translated by Cedric Belfrage, Monthly Review Press, 1997.

Gandhi, Leela. *Postcolonial Theory: A critical introduction*. Allen & Unwin, 1998.

Gandhi, M. K. *Hind Swaraj or Indian Home Rule*, Navajivan Publishing House, 1909.

Geertz, Clifford. 'Religion as a Cultural System'. *The Interpretation of Cultures: Selected Essays*, edited by Clifford Geertz, Fontana Press, 1993, pp. 90–91.

Gellner, Ernest. *Nations and Nationalism*. Cornell University Press, 1983.

Gikandi, Simon. "Walcott's Postcolonial Aesthetics." *Research in African Literatures*, vol. 23, no. 3, 1992, pp. 3-15.

Gramsci, Antonio. *Selections from the Prison Notebooks*. Edited by Quintin Hoare and Geoffrey Nowell Smith, International Publishers, 1971.

Greetz, Clifford. *The Interpretation of Cultures*. Fontana Press, 1993.

Grewal, Inderpal. *Transnational America: Feminisms, Diasporas, Neoliberalisms.* Duke University Press, 2005.

Guha, Ranajit. *Dominance without Hegemony: History and Power in Colonial India.* Harvard University Press, 1998.

Guru, Gopal. "Caste as a Problem: A Theoretical Exploration." *Sociological Bulletin*, vol. 50, no. 2, 2001, pp. 173-194.

Hall, Stuart. "Cultural Identity and Diaspora." *Identity: Community, Culture, Difference*, edited by Jonathan Rutherford, Lawrence and Wishart, 1990, pp. 222-237.

Hargreaves, Alec G., editor. *Memory, Empire, and Postcolonialism: Legacies of French Colonialism.* Lexington Books, 2005.

Held, David, and Henrietta L. Moore, editors. *Globalization and Nationalism: The Changing Relationship.* Routledge, 2002.

Hitchcock, Peter. *The Long Space: Transnationalism and Postcolonial Form.* Stanford: Stanford UP, 2010.

Hitler, Adolf. *Mein Kampf.* Translated by Ralph Manheim, Houghton Mifflin, 1943.

Hooks, Bell. *Feminist Theory: From Margin to Center.* South End Press, 1984.

Hulme, Peter. *Colonial Encounters: A Comparative History of the Colonization of Africa and the Americas.* Routledge, 1992.

Ilaiah, Kancha. *Why I Am Not a Hindu: A Sudra Critique of Hindutva Philosophy, Culture, and Political Economy.* Samya, 1996.

Ilaiah, Kancha. *Untouchable God: A Novel.* Samya, 2009

Ilaiah, Kancha. *Buffalo Nationalism: A Critique of Spiritual Fascism.* Samya, 2004.

Ilaiah, Kancha. *God as Political Philosopher: Buddha's Challenge to Brahminism.* Samya, 2012.

Ilaiah, Kancha. *Buddha's Challenge to Brahminism.* Samya, 2019.

Innes, C.L. *The Cambridge Introduction to Postcolonial Literatures in English.* Cambridge University Press, 2007.

Irele, Abiola. "Negritude: Literature and Ideology in Africa and the Caribbean." *The Journal of Modern African Studies*, vol. 3, no. 4, 1965, pp. 499-526.

Jackson, Ashley. *The British Empire: A Very Short Introduction.* Oxford University Press, 2013.

Jeyifo, Biodun. *Wole Soyinka: Politics, Poetics, and Postcolonialism.* Cambridge University Press, 2004.

Juang, Richard M., and Noelle Morrissette, editors. *Africa and the Americas: Culture, Politics, and History.* CLIO, 2008.

Kaviraj, Sudipta. *The Idea of Freedom in Asia and Africa,* Springer, 2019.

Keay, John. *The History of India.* Grove Press, 2000.

Kennedy, Michael D. "The City, Culture, and Collective Memory." *Cultural Anthropology*, vol. 15, no. 3, 2000, pp. 457-484.

Kincaid, Jamaica. *A Small Place*. Farrar, Straus and Giroux, 1988.

Kipling, Rudyard. "The White Man's Burden." *The Works of Rudyard Kipling*, vol. 3, Macmillan, 1903, pp. 250-252.

Lacan, Jacques. "The Mirror Stage as Formative of the I Function as Revealed in Psychoanalytic Experience." *Écrits: A Selection*, translated by Alan Sheridan, W.W. Norton & Company, 2006, pp. 1-7.

Lahiri, Jhumpa. "A Temporary Matter." *Interpreter of Maladies*, Houghton Mifflin, 1999.

Lahiri, Jhumpa. "Interpreter of Maladies." *Interpreter of Maladies*, Houghton Mifflin, 1999.

Lahiri, Jhumpa. "The Third and Final Continent." *Interpreter of Maladies*, Houghton Mifflin, 1999, pp. 173-198.

Lahiri, Jhumpa. *The Namesake*. Houghton Mifflin, 2003.

Lahiri, Jhumpa. "Hell-Heaven." *Unaccustomed Earth*, Alfred A. Knopf, 2008.

Lahiri, Jhumpa. "Unaccustomed Earth." *Unaccustomed Earth*, Alfred A. Knopf, 2008, pp. 187-216.

Lahiri, Jhumpa. *The Lowland*, Alfred A. Knopf, 2013.

Lahiri, Jhumpa. *In Other Words*, translated by Ann Goldstein, Alfred A. Knopf, 2016.

Lee, Dennis. "Cadence, Country, Silence." *Liberté*, 14(6), 1972, pp. 65-88.

Lee, Dennis. *Civil Elegies and Other Poems Anansi*. 1972.

Lenin, Vladimir. *Imperialism: The Highest Stage of Capitalism*. International Publishers, 1939.

Lopez, Alfred J. *Postcolonial Whiteness: A Critical Reader on Race and Empire*. 2005.

Luke, Timothy W. *Cultural Hegemony: A Critique of the Concept*. University of Minnesota Press, 1998.

Macaulay, Thomas Babington. "Minutes on Indian Education." 2 Feb. 1835, British Parliament.

Mazrui, Ali A. *The Africans: A Triple Heritage*. Little, Brown and Company, 1986.

Mbembe, Achille. *On the Postcolony*. University of California Press, 2001.

Mbembe, Achille. "Necropolitics." *Public Culture*, vol. 15, no. 1, 2003.

Mbembe, Achille. "Sovereignty and Necropolitics in the Postcolony." *Theory and Event*, vol. 22, no. 3, 2019.

Mbembe, Achille. *Critique of Black Reason*. Translated by Laurent Dubois, Duke University Press, 2017.

McKittrick, Katherine. "Mapping Blackness: Cartographies of Race and Social Justice." *Antipode: A Radical Journal of Geography*, vol. 40, no. 5, 2008, pp. 980–1002.

Memmi, Albert. *The Colonizer and the Colonized*. Translated by Howard Greenfeld, Beacon Press, 1991.

Mezlekia, Nega. *Notes from the Hyena's Belly: An Ethiopian Boyhood.* Curley & Associates, 1997.

Morawska, Ewa. *Transnationalism: A New Paradigm for Understanding Globalization.* Routledge, 2009.

Morris, Rosalind C. *Drawings from the Underground.* Seagull Books, 2019.

Mullaney, Julie. *Postcolonial Literatures in Context.* Continuum, 2010.

Mungazi, Charles C. *Ngũgĩ wa Thiong'o: The Politics of Language and Liberation.* Peter Lang, 2000.

Ndlovu-Gatsheni, Sabelo J. *Epistemic Freedom in Africa: Deprovincialization and Decolonization.* Routledge, 2018.

Ngũgĩ wa Thiong'o. *A Grain of Wheat.* Heinemann, 1967.

Ngũgĩ wa Thiong'o. *Petals of Blood.* Heinemann, 1977.

Ngũgĩ wa Thiong'o. *Decolonising the Mind: The Politics of Language in African Literature.* James Currey, 1986.

Nixon, Robert. *Slow Violence and the Environmentalism of the Poor.* Harvard University Press, 2011.

Nkrumah, Kwame. *Neo-Colonialism: The Last Stage of Imperialism.* International Publishers, 1966.

Ortiz, Fernando. *Cuban Counterpoint: Tobacco and Sugar.* Duke University Press, 1995.

Orwell, George. *Shooting an Elephant and Other Essays.* Harcourt, 1950.

Peluso, Nancy. "Counter-Mapping: Cartography that Transcends the Boundaries." *Antipode: A Radical Journal of Geography,* vol. 4, no. 2, 1995, pp. 384-394.

Pieterse, Jan Nederveen. "Globalization and Culture: Three Paradigmatic Views." *International Sociology,* vol. 18, no. 3, 2003, pp. 43-49.

Porter, Andrew, editor. *The Oxford History of the British Empire: Volume III: The Nineteenth Century.* Oxford University Press, 1999.

Potts, Donna L. *Contemporary Irish Writing and Environmentalism: The Wearing of the Deep Green.* Palgrave Macmillan, 2018.

Pritchett, Frances. "Letters to Margaret." 1834. (franpritchett.com/00generallinks/macaulay/txt_letters_margaret.html). Accessed 3 Sept. 2024.

Punter, David, and Simon During, editors. *The Postcolonial Imagination.* Routledge, 1996.

Quayson, Ato. *Relocating Postcolonialism.* Routledge, 2002.

Ramone, Jenni. *Reading Victorian Novels: The Ethics of Reading and the Representation of the Other.* Palgrave Macmillan, 2017.

Rao, Anupama. "Revisiting the Telangana Rebellion: Gender, Caste, and the Social Question in Kancha Ilaiah's Work." *Economic and Political Weekly,* vol. 53, no. 22, 2018, pp. 36-44.

Richardson, Laurel, and Ernest Lockridge. *Travels with Ernest: Crossing the Literary/Sociological Divide.* AltaMira Press, 2004.

Russell, Bertrand. *Why I Am Not a Christian.* Simon & Schuster, 1927.

Said, Edward W. *Orientalism*. Vintage Books, 1979.
Said, Edward. *Culture and Imperialism*. Vintage Books, 1993.
Said, Edward. *Reflections on Exile and Other Essays*. Harvard University Press, 2000.
Satyanarayana, K. "Story of a Social Scientist: Kancha Ilaiah Shepherd." *Deccan Chronicle*, 20 Apr. 2014, pp. 12-15.
Schoultz, James A. *Indentured Labor in the British Empire*. Routledge, 2002.
Serpell, Namwali. *The Old Drift*. Hogarth, New York, 2019.
Shakespeare, William. *Othello*. Edited by E.A.J. Honigmann, Bloomsbury Arden Shakespeare, 1997.
Singh, Namvar. "Decolonizing the Indian Mind." *Indian Literature*, vol. 35, no. 5, Sep.-Oct. 1992, pp. 145-156.
Soyinka, Wole. "Telephone Conversation." *Three Plays*, Oxford University Press, 1963.
Soysal, M. "Scapes and Flows: Situating Appadurai's Anthropological Concepts in the World of Globalisation." *Sociological Review*, vol. 48, no. 2, 2023, pp. 280–295.
Spivak, Gayatri Chakravorty. *A Critique of Postcolonial Reason: Toward a History of the Vanishing Present*. Harvard University Press, 1999.
Spivak, Gayatri Chakravorty. "Can the Subaltern Speak?" *Marxism and the Interpretation of Culture*, edited by Cary Nelson and Lawrence Grossberg, University of Illinois Press, 1988.
Spivak, Gayatri Chakravorty. "Draupadi" by Mahasweta Devi. *Critical Inquiry*, vol. 8, no. 2, 1981, pp. 381-402.
Spivak, Gayatri Chakravorty. "Three Women's Texts and a Critique of Imperialism." *Critical Inquiry*, vol. 12, no. 1, 1985, pp. 243-261.
Spivak, Gayatri Chakravorty. "Scattered Speculations on the Question of Value." *In Other Worlds: Essays in Cultural Politics*, Routledge, 1987, pp. 154-175.
Spivak, Gayatri Chakravorty. "The Politics of Translation." *Outside in the Teaching Machine*, Routledge, 1993, pp. 179-200.
Spivak, Gayatri Chakravorty. *The Spivak Reader: Selected Works of Gayatri Chakravorty Spivak*, edited by Donna Landry and Gerald MacLean, Routledge, 1996.
Sunder Rajan, Rajeswari. *Stories of Women: Gender and Narrative in the Postcolonial Nation*, Manchester UP, 2005.
Tagore, Rabindranath. *Nationalism*. Macmillan, 1918.
Taylor, Diana. *Performing Cultural Memory in the Americas. The Archive and the Repertoire*. Duke University Press, 2003.
Tesfai, Alemseged. *Eritrea: Coming of Age*. Red Sea Press, 1997.
Tomlinson, John. "Globalization and Culture." *Globalization and Culture*, University of Chicago Press, 1999, pp. 105–107.

Valmiki. *Ramayana*. Translated by C. Rajagopalachari, Bharatiya Vidya Bhavan, 1957.

Varughese, Emma Dawson. *Beyond the Postcolonial: World Englishes Literature*. Palgrave Macmillan, 2012.

Viswanathan, Gauri. *Literary Study and British Rule in India*. Oxford University Press, 1989.

Viswanathan, Gauri. *Masks of Conquest: Literary Study and British Rule in India*, Columbia University Press, 1989.

Viswanathan, Gauri. *Outside the Fold: Conversion, Modernity, and Belief*, Princeton University Press, 1998.

Viswanathan, Gauri. *Power, Politics, and Culture*, Routledge, 1998.

Vyasa, Ved. *Mahabharata*. Translated by C. Rajagopalachari, Bharatiya Vidya Bhavan, 1957.

Walcott, Derek. "A Far Cry from Africa." *Selected Poems*, Farrar, Straus and Giroux, 2007, pp. 12-14.

Warraq, Ibn. *Why I Am Not a Muslim*. Prometheus Books, 1995.

Young, Robert. *Postcolonialism: An Historical Introduction*. Blackwell Publishing, 2001.

Index

A

abridgements, 114
Abrogation, 2
absolutist, 191
absurdity, 171
African, 85
African civilization, 162

B

baby monster, 163
barbaric, 173
black, 59
blackness, 85
bloodshed, 135
blurring, 186

C

caste, 15
clansmen, 153
classification, 11
collective, 175
colonial, 96
colonial oppression, 177
colonialism, 41
colonialism f, 8
craftsmanship, 177
cultural preservation, 160

D

diaspora, 24
discourse, 25

E

essentialise, 49
ethnographic, 15
Eurocentric, 41, 185

H

hegemony, 20, 46

I

Igbo culture, 158
imperialism, 42
international, 129

L

linguistic, 28

M

mainstream, 5
mimicry, 25
multiculturalism, 10
multidisciplinary, 1
multilingual, 131
myths, 159

N

narrative, 158
nationalism, 189
Negritude movement, 173

P

parochialism, 60
postcolonial, 96
postcolonial identity, 186
Postcolonial Indian Literature, 185
Postcolonial reading, 34
Postcolonial studies, 42

R

racial bigotry, 170
racialization, 4
racism, 170
rallying, 172
ramifications, 58
resistance, 172
rudimentary, 155

S

satyagraha, 187
savages, 6
silence, 60
slavery, 12
slavish, 159

T

Third Space, 72
transculturation, 37
transnational, 109

U

universalism, 60

V

validate, 74
vanguards, 190
vantage, 50
venomous, 219
version, 21
vestiges, 22
voiceless, 47
voluntarily, 12
voracious, 6
vulnerability, 198

W

worldview, 16
wrapping, 166
wreaked, 196
writing back, 147
wrongdoings, 143

X

xenophobia, 30

Y

Yam, 154

www.ingramcontent.com/pod-product-compliance
Lightning Source LLC
Chambersburg PA
CBHW072138290426
44111CB00012B/1911